THE TRADITION OF RETURN

The Tradition of Return

The Implicit History of
Modern Literature

• • •

JEFFREY M. PERL

Princeton University Press
Princeton, New Jersey

Published by Princeton University Press, 41 William Street,
Princeton, New Jersey 08540
In the United Kingdom: Princeton University Press, Guildford, Surrey

Library of Congress Cataloging in Publication Data will be found
on the last printed page of this book

ISBN 0-691-06621-3

Publication of this book has been aided by The A. C. Smith Fund
of Princeton University Press

This book has been composed in Linotron Sabon
Clothbound editions of Princeton University Press books are printed on acid-
free paper, and binding materials are chosen for strength and durability

Printed in the United States of America by Princeton University Press
Princeton, New Jersey

They that sow in tears
Shall reap in joy.
Though he goeth on his way weeping that beareth the measure
   of seed,
He shall come home with joy, bearing his sheaves.
Psalm 126: A Pilgrim Song

And ye shall eat old store long kept,
and ye shall bring forth the old from before the new.
Leviticus, 26:10

• CONTENTS •

• PERMISSIONS •

· ACKNOWLEDGMENTS ·

The Tradition of Return has been writing itself for a third of my life and its composition has been at once a scholarly project and a deeply personal one. I am very glad for the opportunity to acknowledge debts incurred at either level.

First, there are my teachers. My debts to Dame Helen Gardner and to Richard Ellmann should be obvious to anyone who reads this book. Also in Oxford, I wish to thank John Creaser, and I think with fondness and gratitude of the late J. C. Maxwell, whom I had hoped to please with this study. At Stanford, I want to thank William Chace, and at Princeton, Alvin Kernan and Joseph Frank, who read early drafts of several chapters. A. Walton Litz and Robert Fagles require my special and most immediate thanks for continuing access to their encouragement, criticism, and resourcefulness. I also wish to acknowledge as my teacher a man I have never met—Hugh Kenner; his emphasis on Pound Era archaeology and his depiction of modernism as "Renaissance II" enabled me to locate my own interests.

In addition, thanks are due to Mrs. T. S. Eliot, for permission to examine restricted materials and for generosity with her time; to Marjorie Sherwood of Princeton University Press, for her counsel and kindness; to the Columbia University Department of English and Comparative Literature, for funding research and clerical assistance; and to the National Endowment for the Humanities, the Columbia University Council for Research in the Humanities, and the Whiting Foundation of New York, for their well-timed fellowship support.

I am happy to acknowledge my friends for their support, moral and otherwise. Among many, I must single out a few who saw me through my years in New Jersey: Jeannette Mirsky, William Rivers, and Cristina Thorson—respectively, they have taught invaluable lessons about Humanity, Hard Work, and Tone. Suzanne Mizera made expert suggestions about matters of translation. Andrew Tuck, in particular, has influenced the direction of this study: my thinking about the "process of return," and especially my writing of chapter two and the prologue, evolved during conversations with him, and the whole text has benefited by his critical readings.

As for my family, what can I say at all? They know who they are, know what they mean—and this book is devoted to them.

J.M.P.

NEW YORK CITY

THE TRADITION OF RETURN

· PROLOGUE ·

IF the explanation of texts were the actual function of criticism, then works of criticism should require no explanation. But this does not seem to be the case. Most critical works exhibit a self-explanatory reflex. Some critics even feel a need to launch their books in the manner of a pre-emptive strike:

> I am not intending to say in prefacing this book anything that is not said in the body of it. But it is desirable, if only for the sake of the purpose I do entertain, that no reader shall expect something of a kind that is not offered, or impute to me an expectation that is not mine. . . . My point is that what I have in view entails a radical challenge to modern habits of assumption.[1]

The variety of approaches available to critics is wide, the presuppositions dividing them are deep, and the level of interested mutuality is not high, yet critics' "habits of assumption" are both more and less diverse than this quotation, from F.R. Leavis, allows. We explain ourselves to one another in order to specify our differences but also to affirm our allegiance to a shared self-definition. The critic's tendency toward self-explanation—the fact that we debate so intently over methods and vocabulary—signals our unconscious agreement that literary texts are not simple phenomena and that our task is not to simplify them.

To this agreement there are some notable exceptions, though more interesting than the exceptions to this rule are the methodological paradoxes connected with it. Much Anglo-American criticism, of virtually every "school," seems wedded to an explanatory tone and a procedure that exalt clarity of outline over richness of context, hypothesis above exhaustive demonstration, and lexical definition over definition by the accumulation of significant detail. The primary aim is to state an interpretation at the outset of a project and to present only as many examples or quotations as are essential to clarify the thesis. These professional standards are an odd complement to the belief that literary texts should not be simplified, that they cannot be summarized—and this paradox is probably a legacy of the New Criticism, though much "historical" criticism also exhibits these contradictory tendencies. The standards and tonalities of Anglo-American criticism resemble somewhat those of Anglo-American philosophical writing, to whose goals they are well suited, but literary texts, unlike philosophical ones, are not explanatory by nature and, except in contexts thick-with-complexity and more-than-literary, cannot themselves be explained.

A controlling principle of the present study is that, while it is the calling of the theoretician to explain and thereby simplify, it is the profession of the critic to contextualize and thereby complicate. A prefatory word of explanation seems inappropriate but necessary to a work that proceeds from this assumption. To maintain that the critic's job is to complicate texts is not to reject explanation or interpretation. It is intended, instead, to blur the radical distinction we often assume between an explanation and a "context." The former is commonly thought to give us meaning; we are unsure of what, if anything, the latter gives us. But "meaning" is no longer so privileged an item of vocabulary, even in philosophy, and if we substitute for it "significance"—a word that circumvents the cash-value sense of "meaning"—then explanation and contextualization might seem less distinct: explanation might even seem a mode of providing context. Friedrich Schlegel called criticism the "divine discipline" precisely because it is a balancing act between the claims of explanation and context, analysis and *mimesis*, theory and history, philosophy and poetry—because it is the meeting place *par excellence*, and hence the most likely place for reconciliation, of the misleading antinomies that dominate Western philosophy and theology.

The organization and composition of this book are meant to reflect agreement with Schlegel's assessment. Most of the book (all of part two) is devoted to case studies, each of which constructs an historical context for a large generic or extra-literary phenomenon but centers on a reading of a group of texts by one or two modern writers. A majority of chapters consist of what Clifford Geertz means by "thick description"—perhaps the whole book, and certainly the two chapters called "Novel and Epic," comprise a thick description of Joyce's title, *Ulysses*—but chapter two offers a purposively thin, even naïve reading of *La Nouvelle Héloïse*. In the same way, the crucial term of this study, *nostos* or return, undergoes an "associative" definition, a definition by historical reference and literary allusion, in chapter one, and a systematic definition in chapter two, but the term in fact acquires its full significance by the accumulation of its uses in the varying contexts of the eight chapters. Two basic types of return are described in the first chapter and, viewed from a different perspective, six types are elaborated in the second and third chapters, but the case studies that make up part two are not ordered according to either typology. Such a procedure could have strengthened the reader's sense of a thesis or argument but would have distorted the grainy facts of the individual cases.

This prologue is thus meant to explicate the method and to underscore the morals of a book whose morals, because of its method, may appear to an uninitiated reader opaque. The method has affinities, as already noted, with the thick description proposed in Geertz's book, *The Interpretation of Cultures*, but also with the narrative technique of Michel Foucault's early studies, *Madness and Civilization* and *The Order of Things*, and with the historicist premise of Richard Rorty's *Philosophy and the Mirror of Nature*. All four works resist the reduction of complex intellectual and cultural situations to mnemonic formulae, and they share as an operational motive a principled mistrust of theoretical statements. This "avant-garde" reliance, in non-literary scholarship, on the arts of elaboration—the arts of unfolding—has distinguished precedents in literary criticism. M. H. Abrams has observed that the "post-Wittgensteinian" concern for genre rules, standards of taste, and the conventions of language use are precisely the concerns, albeit unself-conscious, of the most old-fashioned varieties of literary criticism and literary history. Wayne Booth has shown how Abrams' own methodology, sometimes labeled "antiquarian," could serve as a model for the most forward-thinking modes of "counter-theoretical," "narrational" scholarship; and the same could be shown, perhaps even more cogently, of most German literary criticism in the line descending from Friedrich Schlegel to E. R. Curtius and (in some degree) Erich Auerbach.[2] This book deals with the perception of coincidence between old and new, and if its methodology seems old-fashioned to some readers and new-fangled to others, its author cannot be displeased.

But whatever the parallels in literary criticism, old or new, the elective affinities of this study are not literary, even in the broadest sense, though their source is the same one that nourished the German critics. Schlegel, Herder said, wished to be the Winckelmann of poetry, and it is arguable that the fount of modern humanistic scholarship has been the discipline of art history. In any case, art history may be destined to acquire a special importance for our own time because its traditional methods have largely been exempt from what George Steiner calls "the language revolution." Pictures, unlike words, have not often been talked about as if they make theoretical statements concerning the nature of reality. It would be obvious nonsense to say that Holbein's portrait of Erasmus offers us a theory of personality, while it would be unobvious nonsense to say the same of Henry James's *Portrait of a Lady*. The literary critic, like the philosopher, had to discover that theoretical discourse is "merely" language about language—and, like some philosophers, many critics have been blinded by the light of a revelation that should have resulted neither in abdication nor in license. As a kind of therapy, Wittgenstein invited theorists to "compare a concept with a style of painting," but art history has never needed to deal with concepts in any other way.[3]

Hence art-historical scholarship may serve as a model for what can be said, responsibly and with interest, about literary works, and Schlegel describes that model as a kind of "contextualism": "In art history," he says, "one mass explains and illuminates the other. It is impossible to understand a part by itself." But the traditional approach of art history is contextualist in a specific sense; it enjoins that art works be set in contexts of a specific sort. As the founder of modern literary criticism writes about the founder of modern art history:

> The systematic Winckelmann who read all the ancients as if they were a single author, who saw everything as a whole and concentrated all his powers on the Greeks, provided the first basis for a material knowledge of the ancients through his perception of the absolute difference between ancient and modern. Only when the perspective and the conditions of absolute identity of ancient and modern in the past, present, and future have been discovered will one be able to say that at least the contours of classical study have been laid bare and one can now proceed to methodical investigation.[4]

This is one of Schlegel's more paradoxical formulations but elsewhere he makes clear its moral for literary scholarship: proper criticism, he says, is the result of a "ceaseless, ever repeated reading of the classical works," and he insists that only "an ever renewed study of the *whole* cycle" can "really be called reading." The art historian's attention is fixed on tradition and its varieties, on conventions and the causes of their mutation, on the always changing standards of taste and genre, on iconography, quotation, founding monuments or models, classicisms, and renascences. The focus is, in the anthropologist's sense, cultural: even at their most sophisticated, the art historian and the connoisseur deal with the highest products of high civilizations as the anthropologist would deal with primitive myths and sacrificial implements. All are parts of a tradition-bound cultural system. Books, too, are the products of civilizations and are understood most thoroughly and responsibly as elements in the complex fabric of a culture.

Like the work of many art historians, this book attempts to treat civilization as culture, and the points from which it views the development of modernity should not seem foreign to a reader of Erwin Panofsky, Jean Seznec, Francis Haskell and Nicholas Penny, or, for that matter, most other writers on Renaissance and post-Renaissance art. In fact, this study may be read as a gloss on a line from Panofsky's book, *Renaissance and Renascences in Western Art*—or rather, as a response to its invitation: "the Renaissance was permanent. . . . the role of classical antiquity after the Renaissance is somewhat elusive but, on the other hand, pervasive."[5] Every generation has its standard literary history and, from the perspective of our own, Panofsky's remark is imperfectly intelligible. The art historian's sense of period boundaries, much as his sense of national borders, is more fluid than the literary historian's: art history does not take "classicism" to be a period designation any more than it sunders itself, after the fashion of academic literary criticism, into departments of English art, French art, Italian art, and comparative art. Our standard literary history assumes that the classical revival of the fifteenth and sixteenth centuries was extended, in pseudo- or neoclassical form, into the seventeenth and eighteenth centuries, that it was largely restricted to France, and that it was extinguished in the radically new phenomena of a romanticism that extends, roughly, from 1789 to the present.

Books that serve to blur these period boundaries appear from time to time: examples include E. M. Butler's *The Tyranny of Greece over Germany*, the volumes of Donald Bush on the classical allusions in English poetry, Harry Levin's study of romantic Hellenism, and, recently, M. I. Finley's collection of essays, *The Legacy of Greece*, and the Chapel Hill collection, *Nietzsche and the Classical Tradition*, as well as the books of Richard Jenkyns and Victor Turner on the Victorian fascination with Greek antiquity. It is unfortunate that such books are often read as compendia of interesting and curious sidelights on modern high culture. But attention to historical ideology—to the principles that fuel the obsession these works trace—should encourage us to view the persistence of "classicism," "renascence," and "nostalgia" with considerably less complacency or condescension: Return may well be the equal-and-opposite partner of Progress in the engines of modernity.

Yet for all its attention to history, this book is not an Hegelian study of the *Zeitgeist*; it is not an attempt to expose the underlying spirit of our time. On the contrary, its aim is to show how the philosophy of history, the ideologizing of historical trends, led to deliberate attempts to make the modern centuries cohere to a preconceived idea. In the work of modern historians there is an ideological or even artistic patterning of history, and it is this which five centuries of controversy about classicism and Renaissance have most concerned. For hundreds of years it had been presupposed, and during the last century and a half it has been explicitly argued, that Western history falls into three stages—ancient, medieval, modern—and that the third stage is a kind of re-creation of the first, commencing with a Renaissance or rebirth. Periods have thus been balanced off one another aesthetically, and historical analysts have even looked at time as though it naturally possessed a circular or elliptical shape. Modernity for these thinkers is not merely an historical period; its positing implies a reordering of human experience according to normative principles that the historians themselves set down. They agree that the source of our culture was better than the state it has reached, though they locate that source in different times and places. They agree that the source possessed certain necessary qualities we have lost and, for the past two centuries, most have admired those ancient cultures that appear to have maintained a unity of mind and body, spirit and letter, Ideal and Real. The patterning of history according to such normative principles is closer to the prophetic statements of the Hebrew Bible on the destiny of Israel than to anything else in the Western experience, and it is important to emphasize at the outset the extreme strangeness of such a conception attaining presuppositional status.

"Classicism," as T. S. Eliot noted, "is in a sense reactionary, but it must be in a profounder sense revolutionary."[6] Classicism reappears throughout the modern centuries in a variety of guises, though usually—as in the image of Eliot in bowler hat, with umbrella—those guises are highly conservative ones and, like the classicist French Academy and British public schools, they often are closely tied to the cultural status quo.

Yet classicism, in whatever guise, has been extraordinarily destabilizing as a cultural ideology. Each generation of "return ideologists" accused preceding generations of inauthenticity, and the pattern of definition/de-definition/redefinition seems inevitable so long as authenticity is the standard of judgment, and so long as the phenomenon according to which our culture is being judged authentic or inauthentic is buried, literally, beneath the sands of time. As more and more of the Greek, Hebrew, Trojan, and Roman worlds have been dug up and evaluated, more and more theories of what constitutes the authentic source of our culture have arisen. The type of classicism initiated by the Renaissance and the type of Hebraism initiated by the Reformation depend less upon tradition and cultural continua than their medieval precursors did. They care mainly for authenticity and the return to authenticity; their concern is with legitimacy. On the other hand, the challenged traditions of Catholic Christendom could be traced, through a circuitous route, back to the source about which humanist classicists cared. It is ironic that the contemporary products of a line descending from Athens, through Rome and Judea, to Florence should have their legitimacy impugned, since this radical mania with classical authenticity undermined the legitimacy of modern culture still more. As Jean Seznec points out, the humanists' insistence on a return to classical authenticity has made the ancient world "irrevocably detached from our own; it is an enchanted isle, lost beyond a luminous horizon, forever invisible."[7]

One reason for this prologue, therefore, is to sound a note of warning about taking our historical theories for more than they are, or can be. Recent trends in literary scholarship have been, from this point of view, disturbing: they participate in the centuries-old obsession with legitimacy and historical dissociation—with assigning a commencement date to modernity and thereby defining the essential attributes of our own era. The ideological stakes are high and, often, overtly political. If the modern period is seen to begin in the fifteenth century, then "the modern" has to do with Christian humanism, *literae humaniores*, the new sciences, and the new social class—and romanticism, like neoclassicism before it or like modernism after, must be a phase in this development. But if modernity is seen to commence in the later eighteenth century, then romanticism and the revolutionary tradition comprise the essence of all future developments, and the anti-romantic element in modernism must be waved off as rhetorical or else condemned as counterrevolutionary. The debate about romanticism and classicism, which raged from the time of Goethe to that of Eliot, is to some extent replicated today in the strong preference of "post-modern" canon-makers for romantics and proto-romantics over modernists and ancients.

The third chapter of this book ("Classicism, an Historical Explanation") outlines the dialectic among varying definitions of classicism in the post-Renaissance period, and it recounts the classicism/romanticism battles of the twentieth century—Eliot and company claiming that modernism is classicist; their assailants countering that Eliot is a romantic; Eliot contending that romanticism was a late and impure variety of classicism. Many critics today want to argue that modernism was a late but inferior variety of romanticism and, just as this postmodern view deepens the gulf between early and late modernity, between the classicistic *ancien régime* and the *nouvelle ordre* of romanticism, so it effects yet another historical break— this time, in our own century—by mandating several unthinkable exclusions from its literary canon. If we are to accept any major disjunction in the history of our culture, perhaps we should leave it at the Renaissance, precisely because the urge to extend or relocate the period of dissociation has its roots in Renaissance humanism. Much of modern culture was determined by the emphasis on authenticity and legitimacy that characterizes aspects of the Renaissance and the Reformation. If a unity exists among the various post-Renaissance movements that seem so opposed to one another, then that unity descends from the radical historical discontinuity that all those movements or currents assume. With the Renaissance begins the tendency to posit historical dissociations, and it is this tendency that the various modern experiments have in common. The ideology of return is what makes those experiments, in effect, modern.

This same generalization applies to the modernists per se. The modernisms of the late nineteenth and early twentieth centuries are too often viewed as, in Auerbach's words, an "odi et amo hodgepodge." This may be due to the divided state of scholarship about the modernists. To some critics, modernism was a massive cultural deconstruction; other scholars have argued that modernism was entirely a creative phenomenon. But there is no reason why modernism should not seem affirmative to some and critical or even nihilistic to others—though this observation does not preface a sermon on diversity. This study presupposes not only the unity of most trends in modernism but also a loose kind of unity for all the great cultural trends in the post-Renaissance era. In any three-period, A–B–A scheme for history, many centuries of human experience will be called into question or negated, and the religio-cultural principles that underwrite the unsatisfactory B phase will be found wanting—were found increasingly wanting as the modern centuries wore on. If there is an historical return, after all, there must be a founding epoch and a *nostos*, but also a period of wandering in between them which calls for explanation.

The central question faced by the modernists was, historically speaking, What is the meaning of the middle period? or, put in its most usual form, What is Christianity? What purpose did it or does it serve, and has it a future? In the twentieth century, we are all post-Christians, even if some of us—Eliot, for example—are Christians as well. We no longer *assume* Christianity. In general, the modernists attempt to deconstruct Christianity and its cosmology at the same time that they attempt to construct a post-Christian cosmology based on pre-Christian ones. The modernists tend to share constellations of objections to Christianity: it is life-denying (it centers on crucifixion), its view of human nature is incorrect (it cleaves the soul from the appetites), it is dangerously *telos*-oriented. The modernists demand, by and large, the opposite of these principles as guides for living, and they pair their fledgling post-Christian cosmology with venerable pre-Christian ones. Hence the association of Freud with the Greeks (as by E. R. Dodds, and by Freud himself), or of Kant with Aristotle (as by Johann Gottfried Hermann) and of Bradley with Aristotle (as by Eliot), or the association of Einstein and Freud with Homer (as in *Ulysses*). The present is thereby made livable and, quietly or noisily, it is made legitimate.

Virtually every major modernist, at one time or another, used the past as a stick with which to beat the present (this book examines some instances in case studies), and in this way, even the most "affirmative" modernists may be said to have had nihilistic tendencies. There is, for instance, the unending debate over whether James ("I said yes I will") Joyce was ironic or sincere in the affirmations of *Ulysses*. But, in the process-of-return structure, irony and even "nihilism" are merely the tribute paid by a deracinated convention to its first and final causes. The association of the first and last terms of the A–B–A scheme, even when it is projected onto history, is best understood in the terms of psychological process—as a way of perceiving, or making sense out of, experience. In this psychological process, stage one would be something like "convention," unconsciously or unquestioningly followed. Stage two would be rebellion against the convention, usually because it has become ossified into a questionable concept or a risible cliché. Stage three would be an apocalypse of the clichéd convention and it would involve, as the word suggests, neither acceptance nor negation but revelation and rededication. Some of the modernists—Eliot, for example, and, in some moods, Joyce—take this A–B–A scheme to signify that the "conventional" and the "ultimate" are one, but almost every modernist would agree that the conventional and the ultimate are indistinguishable to the psyche that has undergone the whole progress of return from stage one to stage two to stage three. The modern obsession with historical-return ideologies may have been, all along, a matter of making present conditions ultimate: for some, a matter of progress from conventionality to ultimacy and, for others, a technique for revealing the ultimacy that is latent in the mundane.

This application of the process of return could almost stand as a definition for modernism. From Joyce's notion of "epiphany" to Freud's theory of "catharsis," from Pound's slogan "Make it new" to the Russian Formalists' principle of "estrangement," from Picasso's monumental, three-nosed figures to Eliot's insistent redemption of literary clichés, Christian beliefs, and Tory proprieties—modernism seems to be an attempt to prove (above all, to the modernists themselves) that contemporary existence, looked at and lived with properly, is as natural to man and as close to Nirvana, as rich and strange, as any sort of existence whatever. For the modernists, the process of return was not only a means of understanding history and not only an artistic technique, it was a condition of the psyche and (perhaps the same thing) a world view. It could be objected that the West has always been "past"-oriented, and the process-of-return vocabulary has had, doubtless, a more extensive career than the one narrated in this book. But one has to begin somewhere and, consistent with its subject matter, this study begins at the end.

· PART ONE ·

Ideology and History

Nostos: An Introduction

But come now, we are all at leisure
here, let us take up this matter of
his return.
            Odyssey Book 1

AT THE BEGINNING of the *Odyssey*, the council of the gods is
in session and the subject of discussion is Odysseus' return.
But who is Odysseus to the gods? And to what, or from
precisely where, is he returning? Every odyssey presupposes
an Iliad, and Homer presumes we know all about his hero.

Odysseus, of course, is one of the consortium of Greek
warlords who undertook to recapture from Asian hands the
most beautiful woman on earth. The exploit has been a success—Helen has been recovered—but the highest civilization
of the eastern Mediterranean has been burned to the ground
and the Western troops have been decimated, disillusioned,
and scattered. Odysseus himself, having lost all his men at
sea, has been trapped for eight years, by an adoring island
nymph, in literature's most ennui-ridden thraldom. During
this time, the great adventurer has grown less fond of experience and novelty for their own sake—he sheds tears for his
wife and son, for his patrimony and boyhood. Meanwhile,
upstarts are plaguing Odysseus' house and kingdom: making
suit to his wife, taunting his progeny, usurping his legitimate
ancestral rights. In nearby Argos, the commander in chief of
the combined Greek armies, upon making the return from
which Odysseus is prevented, has been murdered by a trea-
sonous cousin and his own adulterous queen.

In the *Iliad*, we find Western Europeans sailing after beauty:
after the Ideal. That is always the tendency of Western Europeans, but this time they have gone too far. The Greeks
have left behind them the fundamentals of human life and,

afflicted with the perversions and ennui which follow on root-lessness, they have come to recognize the real meaning and surpassing value of fundamentals. Odysseus, for one, will pay any price, fight any battle, to return home. The venturing forth from home, which is the subject of the *Iliad*, has disrupted the natural flow of human lives—the time is out of joint and the gods are determined to have men set it right. The Olympians dispatch their messenger to send Odysseus on his way, and the goddess of wisdom, Odysseus' patroness, flies from her father's side down to Ithaca, where she is charged "to put more courage" in Odysseus' son by aiding him to locate his heroic progenitor and to identify with him. The immediate past, it appears, is being rejected in favor of a more distant and noble one.

In the *Odyssey*, the benefits of return are seen as the fruits of departure. The appreciation for fundamental principles, to which wandering leads, is itself of such great value, that the interregnum period—the rending pursuit of the Ideal, the boring pursuit of novelty—is thought to be valuable as well. Odysseus sails for home with pleasure and relief, but he recounts his wanderings with relish and he would not relinquish anything he has gained by the experience. He has, in fact, gained a good deal: he has learned, for example, to take nothing for granted (he tests his wife's fidelity in Book 19, his father's in Book 24), and he has developed a keen sense that there is a time to venture forth and a time to sail for home. The Odyssean *nostos* is complex: it is a return to something old but also a new beginning; it is a meeting of oldest and newest, yet it is in addition the seemly conclusion of an unbroken continuum. Odysseus' history divides into three stages—*ante bellum*, adventures, *nostos*—but the first period (home) and the third (homecoming) are neither exactly congruent nor absolutely distinct. In Book 13, Odysseus arrives on Ithaca and does not recognize it as his home:

> Meanwhile, on his island,
> his father's shore, that kingly man, Odysseus,
> awoke, but could not tell what land it was

after so many years away. . . .
The landscape then looked strange, unearthly strange
to the Lord Odysseus: paths by hill and shore,
glimpses of harbors, cliffs, and summer trees.
He stood up, rubbed his eyes, gazed at his homeland,
and swore, slapping his thighs with both his palms,
then cried aloud:
   "What am I in for now?
Whose country have I come to this time? . . ."[1]

Odysseus thinks his landing at Ithaca is the commencement
of a new adventure—as indeed it will prove to be. Half a
lifetime's odyssey has been required for Odysseus to discover
that life's signal adventure is the discovery of home.

• • •

CRITICS and historians of taste sometimes observe how, in the
nineteenth and twentieth centuries, the *Odyssey* surpassed the
Iliad as the most popular poem of Homer and the most be-
loved literary work of Europe. The Harvard "Five-Foot Shelf"
of classics (1910) comprised fifty volumes but ignored the
Iliad, while the translations of Lamb, Butcher and Lang, Morris, Butler, T. E. Lawrence, Graves, Lattimore, and Fitzgerald,
together with the adaptations of Tennyson, Joyce, and Pound,
represent the groundswell of affection for the *Odyssey* in English-speaking countries alone. The causes of Ulysses' popularity are not far to seek. The picture of Odysseus in Book
13, staring in puzzled anguish at his "strange, unearthly"
home, could be an emblem for the condition of the modern
European; the action of the gods in Book 1 could serve as
emblem for modern notions about the operation of historical
destiny. As the *Odyssey* opens, we are privileged to watch
destiny in action. Telemachus, there, is a representative of the
present life of Greece, and the elder figures of the poem (Nestor, Menelaus, Helen, Odysseus), representatives of its Iliadic
past. By encouraging the present to search out the past, and
by unleashing the past to home towards the present, the Olympian council determines a longed-for future. In the process,

all past and present action—conquest, exploration, suffering, boredom—will come to seem justified by its subsumption into a pattern both aesthetically pleasing and experientially satisfying.

Modern philosophers of history, both professional and amateur, tend to view Europe's past, present, and future in similar terms. Like the life of Odysseus, the history of Europe is very often divided into three stages: a youthful stage (antiquity), a period in pursuit of the Ideal (the Middle Ages), and a time of return to first principles (modernity). The idea of modernity has, since the Renaissance, been intimately tied to the notion of a classical rebirth. The ancient/medieval/modern scheme, which we associate with nineteenth- and twentieth-century philosophers of history, was already latent in the fifteenth-century humanist and sixteenth-century Reformation rejection of the "Gothic" deviation from classical and Biblical norms. Humanists and Reformers asserted that the task of their era was to restore and revive the neglected or misunderstood monuments of antiquity. Giorgio Vasari, writing (in 1550) in support of that historical outlook, provides us with terms in which we can measure the profundity of the perceptual revolution that Renaissance humanism represented:

> having seen in what way art . . . climbed to the greatest height, and how from a state so noble she fell into utter ruin, and that, in consequence, the nature of this art is similar to that of . . . human bodies, [which] have their birth, their growth, their growing old and their death; they will now be able to recognize more easily the progress of her second birth and of that very perfection whereto she has risen again in our times. . . .[2]

From the time the "Pauline synthesis" of paganism and Hebraism took root, during the latter days of the Western Empire, post-classical culture, including medieval culture, was perceived as an organic development—a "growth," a "growing old"—of classical civilization. With the Renaissance, however, the metaphors used to describe the relation of past and present altered radically. The relation of antiquity to modernity—of antiquity to the Renaissance—did not lend itself to organic metaphor. In order to characterize the classic revival of his own time, Vasari had to resort to the language of miracle, to the vocabulary of resurrection ("second birth," "risen again"). The humanists presented their classical renascence as if they had accomplished it with divine aid. Like the Odyssean *nostos*, this historical return was the handiwork of destiny.

The historical viewpoint of the Renaissance is the outlook with which modern culture begins. However, the humanists were not, strictly speaking, philosophers of history—though a large literature has grown up around their use of the terms *medium aèvum* and *media aetas*.[3] The humanists were not concerned so much to construct comprehensive historical schemes as to assert the supernatural importance of their own era: Boccaccio wrote, for instance, that the classical rebirth of his day indicated that God was putting souls "like those of the ancients" into contemporary Italian bodies. It remained for later historians to draw out and underscore the principles that were implied by the humanist approach to history. In *Man on His Past*, Herbert Butterfield documents how "From the time of the Renaissance some such term as 'the middle ages' would occasionally appear, but it did not occur to people to follow out the logical consequences of this and to divide world-history into three great periods" until the mid-nineteenth century.[4] The first, fully self-conscious ideologies of return are, possibly, those of the *philosophes* or, more probably, those of Vico and Rousseau, Hegel and Michelet; but it is to Jacob Burckhardt's study of the Italian Renaissance (1860) that we must turn for the purest and most radical expression of a *nostos*-oriented philosophy of history. Burckhardt was perhaps the first to trace in detail the Renaissance obsession with antiquity, while at the same time pointing to the indisputable fact that the classics were extremely influential throughout the Middle Ages. Burckhardt states succinctly that the Renaissance was unique not because of its revival of interest in the antique, but because it revived antiquity "as a whole" and was "not a mere fragmentary imitation or compilation" of antiquity, "but a new birth."[5]

Accordingly, Burckhardt saw the Renaissance ("a new birth") as the dissolution of "the fantastic bonds of the Middle Ages" and as the beginning of a new age.[6] But the new epoch did not live up to its commencement and Burckhardt's writings are full of vituperation against the failure of post-Renaissance moderns. The new era was meant to be a return to antiquity "as a whole" and Burckhardt's celebration of the fifteenth century was a reminder to nineteenth-century Europeans that— as he wrote in his notes on the history of Greek culture—the development of an art or a civilization is determined "by the manner of its origin."[7] The very idea of "the Renaissance" as an historical entity became possible and necessary only during Burckhardt's lifetime. Winckelmann and the romantics seemed to have proven that the official Christian humanism of the modern centuries was not authentically classical and, worse, that it did not live up to the standards for cultural excellence set by the fifteenth and early sixteenth centuries in Italy. Ideologists of return began to wonder whether modernity as a whole might never become the revival of antiquity that the humanists had proclaimed. As a result, Burckhardt and his spiritual heirs came to cherish two special treasures: nostalgia for the fifteenth-century Florentine revival, and an urgent intuition that a new and lasting renascence might yet occur in the nineteenth or twentieth century. Modernism was meant to reassert and vindicate the humanists' understanding of modernity—the twentieth century was meant to be a renascence of the Renaissance. Both "the Renaissance" and "modernism" were produced in the nineteenth century out of an ambivalent commingling of feelings: expectation, awe, and the hatred born of disappointment.

Burckhardt's attitude toward post-Renaissance modernity is instructive. The cultural theoretician approaches the unfinished odyssey of history with an artistic entelechy in mind— this much, at least, Hayden White's controversial study, *Metahistory*, appears to have demonstrated.[8] Whether the patterns of development that the theoretician finds are drawn from the historical "text" or imposed upon it is an open question to which we shall return, but certain facts are clear. The thrust of modern culture after the Renaissance appears to run counter to the humanist evaluation of modernity as a return to antiquity. The bourgeois progressivism and technological novelty-seeking of the Protestant era seem to have little in common with the aristocratic, Latin institutions that Italian humanists had expected to revive and purify. The humanist theoretics of modernity (which is, perhaps, what is meant by our curious term *modern-ism*) and modernity itself are, in Burckhardt's view, irreconcilable opponents. For Homer, the old and new orders—Odysseus and the suitors—are indeed irreconcilable, and the former, returning to his legitimate place with the help of the gods, makes quick work of the latter. Burckhardt is the first in a distinguished line of theorists who feel about bourgeois materialism and Christian spirituality as Odysseus felt about Antinoös and the other young men occupying his dining room.

Certainly the three-epoch, *A–B–A* periodization of history implies, by definition, an attitude like that of Burckhardt. Prior to the Renaissance, the predominant historical divisions were either dual (B.C., A.D.) or quadruple (the "Four Empire" theory, based on the Book of Daniel) and had reference to Biblical events. The triple division has no basis in orthodox Christianity (though the apocalyptic character of many *nostos* schemes may be related to the three-epoch divisions made in certain Christian heresies).[9] And in an historical division where the first epoch is pre-Christian and the second is a kind of temporal Christendom, symmetry demands that the third or modern era carry with it uncomfortable intimations of post-Christianity. Further, the *A–B–A* division of history is founded on value judgments rather than objective historical events, and the middle epoch necessarily suffers from a negative resonance. The Middle Ages begin with the collapse into barbarism of the classical world order and close upon what the Göttingen historians term the "revival of literary culture" in the fifteenth century. The Middle Ages are defined as a relatively illiterate period of un-classicism between two supremely literate and classical eras—and the cultural-intellectual legitimacy of Christianity is thus called into question. Moreover, as already noted, medieval Christianity was not alone in facing condemnation from the ideologists of return. Burckhardt sees the seventeenth, eighteenth, and nineteenth centuries as a deviation from the promise of return embodied in the fifteenth and sixteenth: he views modernity as a new age *manqué*. The bourgeois materialism, progressivism, and pursuit of novelty that dominate the modern era—just as much as Christianity's pursuit of the Ideal—are constituents of the unsavory middle period in Burckhardt's three-epoch scheme. The Renaissance is an island of light in a sea of darkness.

Yet Burckhardt's objections to Christianity and to bourgeois values are not exclusively conditioned by an historicist dogma. Burckhardt's praise for the men of ancient Greece or Renaissance Italy, and his contempt for the men of medieval and modern Europe, are rooted in a specific view of human nature. The middle epoch is rejected because its thinkers refused to accept man as he is—they insisted on theorizing and idealizing humanity. In reaction, Burckhardt endorses the Homeric Greeks' strong personalities, their refusal to recoil from the gruesome, their lack of inhibitions and guilt feelings, their easygoing response to bodily needs or desires, and their innocence of dividing passions.[10] The Italians of the Renaissance are admirable for the same characteristics, though the ancient conception of "the full, whole nature of man,"[11] reasserted under modern conditions, led to a moral crisis for Christianity. Burckhardt details the murder, rapine, incest, adultery, cruelty, sacrilege, and treason in the court of Rimini, but he excuses Sigismundo Malatesta's career because it occurred "through an historical necessity." Sigismundo's behavior was "neither good nor bad, but necessary," for

> within it has grown up a modern standard of good and evil—a sense of moral responsibility—which is essentially different from that which was familiar to the Middle Ages. . . . the Italian of the Renaissance had to bear the first mighty surging of a new age.[12]

The fifteenth-century "discovery of the outward world" necessitated, Burckhardt thought, a new type of morality—it

brought Europe to the verge of "a new age." Whatever we
think of Renaissance morals, it is clear that, with this assertion
of Burckhardt, European morality had entered the era of *Beyond Good and Evil*—a book that made obvious the implications of Burckhardt's historical scheme. Nietzsche, an ad-
mirer of Burckhardt's and a colleague on the Basel faculty,
attributed the revaluation of morality, as Burckhardt had, to
a revival and revaluation of antiquity. The archaic Greeks
were, for Nietzsche, neither materialists nor idealists but *human beings*, and he pits them, to startling effect, against modern men. In an early fragment (1872) on Homer, Nietzsche
assumes that, since man is "wholly nature and embodies [na-
ture's] uncanny dual character,"[13] Christians (and moderns
in general) cannot be thought human beings in the Homeric
sense—their lives are too much controlled by "a disgust with
existence."[14] But Nietzsche believed that Europe was, in his
day, making an odyssey back to a more Homeric understanding of humanity, where "the most humane men . . . have a
trait of cruelty, a tigerish lust to annihilate."[15] The new age—
the twentieth century—would be free of the "wholly erroneous distinction" between spirit and matter, mind and body,
and free also of the overly genteel distinction between civilized
or human, and barbaric or animal, impulses.[16] Human history
is psycho-history—this was true for Nietzsche, but also for
Burckhardt before him and for most other *nostos* theorists
after him. Ideologists of return share the assumption that man
possesses a unified sensibility, and the historical divisions they
posit tend to correspond with supposed dissociations or reas-
sociations in the cultural psyche.

However, *nostos* theorists part company in their attitudes
toward those psycho-historical divisions. As we have seen, the
impulse to slaughter suitors is a reflex inherent in any return-
oriented historical philosophy. Burckhardt and Nietzsche
originate a line of theorists who view the middle epoch, the
period of psychological dissociation, as a failure or a cheat,
deserving of annihilation. But there is another and more subtle
reading of the odyssey of history, a second line of *nostos*
ideologists. At the conclusion of Homer's epic, the men of

Ithaca rise up against Odysseus' family to defend the *status quo* against the *status ante bellum*. Odysseus' party—the party of the *nostos*—prepare to "cut the enemy down / to the last man, leaving not one survivor," but the gods intervene suddenly to impose "terms of peace." The apparently irreconcilable opponents are reconciled. They have, after all, much in common: the suitors' families are Ithacan and Odysseus is king of Ithaca. In T. S. Eliot's words, the combatants have been "United in the strife which divided them. . . . / And are folded in a single party." This, certainly, is the viewpoint of the gods—as also of those men, like Odysseus and Halitherses Mastorides, who can see "the field of time, past and to come" (24.421). In other words, providence and the philosopher of history can agree: the battle of past and present is a fine way of bringing past and present into intense relation, and all is part of a theodicean design whose wholeness lends significance to every part. Moreover, from this point of view, dissociations or discontinuities are less interesting, in the end, than that design and its significance.

The most transparent and paradigmatic of these "theodicean" histories in the nineteenth century is probably that of Walter Pater, whose approach, like Burckhardt's historical philosophy, is embodied in a study of the fifteenth- and sixteenth-century renascence. The relevant section of *Studies in the History of the Renaissance* (1873) is the chapter on Winckelmann, in which Pater traces the fortunes of the classical revival during the seventeenth, eighteenth, and nineteenth centuries.[17] Pater, again in harmony with Burckhardt, thinks that northern Europeans of the post-Renaissance period perverted, dampened, or falsified the new understanding of antiquity that the Italian humanists had established—and Pater likewise prefers the culture of Renaissance humanism to that of medieval Christendom. Unlike Burckhardt and Nietzsche, however, Pater views the deviations from the standards set by classical Greece as less interesting than the continuities. He calls the outlook that we have associated with Burckhardt "the superficial view," and he writes that the deeper view is that which preserves the identity of European culture. The two [classical and post-classical culture] are really continuous: and there is a sense in which it may be said that the Renaissance was an uninterrupted effort of the middle age, that it was ever taking place.[18]

Pater reasons that the Greek achievement has always been present as "a conscious tradition" in "our intellectual life," and that it has had "an underground life" even in periods that appear, like the Middle Ages, to be unclassical. Out of this underground life, "from time to time [the Hellenic element] has started to surface" so that culture can be "drawn back to its sources to be clarified and corrected."[19] Hellenism remained underground during the formative period of Christianity, for the pursuit of the Ideal was inimical to the Greeks' "happy limit" and "perfect animal nature."[20]

On the other hand, in Pater's view, a proto-Christian pursuit of the Ideal had already commenced at the high point of Greek civilization. Though "the mind [had] not begun to boast of its independence of the flesh," and though man was still "at unity with himself, with his physical nature, with the outward world," the Greeks were already committed to a train of reflection that would end in "a defiance of form, of all that is outward, in an exaggerated idealism."[21] After Christianity had become secure enough so that it could "compromise" its idealist severities, the Hellenic element began to assert itself—in the classical influences on Gothic architecture, for example. But despite his insistence on cultural continuity, Pater acknowledges that "When the actual relics of the antique were restored to the world, it was to Christian eyes as if an ancient plague-pit had been opened." The Renaissance represented a crisis for Europe because "all the world took the contagion of the life of nature and the senses":[22] Hellenic paganism and Christian idealism were seen to be more than somewhat at odds.

Heinrich Heine, some years before Pater, placed this problem in a "theodicean" historical framework, asserting that

Christianity (a religion Heine did not in his early years admire) had been necessary because of the excessive materialism rampant in late antiquity: "The flesh became so arrogant in this Roman world that it required Christian discipline to chasten it. After the banquet of a Trimalchion such a hunger-cure as Christianity was a necessity."[23] Following Heine's lead, Matthew Arnold, in the influential essay, "Hebraism and Hellenism," argued that, just as Catholicism had served to counter Greek and Roman immorality, so Protestantism in the modern period served to discipline the excesses of the Renaissance. For these mid-century theorists, it was as though history had arranged itself dialectically, into waves of materialism and idealism, in order to produce in the end a unified cultural sensibility. Pater's "theodicean" history was less programmatic and more Odyssean. He conjectured that the middle epoch (the Christian centuries) came about so that the cultural mind could "repose, that it might awaken when day came, with eyes refreshed, to those antique forms": the years of wandering, in effect, were leading toward an intenser appreciation of home.[24]

The question that remained for Pater, as for all subsequent *nostos* theorists, was how, in the era of return, to bring ancient patterns "into the gaudy, perplexed light of modern life"— to "work out a supreme *Dénouement*" to the "problem of moral order versus natural law."[25] Pater's notes toward a solution illuminate the various solutions that succeeded his. He proposed that the romantic temper of the modern era— "its adventure, its variety, its deep subjectivity"—was precedented "within the limits of the Greek ideal itself."[26] That is to say, "the gaudy, perplexed light" of modernity was already, in large degree, "classical." Pater would prefer that the romantic temper embrace a few more Hellenic qualities ("transparency," "rationality"); he would prefer that modern culture be born to a "marriage of Faust and Helena."[27] But it is crucial to emphasize that, unlike the Burckhardtian line, the theodicean ideologists contended that post-Renaissance modernity continued to parallel the ancient world in numerous and important respects. Some theorists of return—Yeats, for example, in his essays on the theater—chose to underscore and defy the gulf between the modern and the ancient. At the other extreme, Hegel—possibly our first theodicean historicist—did not contend that the novel, born at the height of the sixteenth-century *nostos, ought* to become a kind of epic, but that that quintessentially modern and bourgeois genre *is* a kind of epic.

More than half a century after publication, Joyce's masterpiece is still a generic puzzle for critics. Is it a novel? Is it an epic? We only know for certain that the book contains no truly epic heroisms, many novelistic trivialities—and that its author entitled it *Ulysses*. In similar fashion, T. S. Eliot and T. E. Hulme argued not so much that modernist aesthetics must become classicist, as that modernist aesthetics *had become* or were in the process of becoming classicist. Outside the arts, too, many emphasized what they perceived to be parallels between antiquity and modernity: E. R. Dodds, for instance, in his comparison of the Hellenic and Freudian psychologies, or George Thomson, in his work on the bourgeois character of Aeschylean Athens. And today, Claude Lévi-Strauss maintains, more radically, that the most advanced conclusions of the sciences, hard and soft, have brought modern culture full circle with *la pensée sauvage*.

The interaction between the Burckhardtian and theodicean types of historical thinking—often within a single mind—has been hugely productive in the nineteenth and twentieth centuries. The congeries of individuals and movements we call "modernism" have been intimately involved with both varieties of *nostos* ideology. Those historical theories are not the sole determinants of the nature of modernism but, of its principal components, they have been the least acknowledged and studied. Part of the reason may be the extraordinary complexity, unevenness, inconsistency, and unsystematic character of the return ideologies. Sometimes Yeats or Pound will appear to be using the *nostos* myth as if merely to provide his verse with a structuring device or a cache of metaphors: examples might be Yeats's *A Vision* and Pound's lyric, "The Return," which Yeats mentions there. At other times, however, both Pound and Yeats take that myth with the deadliest kind of seriousness—their reactionary social criticism can be read as the application of a return-oriented, Odyssean structure to matters of history and politics. It is difficult, modernist by modernist, to measure the sincerity of such applications. Furthermore, there is a great diversity—or confusion—of antiquities, and the anatomist of modernism must make his peace with them. Even within the Hellenic context, the precise character of the *nostos* diverges widely: Maurras would offer sacrifice to Athena at the Parthenon, Nietzsche to Dionysus at the foot of the Acropolis, and Rousseau to some pastoral deity at his shrine in suburban Sparta. Others have set their course for a destination farther east in the Mediterranean—have hoped to moor their vessels in an ancient Israelite harbor. And the *nostoi* of Lawrence and Lévi-Strauss are to still more archaic (and unclassical) worlds.

Yet in the recognition of diversity, often, there lurks a discovery of some deeper kind of identity. The various *nostoi* of modernity, however different or diffident, are linked by that kind of identity: each perceives an essentially psychological patterning in, or imposes a psychological structure upon, the history of culture. Whether the structure be perceived or imposed is immaterial to this generalization—the psychoanalytic term "projection" will do for both. The phrase, "the mind of Europe," was popularized by modernists and frequently used by them in their explanations of the historical *nostos*:

> An extraordinary shudder ran through the marrow of Europe. She felt in every nucleus of her mind that she was no longer the same, that she was no longer herself, that she was about to lose consciousness, a consciousness acquired through centuries of bearable calamities. . . .
> So—as though in desperate defense of her own physiological being and resources—all her memory confusedly returned. Her great men and her great books came back pell-mell. . . .
> And in the same disorder of mind, at the summons of the same anguish, all cultivated Europe underwent the

rapid revival of her innumerable ways of thought . . .
illuminating with a strange and contradictory glow the
death agony of the European soul. . . . she sought refuge,
guidance, consolation throughout the whole register of
her memories, past acts, and ancestral attitudes. Such are
the known effects of anxiety. . . .[28]

In an increasingly post-Christian and secular world, the men
of Christendom quite naturally looked to their own pre-Christian past (among other places) for examples of a non-Christian, but nonetheless civilized, social order. There is nothing
surprising in the phenomenon Valéry describes; what is remarkable is the language he uses to describe it. The cultural
"mind" is depicted as engaged in a specific type of psychological dynamic, in what might be called the "process of return."

As Valéry explains, that process begins with anxiety about
the present and future. There is dissatisfaction about an unstable present that, less and less, has a meaningful connection
with authentic selfhood and authentic memory. What follow,
in this "disorder of mind," are a self-motivated self-analysis
and an evaluation both of the interrelations of memories and
of the patterns they form. Ideally, the process will conclude
with a return, a psychological reintegration. In this sense,
"return" means the reconciliation with, and revitalization (or
even reification) of, present conditions and conventions. We
are familiar with this process from its relation to classic psychoanalytic theory, but we also have seen the pattern where
Freud first saw it: in various underworld-journey myths and
in more sophisticated works of literature. To say that the
ideologies of historical *nostos* are based upon a psychological
process of return is no more than to remark, as we have done,
upon the resemblance of those theories—usually coincidental,
though sometimes, as in *Ulysses* or *The Cantos*, with conscious intent—to the structure of the Homeric *nostos*.

We already have examined the Poundean sociology of the
Odyssey, in which a rich, lazy, bourgeois present is brought
face to face with its heroic past. However, the human activity

of the *Odyssey* begins not with Odysseus but with Telemachus, not with the physical and political movements of the father but with the psychological processes of the son. Telemachus' anxiety about his present and future, in a suitor-dominated Ithaca, is extreme and well-founded. The connection of past and present in his life has disappeared mysteriously, and his sense of selfhood has been lost along with it:

> Telemakhos answered:
> Friend, now that you ask about these matters,
> our house was always princely, a great house,
> as long as he of whom we speak remained here.
> But evil days the gods have brought upon it,
> making him vanish, as they have, so strangely.
> Were his death known, I could not feel such pain—
> . . . Instead, the whirlwinds got him, and no glory.
> He's gone, no sign, no word of him; and I inherit
> trouble and tears. . . .[29]

Accordingly, the goddess of the mind arranges for Telemachus to voyage forth, both in imitation of his father and in pursuit of information about the past. When Odysseus in fact returns home, Telemachus is more than ready for the new/old order that he and his father will inaugurate together.

Harried by a rich, lazy, bourgeois present, numerous educated persons in Europe and America found themselves in the Telemachan position. Athena drove some of them on literal voyages after the past—the Dilettanti and Philhellenists to Greece; Chateaubriand to Rome, Athens, and Jerusalem; Flaubert to Carthage; Schliemann to Troy; James, Pound, and Eliot from the New World to old Europe; the Zionists to Zion. Even Delacroix's expedition to North Africa and Gauguin's to Tahiti were partly inspired by the craving for a natural classicism no longer available to artists in Paris. But many who remained at home experienced the Telemachan ordeal that Valéry describes. Inevitably, we are brought to ask: Is modern history, then, the record of our culture's process of return? The individuals who underwent that process underwent it individually—and, for most of them, coming to terms with aging institutions or values, and with their modern misconstructions, was an intensely personal experience. The process resulted for some, like Joyce or Picasso, in a more or less complete integration into the conditions and conventions of the present; for others, like Nietzsche or Lawrence, the process concluded with an almost complete rejection of the status quo; for still others, like Ezra Pound, the experience ended in silence. Such experiences are not collective, and speculations about historical teleology are best left to accredited prophets. We can, however, examine individual cases in concert and thereby attempt to arrive at a body of illuminating, if unmystical, generalizations. To examine as a continuum our developing concepts of "the modern"—from humanism to modernism—may bring us to see the development of modernity as both less haphazard and more constructive than we are sometimes inclined to see it. In any evaluation of modernity, we must question strenuously all manner of modern assumptions, every variety of historical ideology. Yet at the same time, and out of the same concern for objectivity, we surely must remain open to the modernists' suggestion that the development of a culture can follow a psychological, or even an artistic, entelechy. "The odyssey of history" may be a cliché, but it is not, necessarily, a metaphor.

· II ·

The Process of Return

And in the end
That is the completion which at the beginning
Would have seemed the ruin.
      T. S. Eliot, *The Family Reunion*

THE IMPULSE to "return" is rooted in the intuition that problems have origins. That intuition is probably less modern than human and has long been part of our cultural apparatus. The classical myth of the Golden Age and the Christian myth of the Fall both express yearning for an unproblematic ur-state—and the relations between the myth of *nostos* and the emotion of *nostalgia* extend even to etymology. Modern versions of those myths imply that our cultural and personal dilemmas are the legacy of a trauma in historical, rather than mythical, time: Eliot's "dissociation of sensibility" begins with the English Civil War, Freud's with the terrors of childhood. And the modern varieties, unlike the traditional ones, often assume not only that our dilemmas have specifiable origins but that they are susceptible of ready solutions. Yet the traditional and the modern types of return, despite these distinctions, are not opposed. As Geoffrey Hartman observes of the romantics' return ideology:

> The traditional scheme of Eden, Fall, and Redemption merges with the new triad of Nature, Self-Consciousness, and Imagination—the last term in both involving a kind of return to the first.[1]

Merge is perhaps not the best verb to describe the relation of kinds, but *contrast* would be more misleading. In the same way, the cultural and psychological approaches to return are closely intertwined, as are what we have termed the Burckhardtian and theodicean orientations.

The result of the interaction among the various types of return is a nice complexity which we must attempt to clarify rather than simplify. What is required is a typology of returns that emphasizes the inextricability of types, and one of the most influential of *nostos* theorists has thoughtfully provided us with it. *Julie ou La Nouvelle Héloïse* (1760) of Jean-Jacques Rousseau is among the earliest expressions of the modern spirit of return and remains one of its most careful analyses. In his *Confessions*, Rousseau refers several times to his "plan" for the novel, and he indicates he means by that something more systematic than the usual, plot-centered "placement of details."[2] He explicitly states that this epistolary novel is as bold a departure and as theoretical an exposition as his much more controversial *Émile*: "all that is daring in *Émile* already existed in *Julie*."[3] And, in a personal letter, Rousseau describes *Émile* as "a highly philosophical work" whose purpose is "to show, in the history of the human heart, the origin of all the vices."[4] In the context of these remarks, it is possible to read *La Nouvelle Héloïse* as a systematic examination, in novel form, of the multiple origins of vice in the human soul. The novelist is seeking, in other words, to locate the various points of departure (from a normative state of nature) toward which we must try to return.

But Rousseau's typology, while programmatic, is also dynamic: a point which, as Paul de Man observes, has eluded readers as subtle as Starobinski.[5] Rousseau plots a convincing *process* of return by raising, defeating, and transfiguring our expectations. He quickly orients his readers to the fictional landmarks of *Julie*: a *petit-bourgeois* male tutor, an upper-class female pupil—and, connecting them, a fervent love; dividing them, a class-conscious, convention-bound society. Rousseau uses every device of the *tradition de refus*, every trope from the dialogue-of-body-and-soul literature, in order to make his readers comfortable in a familiar set of expectations. In their first exchanges of letters, Saint-Preux's passion is contrasted with Julie's tomblike adherence to the strictest social conventions. Even after she admits her own overwhelming passion, even after their love is consummated, Saint-Preux is forced to play the role of Julie's passionate shepherd. He is moved to ask all the traditional questions: "But where did this bitter alternative come from, and why render incompatible things which nature desired to reunite?" (p. 25).[6]

As soon as Rosseau has situated his readers among the *topoi*, he begins to complicate this traditional story of separated lovers. Social convention, in this novel, has sundered more than a well-matched couple. By the end of Book 1, Saint-Preux has become a representative of the Platonic realm of the Ideal; and Julie, a citizen of the Real world. Saint-Preux writes to Julie that "I was happy in my dream world [*dans mes chimères*]; my well-being left with it; what am I to be in the real world [*en réalité*]?" (p. 49), and the lovers debate incessantly over his impatience with all concern for appearances, with even the most hallowed social conventions. He sees nothing problematic in their love affair or its consummation and he views marriage as a mere ceremony—a matter of public relations (bk. 1, chap. 32). When Saint-Preux enters Parisian society "with a secret horror in this vast desert, the world" (p. 163), Julie berates him for failing to recognize that the phenomenal world contains many honest and worthwhile persons. And Rousseau's long note on this anti-social letter (bk. 2, chap. 14), while written ostensibly to express disagreement with Saint-Preux's viewpoint, instead serves to draw our attention to the nature and importance of Saint-Preux's remarks.

We are asked to see Saint-Preux in radically anti-social terms; for him, the Ideal can have no phenomenal embodiment, and he contemplates suicide (complete disembodiment) because engagement in the life of this world pollutes the purity of human nature and is the source of all our ills (bk. 3, chap. 21). Julie, on the other hand, is a this-worldly creature with social responsibilities and family ties. As Saint-Preux writes to her, contrasting their states of being:

> Yet, please observe, what a difference there is between your world and mine! I am not speaking of rank or fortune. . . . But you are surrounded by people whom you

cherish and who adore you: the attentions of a tender mother, and of a father who loves you as his only hope; the friendship of a cousin who seems to breathe only for your sake; a whole family which sees you as its adornment; an entire town proud to have witnessed your birth—all these occupy your emotions and divide them. And what remains for love is but a small part compared with that which is ravished from you by the demands of blood and friendship. But I, Julie—alas!—wandering, without family, virtually without a country, I have no one but you upon earth, and I am possessed of nothing save my love. (p. 41)

The marriage of these opposite types would be the most perfect union that ever existed; their separation is catastrophic: "O my Julie! What unforeseen catastrophes could have occurred, in the space of a week, to dissolve forever the world's sweetest bonds!" (p. 38). Saint-Preux writes Julie, in words loaded with philosophical baggage, that he needs her in order for his insubstantial dreams ("*des chimères*") to be made real ("*bien réaliser*") (p. 68). The separation of these lovers marks a division between Real and Ideal, the conventional and the romantic, the social and the anti-social, letter and spirit, body and mind. Cut off from Saint-Preux, Julie feels her self divided, her sensibility dissociated. She says her *heart* belongs to Saint-Preux but that she must allow her father to assign her *hand* to another suitor, and her secrecy about the liaison with Saint-Preux causes her to feel an interior/exterior, appearance/reality disjunction she has not known before (bk. 1, chap. 37). Saint-Preux sees such dissociations everywhere: in Paris, for example, he is horrified to find that a moral philosopher could be capable of writing one thing, acting in a second way, and having polite conversation in a third (p. 166).

If there is to be a *nostos*, in this context, the return will be from disunion to wholeness. Hegel would describe that process of return as follows:

The spiritual is distinguished from the natural . . . in the circumstance that it does not continue a mere stream of tendency, but sunders itself to self-realization. But this position of severed life has in its turn to be suppressed, and the spirit has by its own act to win its way to concord again. . . . The hour when man leaves the path of mere natural being marks the difference between him, a self-conscious agent, and the natural world.[7]

As Geoffrey Hartman summarizes this outlook: "the way back to Eden is via contraries."[8] But the way back is blocked by petty social conventions, thrown up specifically to maintain the unsatisfactory status quo. Lord Edouard sees the situation of Julie and his friend, Saint-Preux, in precisely these terms:

These two fair souls were made for each other by the hands of nature. In a serene union . . . , at liberty to exercise their talents and their virtues, they might have illumined the world by their example. Why should an absurd prejudice change the eternal course of nature and subvert the harmony of two thinking beings? (p. 134)

Since social prejudice prevents the reunion of spirit and matter, the spiritual principle is exiled from the world of men to a proto-Goethean, proto-Byronic life of romantic agony. Rousseau's Saint-Preux, like Byron's Manfred and Wordsworth's Wordsworth of a generation or two later, ascends into the purifying chill of the mountains to contemplate the corruption of the phenomenal realm (bk. 1, chap. 23). The only solution to this romantic dilemma—the obvious solution to the romantic formulation of the process of return—is for social convention to be thrown aside and the magnetic contraries to be fused.

This is not Rousseau's solution: in *La Nouvelle Héloïse*, social convention is enforced. However, this book is not a tragedy, despite its Romeo-and-Juliet apparatus. Baron D'Étange compels his daughter to marry the nobleman Wolmar and a predictable crisis follows—Julie contracts smallpox and Saint-Preux rushes to her bedside in order to share it. But Julie recovers, she marries Wolmar, and much to our surprise (and to the shock of the characters themselves), Julie is not only happier with Wolmar than with Saint-Preux, but their marriage brings about the return to wholeness that Rousseau's allegorical insinuations had led us to believe only her union with Saint-Preux could effect. Immediately after her wedding, Julie discovers with relief that her love for Saint-Preux is not an obstacle to her marital happiness, and the discovery brings her to embrace fully a conventional life at Clarens with her dispassionate husband. Julie no longer perceives the separation of herself and her lover as a division of Real and Ideal, or of matter and spirit. She writes to Saint-Preux that their premarital affair had been immoral and that it had in turn been the cause of much unclear thinking, of many self-serving formulations:

> If this confidence led us astray, nevertheless the principle on which it was founded is alone capable of restoring us to virtue. Is it not unworthy of a man to be always at variance with himself, to have one rule for his actions, another for his opinions [*ses sentiments*], to think as if he were without a body, to act as if he were without a soul . . . ? For my part, I find that one is best off with ancient principles [*nos anciennes maximes*], at least when they are not confined to idle speculation [*de vaines spéculations*]. (p. 267)

Julie now believes that she and Saint-Preux could have entered upon an illicit love-affair only after each had become a divided personality. Each, she believes, has behaved as if he were soulless and reasoned as if he were bodiless.

The remedy Julie prescribes for this dissociation is a return to "*nos anciennes maximes*"—a phrase which refers to the tried-and-true clichés of European culture, but which also may refer to the precepts of those non-Socratic ancients who declined to engage in "*vaines spéculations.*" (An early English-language version of *Julie*, prepared not long after Rousseau's death, translates this phrase as "the maxims of the ancients.")[9] She recommends, in other words, a return to first principles.

More emphatically, Julie urges a reinvigoration of the principles and practices of Christianity. She discovers that her problem all along has been of a religious nature—that the severest disjunction in her life has been that between spirit and letter, in the specifically Christian sense. Following her wedding, Julie swears she will keep the laws of marital chastity imposed by her father's God and, because of that oath, she is brought to her great realization:

> After this short prayer, the first I ever made with true devotion, I found myself confirmed in my resolutions. It seemed so easy and so agreeable to follow them that I clearly perceived where I must look for that power which I need in order to resist my own inclinations, and which I could not find within myself. . . . I had never been entirely without religion; but perhaps I had better been wholly so than to have had an external and mechanical one, which satisfied the conscience without affecting the heart: one which was confined to set forms and which taught me to believe in God at stated hours, in order not to think of Him at any other time. Scrupulously tied to public worship, I nevertheless drew nothing from it for the living [*pour la pratique*] of my life. . . . I had one set of principles for belief and another for behavior [*j'avais des maximes pour croire et d'autres pour agir*]; I forgot in one place what I thought in the other; I was a devotee in church and a philosopher at home. Alas! I was nothing anywhere; my prayers were but words, my reasoning sophistry; and the only light I followed was the false glimmer of wandering flames, which guided me to perdition. (p. 263)

Julie causally relates the spirit/letter dissociation to the far more dangerous split between behavior ("*agir*") and belief ("*croire*"). If Julie is a fallen woman, that is because, first, she has separated public religion from heart-religion and, next, has assumed a related dichotomy between the truths of revelation and the truths of reason. She suggests to Saint-Preux that, like herself, he retire from speculative thinking, presumably because, by definition, self-analytical detachment alienates the thinker from his behavior and results in the kind of divided sensibility that conduces to immoral action. Julie's concern is, above all, for an appropriate mode of behavior. In the typology of *La Nouvelle Héloïse*, Julie's return is "ethical" and, in the connection she emphasizes between sophistical reasoning and unethical behavior, her type of return is conscientiously traditional. The association of learning and corruption is an echo of Genesis 3, and Rousseau frequently exploits the parallel. Saint-Preux is Julie's teacher (she calls him her "*philosophe*") and his subjects of instruction include both, cultural and carnal knowledge. Early in the novel, Julie writes her cousin Claire that she fears, with such a teacher, "to become too wise" (p. 19). Her loss of sexual innocence is presented, metaphorically, as a fall: "I have fallen" she writes to Claire, "into the abyss of infamy from which a girl can never return" (p. 59).

Julie is wrong about the impossibility of reascending to virtue: Rousseau evidently agrees with St. Augustine that a fall is necessarily part of a larger economy of return. In the *Enchiridion*, Augustine argues that the difference between Adam's state in Paradise and man's future state is that between imperfect innocence (goodness, accompanied by the inclination and power to will evil) and perfect righteousness (goodness, without either the desire or the freedom to sin). "God's arrangement," Augustine writes, was to show "how much better" the latter state is than the former—to show why the prodigal son, upon his return, is superior to his brethren.[10] Julie's history follows Augustine's account of a human history shaped by the principle of *felix culpa*. She begins in innocence but, possessing the inclination and freedom to do so, she commits a moral error. As a result, she becomes a "slave to sin" (both Augustine's term and Julie's) for, in the period after the pleasure of indulgence has evaporated, turpitude becomes a mere compulsion.[11] In describing this phenomenon, Julie describes the state of Fallen Man:

That happy time is no more: alas! it can never return.
... Compare that charming condition with our present
situation: such agitation! such terror! what deadly fears!
These extremes of feeling have lost their former sweetness. (p. 63)

In this fallen state, every form of reasoning is entirely cor-
rupt; any reasoned attempt at restoration can only make matters worse. Rousseau departs Geneva, in Book 2 of the *Confessions*, with plans to improve his prospects, but matters worsen
consistently. He discovers, to his great surprise, that only in
Paris, the capital of corruption, can he find any evidence of
human sensitivity or virtue.[12] He concludes that men seek to
improve their lot by rationalizing, formulizing, or perfecting
their condition when, in fact, man can ascend only by following the course in which his (corrupted) nature leads. Rousseau
writes of his *Discours sur l'inégalité*:

I demolished the petty lies of mankind; I dared to strip
man's nature naked, to follow the progress of time, and
trace the things which have distorted it; and by comparing
man as he had made himself with man as he is by nature
I showed him in his pretended perfection the true source
of his misery.[13]

In descent there is ascent. This principle antedates Dante's
downward-pointing, upward-moving Inferno, and it informs
both the ideology of *felix culpa* and Julie's ethical type of
return. Julie descends until she reaches the bottom. Her slavery
to sin becomes increasingly complete until, at last, she collapses into a near-fatal illness: as in the underworld-journey
myths, she symbolically dies to be spiritually reborn. Following an act of divine grace (the sacrament of marriage), Julie's
rehabilitation is sealed by her submission to divine law. Through
the process of descent, she arrives at a state of virtue superior
to virginity, for from this new state she cannot fall. The urge
to sin has been purged from her nature and the memory of

her fallen past guarantees the risen innocence of her present and future:

> I should think that a soul, once corrupted, would remain so forever and never recover by itself. . . . [But] When all its habits are destroyed and all its passions modified . . . , it sometimes resumes its primitive character and becomes like a new being recently transformed by the hands of nature. Then the recollection of its former unworthiness can serve as a preservative against relapse. (pp. 268–69)

The process of descent is the process of return. As Hegel writes of Adam's fall and the possibility of restoration: "the hand that inflicts the wound is also the hand which heals it."[14] Or as Julie writes to Saint-Preux: "Ah! if only my faults could produce the means of their own cure! . . . all I can say of this at present is that love, which was the occasion of our misfortunes, ought to furnish us with relief" (p. 66).

The "ethical" process of return is theodicean, in the sense in which Pater's reading of history is an exercise in theodicy.[15] Julie tends to use words like *carrière* and *progrès* to describe her relation with Saint-Preux—and, like Pater, she emphasizes the process as process because, by viewing individual events as necessary parts of a necessary whole, she is able to justify the gravest mistakes in behavior and the worst afflictions of life. On her deathbed, Julie tells the local clergyman that what matters in the end is not the moment of the end but the whole pattern of the life. She offers that pattern up to heaven and dispenses with last-minute acts of contrition: "I offer up my entire life, full of sins and faults. . . ." (p. 545). The *telos*—the return—is important, yet it is not the point for Julie; more important is the process, the whole entelechy, of falling and returning. But if Rousseau's own view is process-oriented and theodicean, he earns his optimism with greater labor. As a foil to Julie's theodicean perspective, Rousseau poses Saint-Preux's pessimistic—or Burckhardtian—outlook, which cares only for first and final causes. Saint-Preux regards the innocence of his past as something precious, lost, and painfully irrecoverable:

> O time, never to return! time forever past, source of eternal regrets! pleasures, transports, sweet ecstasies, delicious moments, celestial raptures! my loves, my only loves, the honor and charm of my life! farewell forever. (p. 272)

Julie believes that, in mourning for an irretrievable past, Saint-Preux is resisting a natural process. As late as Book 6, she writes that he has terminated his "career" prematurely, that the process of return will not have finished with him until he has married her cousin Claire (bk. 6, chap. 6).

Saint-Preux does not care, much, for process. For him, the nature of things is a static given, and he trusts both in his perception of that nature and in his concepts or nomenclature for defining it: in other words, Saint-Preux is a *philosophe*, despite his objections to contemporary philosophy and his preference for *exempla* over analytical categories. He may be, in fact, a somewhat critical self-portrait of Rousseau. Saint-Preux's social class and profession, his objections to the life of cities (especially Paris), his idealistic theories about friendship, and his readiness to indict social convention for the evils that beset himself and mankind—all these point to a self-conscious parallel between character and creator. Perhaps Rousseau is correcting some of his own views—or, more likely, correcting his critics' understanding of them—in his treatment of Saint-Preux as the "pupil" of Julie. In either case, the salient word is *correcting*. Saint-Preux's perceptions undergo a radical alteration during the course of the novel, and the type of return which his story embodies is best termed "epistemic." Saint-Preux's epistemic return is in certain ways opposed to Julie's ethical type. The ethical return is theodicean; the epistemic, Burckhardtian. The ethical type is traditional (its roots are in underworld-journey mythology and in Augustinian doctrine), while the epistemic is rarely dealt with, at least in European literature and philosophy. In the ethical type, the subject (Julie) at last will relinquish any perception that nourishes an inappropriate mode of behavior; in the epistemic, the subject is willing to alter his behavior (Saint-Preux exiles himself from Julie's vicinity) but clings tenaciously to his mode of perceiving events.

Yet the ethical and the epistemic types of return are as closely connected as Julie and Saint-Preux themselves. They share a point of departure—the love-affair, or "fall"—and also the initial perception that social convention is obstructing the union of Real and Ideal. Further, Julie's ethical transformation triggers Saint-Preux's own, more time-consuming process of return. Her happy marriage to Wolmar demands a response from Saint-Preux at the level of perception. If Saint-Preux's appraisal of events and personalities had been correct, then Julie ought to be inconsolable at losing him, her husband ought to be oppressive and her married life either nightmarish or empty. None of this has come to pass and Saint-Preux remains a mightily confused young man for several hundred pages. Saint-Preux's misery—and he is, by this time, suicidal— has a very curious origin: it derives from his rejection of eight-eenth-century class structure and marriage taboos. Saint-Preux is a *philosophe* and, like most skeptical, ironic intellectuals, he has lost his respect for the conventional world because of its hypocrisies. Conventional man mouths clichéd versions of the truth and, at best, lives a parody of the Ideal: his speech and behavior, in effect, cleave Real from Ideal. Horrified by the cold formulations that conventional man substitutes for the eternal flame, the intellectual rejects conventional for-mulations and institutions.

Saint-Preux's letters from Paris exhibit evidence that his social intercourse is entirely determined by this mechanism of perception. He writes to Julie that the Parisians admire and discuss Homer, as intelligent people should, but that they admire him as connoisseurs or pedants rather than as pas-sionate readers (bk. 2, chap. 17). He feels, in general, that the conventional men and women of Paris demean important ideas by discussing them in mechanical and insincere ways; he seems to assume that clichés subvert and substitute for the idealities they name or misname (bk. 2, chap. 14). Clichés may keep the Ideal in front of us, but at the same time they keep the Ideal from penetrating us:

> I have never before heard such things said: *You may count on my help; my credit, my purse, my resources are at your disposal.* If all this were sincere and taken literally [*pris au mot*], there would not be a nation less attached to property; a commonwealth of possessions would be virtually established: with the richest offering ceaselessly and the poorest always accepting, both would naturally come to the same level. Sparta itself had a division of property less equitable than that which would obtain in Paris. (p. 164)

Saint-Preux equates the Real world (Paris) with clichéd social formulations, and the Ideal (Sparta) with a lost state of nature that those formulations have replaced. Yet the most insincere clichés of modern Paris, *"pris au mot,"* would transform that city into ancient Sparta.

To this assertion, there are a pair of possible responses: that we ought to take Paris at its word, or that we must reject Paris for not being Sparta. A prefigurative Jacob Burckhardt, Saint-Preux takes the latter option, and with disastrous consequences for his morality. His wholesale dismissal of the social order makes inevitable a dismissal of worthwhile ethical principles that happen to find expression in contemporary clichés. Debauchery follows, and the ethicist of this novel, Julie, expends considerable energy in disabusing Saint-Preux of his faulty perception. She responds vehemently to a letter from Saint-Preux in which he tries to justify his moral lapses by accusing the Parisians of shallowness and of Ideal-killing hypocrisy:

> I have tried to suppress the indignation which these maxims inspired in me, in order to discuss them calmly with you. . . . Where are we to look for sane reasoning if not from Him who is its source? and what shall we think of those who, devoted to the ruin of mankind, pervert the sacred flame that He gave to them for guidance? Let us

defy this philosophy of words; let us defy the false virtue
that saps all true virtues and attempts to justify every vice
in order to authorize their possession. (p. 266)

The point which Saint-Preux has missed is that, if the Real
and the Ideal are one, no social convention or cliché can
possibly divide them; hypocrisy can do no worse than obscure
the fact of their perpetual union. "Real" and "Ideal" are merely
analytic categories—sometimes more, and sometimes less, useful. But, as a man whose life is devoted to analytical thinking,
Saint-Preux has confused these analytic or linguistic constructs
with actual states of affairs. His intellectual error derives from
his being an intellectual: Lord Edouard tells Saint-Preux that
his inclination toward speculative analysis and skepticism is
a kind of emotion, endemic to youth, rather than a tool of
the mature truth-seeker (bk. 5, chap. 1). The Real and the Ideal
do not need unifying, because they possess no objective existence: Saint-Preux's formulation, all along, has been a misperception—a kind of linguistic problem. Julie accuses both
Saint-Preux and herself of having played dangerous linguistic
games. They had used the cliché-word *vertu* to mask a host
of vices:

> We have always sensed that, without virtue, there is noth-
> ing; but consider carefully whether this word *virtue*, taken
> in too abstract a sense, has not more flash to it than
> solidity, and whether it is not a term of parade, more
> calculated to dazzle others than to satisfy ourselves. I
> shudder when I reflect that people who harbored adultery
> at the bottom of their hearts should dare to speak of
> virtue. (p. 277)

Ironically, while Saint-Preux is the last to embrace the importance of language to perception, he is the first to notice its
linguistic nature. He notes that, taken literally ("*pris au mot*"),
the verbal clichés of Paris enshrine the loftiest ideals of humanity (bk. 2, chap. 14). Yet Saint-Preux does not conclude
from that observation that the return to ultimacy (from conventionality) might be, at root, a linguistic question.

In her discourse on the word *vertu*, Julie urges him on to that conclusion, for she believes that an epistemic revolution of that order would return Saint-Preux to psychological health:

> Do you realize what this term, so respectable and so profaned, meant to us while we engaged in a criminal commerce? This frantic love, by which we were both inflamed, disguised its transports as religious ecstasies— in order to render them dearer to us and to abuse us the longer. . . . It is time for this illusion to cease; it is time to return from a deviation that has carried us too far astray [*il est temps de revenir d'un trop long égarement*]. My friend, this return will not be difficult. . . . Return to the foundation of your conscience. (pp. 277–78)

Julie and Wolmar invite Saint-Preux to their home at Clarens where, by force of example, they demonstrate that the return to authenticity, from concept or cliché, is merely a problem of etymology. M. and Mme. de Wolmar have traced the roots of marriage back to a natural, even primordial institution, and by living in consonance with its original meaning, they redeem the convention for Saint-Preux. Of that convention in its contemporary state, Saint-Preux had written: "It seems that the whole order of natural sentiments is here reversed. . . . Even love . . . is no less denatured [*denaturé*] than marriage" (pp. 193–94). At Clarens, however, he perceives a natural marriage, yet it is to the eye perfectly indistinguishable from the most cliché-ridden of bourgeois marriages. Julie herself describes life with her husband in the most temperate terms—though at the same time she equates their relationship with "the happy revolution" that has so completely altered the life of everyone around her:

> The sentiment which joins us is not at all the blinding transport of impassioned hearts, but the invariable and constant attachment of two honest and reasonable persons, who, destined to pass the rest of their days together, are content with their lot. . . . We are each made exactly for the other; he instructs me and I enliven him. . . . Even

his slightly advanced age redounds to our common advantage: for, with the passion that was tormenting me, it is certain that had he been younger I should have married him with more pain, and my excessive repugnance might have prevented the happy revolution I have experienced. (pp. 275–76)

Julie and Wolmar enjoy a kind of revolutionary normalcy. The ultimate is latent in all time-honored institutions, however debased they may have become, but ultimacy is manifest only to the perceptual apparatus of the initiated beholder. Julie seems from the start to have possessed an innate genius for perceiving ultimacy in the quotidian and for making the profound appear commonplace (bk. 1, chap. 21). But only the fullest repudiation of a convention, an institution, or a cliché can bring one to feel the force of its meaning or to locate its radical root in human nature. Julie and Saint-Preux rejected and violated the social conventions of premarital chastity and class separation; their stance led Saint-Preux to degradation and nearly to suicide, as it brought Julie to the edge of despair and her parents to emotional and physical extremity. It is only after this initiation of negation that Rousseau's characters realize that the opposite of conventionality is neither nature nor ultimacy, but the Void.

A stance against convention alienates one from nature, since a convention is nothing but a traditional formula for a natural phenomenon. Saint-Preux frets about the overdone and, to him, unattractive cosmetics of Parisian ladies, until he recalls the obvious: that beneath the elaboration which conventionality requires, the natural woman—the *Ding-an-sich*—endures (bk. 2, chap. 21). On the same principle, Saint-Preux later endorses Julie's marriage; he writes a series of very long letters to Lord Edouard, eulogizing the Wolmar household, and he concludes even that he and Julie are happier as friends than as lovers. In a letter to Claire, Saint-Preux heralds the "epoch of my return" (p. 464), and his return is both metaphoric and literal. He has resolved the Real/Ideal problem, as he originally had aspired to do, though not by marrying Julie:

his resolution is at the epistemic level. On the other hand, Saint-Preux and Julie are once again together and under one roof. Wolmar has invited his wife's former tutor to instruct her sons and live in her house. As Harry Monchensey, of Eliot's *Family Reunion*, says of a similar return: "Everything is true in another sense."[16]

The reunion of Julie and Saint-Preux, the disgrace of the Real/Ideal distinction, and the rehabilitation of Julie are all enacted under the auspices of M. de Wolmar. Julie's husband is not as developed a character as either of the young lovers, but his position in *La Nouvelle Héloïse* is pivotal—and, like Rousseau's hero and heroine, he undergoes a species of return. Also like Saint-Preux and Julie, Wolmar is an intellectual of sorts—indeed, his is the only type of return in the novel that is largely "of the intellect." Wolmar's behavior always has been impeccable; his ethics are Christian and he attends church regularly. Nor are his *égarement* and *retour* precisely a matter of nomenclature or perception. Wolmar's process of return is "metaphysical"; it is specifically a question of belief. If Saint-Preux is an intellectual on the model of Rousseau, then Wolmar may be a *philosophe* on the model of Diderot: Wolmar is a classic Enlightenment skeptic. Brought up in the Greek church, he finds its doctrine imbecilic and contrary to reason. On investigation, he finds the Roman rite no less contemptible—a jargon of words without meanings (bk. 5, chap. 5). Wolmar is a metaphysician—he is devoted to the truth—and because Christianity has in some respects distorted the truth, he ceases to be a Christian. Wolmar attempted a return to religion before meeting Julie. He has traveled the road from atheism to agnosticism and has become a practicing (though not a believing) Christian. He has come as far as reason can bring a man toward belief but, as Saint-Preux writes to Lord Edouard, "when at last he came amongst Christians, he had arrived too late; his faith had already been closed to the truth, his reason was no longer open to certainty. . . ." (p. 446).

Consciousness, reason, and will are not the final means of return from skepticism to certitude. For Rousseau, any type of return is a natural, even an unconscious, process—and metaphysical truth is inaccessible to any system of inquiry as artificial as Aristotelian logic. In searching consciously for a religious outlet, Wolmar has reached an intellectual cul-de-sac: reason has led him to a hypocritical double life of conventional, Christian-like behavior and radically disruptive unbelief. So far from effecting a return, reason has led Wolmar to reproduce, in the structure of his own life, the Real/Ideal, exterior/interior disjunction against which the other characters' processes of return were reactions. At the novel's conclusion, Wolmar is at the point of full conversion, but not because of any discovery of logic. With breathtaking equanimity ("My return to God calms my soul") (p. 553), Julie dies her martyr's death—and her husband is impressed by the *telos* of the life of faith. The process of return, for both the epistemic and metaphysical varieties, is tied to the ethical (or "behavioral") type. Just as the Wolmars' exemplary marriage was the catalyst for Saint-Preux's epistemic return, so Julie's exemplary death helps M. de Wolmar to transcend his metaphysical doubts. For Rousseau, behavior has primacy over intellection.[17] It is the analysis of, and consequent alienation from, appropriate behavior that inaugurates the process of return. On the other hand, an exemplary mode of behavior can both correct erroneous perceptions and body forth (or even reveal) metaphysical truths.

But perhaps "exemplary" is not the proper word. The Wolmars' marriage and Julie's "return to God" are, in Rousseau's vocabulary, not so much exemplary as natural—or, in a diction more useful for our purposes, we might say that the various types of return are "normative." The three basic types that pertain to individuals—the ethical, the epistemic, and the metaphysical—are all roads to a single place; all are means of working-through to a place normatively prescribed. These are not necessarily returns to the place from which one began, though an element of this kind is always present. (Saint-Preux, for example, returns to Julie's house in the same tutorial capacity in which her father originally had brought him there.) Nor is the return necessarily to a place one has known or to a condition one has experienced, and it is never precisely to the place or condition one has consciously expected or desired. Yet the three main characters of *La Nouvelle Héloïse*, beginning in very different circumstances and with divergent aspirations, end by living at the same address in a community of shared values.

It is toward this fourth, communal type of return—which we may call "social," "cultural," or even "political"—that the three psychological types have inexorably led. Hence, the issue of cultural versus psychological types of return is something of a non-question. Anita Brookner would have it that Rousseau (and, one extrapolates, subsequent *nostos* ideologists) are essentially psychosomatic theorists, projecting their own malaise onto social history; Lionel Gossman argues that Rousseau imposed categories, which he had drawn from his study of social history, onto the individual psyche.[18] But, to Rousseau, the cultural/psychological dichotomy was no more allowable than the Real/Ideal distinction. The author of the *Contrat social* believed that the psyche was socially conditioned but, as *Julie* demonstrates, he also believed that a social order is the creation of the psyches that live within it.

The social order of Clarens is defined by its citizens and, more particularly, by the experience of *égarement* and *retour* that its leading citizens share. The life of Clarens embodies all that Julie, her husband, and her former lover have learned *en route*. Like the Wolmar marriage, the house is simple and conventional: unornamented and functional, Clarens in Saint-Preux's presentation (bk. 4, chap. 10) recalls Ben Jonson's low-key panegyric on Penshurst or Marvell's on Appleton House. Everywhere the ultimate is conventional and the conventional, ultimate. Saint-Preux finds all the details of organization "simple and sublime" (p. 350), and his detailed letters to Lord Edouard amount to a prescription for normative human life. The normative social order of *Julie* consists in a happy, fulfilling marriage, productive of offspring; a small number of extremely close friends and relatives; a well-run household, partly hierarchical and partly meritocratic; a pastoral economy; a love of nature, learning, and the arts; and a tough-minded, stripped-down Christianity. It is to this normative social life that all human beings, having strayed, must return. The estate includes only one, somewhat unconventional feature, but it clearly marks Clarens as the place of return *par excellence*. Julie has conspired with nature to create a perfect, hidden orchard at the heart of the estate. Saint-Preux calls it "the end of the world" (p. 353)—and, in a social order whose every mundane detail is meant to embody or mediate the ultimate, Julie's *sanctum sanctorum* signifies the presence of unmediated, apocalyptic ultimacy. Clarens is a post-Fall culture but its existence repeals the Fall, and at its core is a new, man-made Garden of Eden.

Moreover, the Wolmars have organized life so that no future fall will be possible, so that the generations brought up at Clarens will never need to endure the process of return which caused their progenitors such intense suffering. The individual *égarements* of Julie, Saint-Preux, and Wolmar share a common impetus: their reaction against a societal *égarement*. The hypocrisies and clichés which obscure, or denature, the natural roots of traditional institutions—and the false dualisms which camouflage, or misrepresent, the simple facts of human life—have no place at Clarens. The children of Julie and Claire will have no cause for rancor against the social order and will feel no urge to depart from the standards society inculcates. They will reason as persons with bodies and feel as persons with minds. Saint-Preux has even developed a special system of education to ensure that none of his charges will embark on the perilous journey from normative to unnatural behavior, perception, or belief (bk. 5, chap. 8). As already noted, Rousseau identified the "message" of *Julie* with that of *Émile*, his utopian educational program, and Saint-Preux's system has much in common with it.[19] *Émile* presents a history of human nature (similar to that in Rousseau's second discourse) that aims to demonstrate how denatured elements enter human habits, concepts, and institutions. And he undertakes this feat in order to show that human corruption has origins—that the social order need not be contrary to the natural order.

In *Émile*, the state of innocence, pre-*égarement*, is associated with nature, and the state of fallen corruption with the social order. The transition from the first state to the second is marked by disapproving self-reflection, analytic skepticism, and experimentation. Or, as Saint-Preux describes that transition in *Julie*: "Nature has done the best that is possible; but we would do better, and so spoil all" (p. 462). For Rousseau, an inherent contradiction exists between nature and society, between stages one and two in the process of return, but this does not imply that stage three could or should be a return to the conditions of prehistory. On the contrary, stage three (the return) is meant to resolve the nature/culture contradiction and to make it possible for natural man to live in society. In stage one, unsocial natural man lives in a state of nature; in stage two, denatured social man lives in a state of society; and in the third stage, as Roger Masters observes, natural man "lives *in* civil society, but . . . is not *of* civil society."[20] This third state is the most desirable of the three—more desirable even than the state of natural innocence—because only in the social state can one human being love another, and because it is necessary to pass through the stage of skepticism and analysis in order to abdicate freely the exercise of skepticism and analysis in behaviorial and ethical matters. At the commencement of stage three, social man (or, as Nietzsche will call him, "theoretical man") re-establishes "all the requirements [*les devoirs*] of natural law,"[21] but now on the basis of independent reflection and long contrary experience. The way back to nature is through civilization—or, in our own terms, the first step toward fully normative behavior, perception, belief, and social order is the departure from them.

Rousseau appears to have written *La Nouvelle Héloïse* to embody this principle at every level, including the aesthetic-generic. *Julie* has a very singular form, and it suggests the contours of a fifth type of return: the "aesthetic" or "formal." To class *La Nouvelle Héloïse* generically requires a good many descriptive terms. Rousseau has confronted his reader with an epistolary, novelistic, bourgeois rendition of the classical pastoral form. In the bourgeois genre of *Clarissa*, Rousseau perceived elements of the aristocratic genre of *Daphnis and*

Chloe (or more immediately, of *L'Astrée*)—and this perception was an imaginative act parallel to Saint-Preux's observation that, taken at its word, Paris would instantaneously become Sparta. As we shall see later, in relation to the epic theory of the novel, a return to the most ancient forms can be effected only by "epiphanizing" the most contemporary. Rousseau's choice of the epistolary mode for his novel points a similar moral. Until the mid-eighteenth century, most novels had had a reliable narrative point of view, and the novel was therefore a relatively "objective" genre. The epistolary mode, on the other hand, permits no vision of events external to the characters' own and consequently engenders the feeling of a less mediated emotional experience. Like Julie's magical orchard at conventional Clarens, the psychological intensity of the epistolary mode infuses the objective world of the novel with subjective energy. The ultimate is attained by exploding the idea of the conventional. Thus we arrive at an intensely charged kind of objectivity, an exceedingly modern type of classicism, and a highly sophisticated sort of primitivism. In a time when many Europeans were beginning to react against their own hyper-sophistication, Rousseau recognized that every convention and every culture contains its own alternative. Even for the Greeks, the pastoral genre, in which characters flee from the *polis* to the green world, was a culture-bound means of transcending culture and a conventional means of overcoming conventionality.[22]

The process of return, of whatever type, is the only means of transportation from convention and culture to their self-contained alternatives. This is so, not because a convention exists at point A in space or time and its alternative at point Z. Rather it is necessary for an individual or a society to traverse the *psychological* distance from A to Z—for only from the privileged position of Z is it possible to understand, having come full circle with A, that unsavory point A and alluring point Z are identical. Crossing this psychological terrain, for an individual or a society, is a process which unfolds in time. The process is, by definition, historical or, more precisely, it is a matter of historical explanation. The story (*l'his-*

toire) that each character in *Julie* tells about his life—and, in the epistolary mode, each character does exactly that—is an interpretive rehearsal of events. Julie, Wolmar, and Saint-Preux struggle to make sense of their lives, to draw out of the events of life a controlling pattern, and each is forced by new data to discard a number of false or partial interpretations along the way. The initiate, whether individual or communal, has reached the end of the process when he, she, or they arrive at an interpretive device which serves to integrate all the previous, discarded interpretations into one "processive" explanation. That is to say, the process of return is over when one recognizes it as a process of return. It is not until Saint-Preux realizes that the conventional and the ultimate are one—not until he has traversed the route from psychological point *A* to psychological point *Z* and recognized he has come full circle—that he attains and integrates his original aims: to unite the Real and the Ideal, and to live his life in company with Julie.

Rousseau thought that human personality could only be defined in this "processive" mode. As Roger Masters writes, in his lucid reading of *Émile*:

> Whatever the philosophical merits of Rousseau's approach, it poses an immediate problem of great theoretical significance: a man, at the beginning of his development (i.e., at birth) is not truly human. Indeed, Rousseau himself defined education broadly as that which provided "everything that we do not have at our birth and which we need when grown." . . . Hence we are faced with a fundamental question: which faculties and attributes of the human adult, although lacking in the child, are acquisitions which are naturally necessary?
>
> One might be tempted to restate the question more simply: what is man? But Rousseau's formulation of this question is different from that of most previous philosophers; it would be more accurate to say: what does man naturally become?[23]

If a man is not truly human at birth, he cannot return to his origins without loss of his most essential identity. "Process of return," then, may be a slight misnomer—the process is actually one of growth, dislocation, and reintegration. The self must reintegrate into its current personality what can be retrieved of its origins and of the various stages of its growth. This formulation of Rousseau's was a revolutionary one for philosophical psychology (its line of influence reaches Freud), but its application to the philosophy of history has had an even more eventful development. In his *Essai sur l'origine des langues*, for instance, Rousseau conjectures that music, as the modern European knows it, descends from the corruption of some more direct and lively expression. But, as Lionel Gossman shows, Rousseau does not argue that we should re-create the more primitive type of expression; he argues instead that we should combine the technical advances of modern music with the vigor and simplicity of the ur-music.[24] The goal of any self, whether individual or cultural, is to integrate the various, and usually contradictory, parts of its processive personality. To the other five types of return, there clearly needs to be added a sixth: the historical. Rousseau often is described as the first citizen of modern history. It is certain that the writing of modern history begins with Rousseau's perception of a cultural personality as the unfolding of a self through time.

· III ·

Classicism, an Historical Explanation

Is Edith, in spite of her romantic past, pursuing stead-
ily some hidden purpose of her own? Are her migra-
tions and eccentricities the sign of some unguessed
consistency?
T. S. Eliot, "Eeldrop and Appleplex"

THE WRITING of modern cultural history begins with the opposition of the terms "romanticism" and "classicism." In its
earliest uses, "romanticism vs. classicism" was less a slogan
than the title of a story—the name appended to an explanation
of historical events. Friedrich Schlegel was perhaps the inven-
tor of the romantic/classic terminology, and late in his career,
he undertook to rewrite, with his youthful invention in mind,
the story of literature and philosophy. Schlegel's *Lectures on
the History of Ancient and Modern Literature* (1832), like
Rousseau's essays, depict Western culture as a process of growth,
dislocation, and reintegration or return. The reintegration,
Schlegel wrote, would occur when Europeans at last came to
accept the paradox that romanticism—Europe's revolutionary
ideology—"opens up a perspective upon an infinitely increas-
ing classicism" and that "the core of the Romantic imagination . . . tends toward antiquity in spirit and even in kind, as
if there were to be a return to it."[1]

For Schlegel, intellectual and cultural history, especially that
of the modern centuries, seemed a parade of misconceived
antinomies or alternatives, and he proposed romanticism/clas-
sicism as its summary statement. Dislocations followed invariably on distinctions: church and state, science and religion,
Papist and Protestant, reason and intuition, nature and society, liberal and conservative, subject and object, *noumena* and

phenomena, Hebraism and Hellenism, art and life. Every thesis was met immediately with its antithesis but, Schlegel believed, a transcendent synthesis was by no means inevitable
and, in the historical process, vast periods of time could elapse
in awaiting its advent. Schlegel, who introduced the term "irony"
into modern criticism, thought that an opposition such as
"romanticism vs. classicism" ultimately must comprise a dynamic whole, that romanticism would one day be seen for the
classicism it was. But Schlegel also believed that it was impossible, at the beginning of the nineteenth century, to transcend the romanticism/classicism opposition: the cultural personality was still unfolding; the process of reintegration had
not yet come full circle.[2] A dialectic of this kind, Schlegel
thought, needs to be played out in the creative medium of
historical chaos.

The terms "romantic" and "classic" began in the confusion
to which they are sometimes said to descend—there never has
been the slightest agreement concerning their definition. Since
the beginning, the battle between "romantics" and "classicists" has been waged near the frontiers of burlesque. The
Lake Poets loved Dryden; J.-A.-D. Ingres, president of the
French Academy, painted some of the nineteenth century's
lushest odalisques; the author of *Young Werther* diagnosed
romanticism as a disease. By the early twentieth century, the
romantic/classical argument moved yet one step closer to the
absurd when artists obviously deriving from the symbolist-
romantic camp took up the classicist banner. Of these, perhaps
T. S. Eliot best understood the irony of professing classicism
in the post-symbolist ambience. When Old Possum described
his "general point of view" as "classicist in literature, royalist
in politics, and anglo-catholic in religion," he may have hoped
we would recall Sainte-Beuve's definition of Restoration romanticism as royalism in politics, Catholicism in religion, and
Platonism in love.[3]

During the last four decades, more and more critics have
perceived these ironies and have reacted sharply against the
tactical revision of literary history in which Eliot, Pound, Hulme,
and lesser theoreticians of classicism engaged. Critics have

reacted so sharply, in fact, that the very notion of a modernist classicism has been ruled out almost entirely. The whole of the last two hundred years is coming to be seen as (in the larger sense) symbolist. M. H. Abrams has traced the roots of the romantic aesthetic to certain eighteenth-century neo-classicists, while Edmund Wilson, Northrop Frye, and Donald Davie have examined the twentieth-century "school of classicism" and have pronounced it a second wave of symbolism. Several recent critics—Harold Bloom, Paul de Man, and Geoffrey Hartman among them—have brought this trend a stage further: modernism not only is derivative of romanticism but also is inferior to it. The "Yale school" may be the revenge of Wordsworth and Shelley on the man who called them "palpitating Narcissi," but Eliot's anti-romantic excesses have met with a bit more than poetic justice. The problem for modernist scholarship is that, for many years, criticism has been to a degree fixated on the rise, continuity, and import of romantic phenomena—and there have been consequent distortions of European literary and cultural history, in both content and form. "The modern," to judge by the anthologies, now begins with Kant and Blake, rather than Erasmus and Petrarch; with the French Revolution, not the Italian classical renascence. Thus, the world we inhabit is, by definition, vernacular and secular, and the reputation of modernists like T. S. Eliot is necessarily held hostage to this "post-modernist" attempt to redefine modernity.

But the revaluation of Eliot (and of modernism) has been a necessary corrective, and, on the whole, it has been tempered with insightful caveats. Thus, Davie:

> it is commonly held that he [Eliot] has . . . re-established continuity with the poetry of the seventeenth and eighteenth centuries. And he really has done so—but only in relatively superficial ways.[4]

and Frye:

> Nor did it [the anti-romantic movement] return to the older construct [of metaphysical imagery], though Eliot,

by sticking close to Dante and by deprecating the importance of the prophetic element in art, gives some illusion of doing so.[5]

and Wilson:

I have noted the similarity between the English seventeenth-century poets and the French nineteenth-century Symbolists. The poetry of T. S. Eliot has . . . brought together these two traditions.[6]

Each critic feels the need to qualify. Yes, admit Frye and Davie, Eliot appears to have restored something of the classical standards of eighteenth-century England or of thirteenth-century Florence. Yes, Wilson concludes, Eliot is a symbolist romantic, but is it not odd how similar Renaissance English poetry is to that of symbolist romanticism?

Wilson does not flesh out his observation but it is nonetheless an acute one: he seems to suggest, as Eliot himself had suggested, that what the modernists inherited, selectively, from the symbolists was "classical" in origin. The notion seems strange—but, perhaps, only because the rhetoric of the anti-romantic movements has trained us to consider romanticism and classicism as polar opposites. The great modernists themselves declined to do so. Eliot once admitted, in a published letter, that Charles Maurras, one of his favorite classicists, was in fact a romantic, but then went on to question whether "the terms 'romantic' and 'classic' are mutually exclusive and . . . antithetical."[7] In 1923, Eliot summarized his view of the classical as follows: " 'classicism' is not an alternative to 'romanticism,' as political parties . . . on a 'turn-the-rascal-out' platform. It is a goal toward which all good literature strives, so far as it is good, according to the possibilities of its time and place."[8] And this position was not merely the product of Eliot's youthful enthusiasm for paradox. Two years before his death, Eliot still approved as "valid" his view of 1933 that, for example, Wordsworth expressed in certain ways a classicism more authentic than the neoclassicists'.[9] Post-romantic modernism, in his view, approached the essence of the classical even more closely. In his notes for a 1916 extension lecture, Eliot states that "The beginning of the twentieth century has witnessed a return to the ideals of classicism,"[10] and in a *New Criterion* editorial of a decade later, he writes that "the modern tendency is toward something, which, for want of a better name, we may call classicism. . . . if this approaches or even suggests the Greek ideal, so much the better."[11]

The twentieth-century debate about classicism and classical authenticity is exceedingly vexed. Eliot claims that his work is classicist; Eliot's critics respond that his classicism is a late variety of romanticism; Eliot replies that romanticism itself was merely a late and impure variety of classicism. The debate is vexed but it is not without precedent. The classicism controversy, in fact, began with the Renaissance and has continued uninterrupted ever since. As distinct from the less historicist, scientific, and exacting classicism of the Middle Ages, or of Rome—a classicism in which the forms of tradition were " 'handed down' and therefore altered"[12]—Renaissance classicism demanded that the authentic essence of the classics be unearthed, restored, researched, and re-created out of original sources. What the humanists' demand led to, in practice, was a centuries-long dialectic of rival classicisms, each founded on the latest conclusions of classical scholarship. Boileau's *Art poétique* is a reconstitution for seventeenth-century France of the canons of Aristotelian-Horatian criticism, and its rules worked for Boileau's generation: a generation that produced, among other imperishable objects, Racine's *Phèdre*. Yet Lessing would find French neoclassicism inauthentic. In a passage that emphasizes the horror, dread, and despair in Sophoclean tragedy, Lessing turns from the analysis of his text and rails against Chateaubrun and the other French neoclassical critics for their failure to understand the terrible essence of Greek drama: "Oh, the folly of the Frenchman," he writes in the *Laokoön*, "who hadn't the sense to consider this nor the heart to feel it!" Lessing goes on to berate the French for their near-exclusion of Homer from the classical canon and for their belief that the French classicist writers had surpassed the Greeks: "As might be expected, the Parisian critics called this 'triumph-

ing over the ancients,' and one of them suggested that Chateaubrun's piece be called '*La difficulté vaincue.*' "[13]

The Lessing/Chateaubrun confrontation is emblematic. Since
the Renaissance, a long series of mutually exclusive classicisms
has been defined in precisely this way: the classical canon (of
which ancient works shall be most honored) is amended and
a new analysis of what makes the canonical works "classic"
is proffered. It is possible that the "classical tradition" has
operated in this fashion from the beginning. In the first century
B.C. Longinus, for example, was already making distinctions
between the tragic and the "pseudo-tragic."[14] But the extraordinary proliferation of period designations during the modern
centuries—the invention of the medieval, Renaissance, Pre-
Raphaelite, Hellenistic, and pre-Socratic epochs—has been, at
least in part, a response to the special exigencies of post-
Renaissance canon-making. In modern canon-making, the
general trend has been away from Latinity, Alexandrian Hellenism, and the Greco-Roman philosophical tradition, in the
direction of classical and archaic Greek literature.

Yet the classicism debate is even more complex than this
analysis—than the Chateaubrun/Lessing model—would suggest. The search for authenticity that the Renaissance set in
motion is not the only manifestation of classicism in the post-
Renaissance era. In addition to the humanist kind of classicism—to the kind of historical outlook we have associated
with Burckhardt—there has been an "evolutionist" type, in
which antiquity is not perceived as a distinct historical period
but as an infinitely elaborative milieu in an authentic continuum. Medieval classicism, with its allegorizing and "modern-
izing" tendencies, belonged to this type, to the variety in which,
according to Panofsky, "The classical world was not approached historically but pragmatically, as something far-off
yet, in a sense, still alive. . . . Antiquity . . . was still around,
so to speak."[15]

According to Jean Seznec, this ahistoricist variety of classicism went into abeyance for a generation or two at the height
of the Renaissance, but was revived in response to specific
and pressing cultural problems:

It is indeed worthy of note that during the most radiant period of the Renaissance . . . there seems to be an interruption in the mythographical tradition, at least in Italy (no Italian history of the gods appeared between Boccaccio and Giraldi). It is as if nothing more was now needed, in order to know and understand the gods, than to look out at the surrounding world and listen to the voice of instinct; as if man had at last penetrated to the inner meaning of mythology, now that he was engaged in rehabilitating, along with physical beauty, the realm of nature and the flesh. But beneath this gaiety and enthusiasm lurks a stubborn diquiet; just because a "pagan" cult of life is now being professed, with the gods as its incarnation, the need is of bringing that cult into line with the spiritual values of Christianity. . . . the Renaissance, in its moment of flowering, is this synthesis—or rather, this fragile harmony. But the equilibrium is disturbed after only a few decades. . . . Zeal is succeeded by admiration grown reticent. . . . [thus the] tradition of the *libri de imaginibus deorum* is born again.[16]

This evolutionist classicism, in which "classical themes . . . [are] anachronistically modernized,"[17] is represented best, in the post-Renaissance period, by the efforts of Greek and Latin tranlators. Pope's Augustan *Odyssey*, Lamb's romantic version, and Fitzgerald's modernist Homer—these landmark translations form part of a "further adventures of Odysseus" tradition which seeks in every age to readjust the classics to the contemporary idiom. The ahistoricist or evolutionist variety of classicism has flourished throughout the modern era alongside the radical historicism of the Renaissance humanists and their heirs: alongside—and very often in more paradoxical and productive relations. Not infrequently, the humanists of a given century have condemned as fanciful inventions the literary products of an evolutionist classicism that the humanists of an earlier century had helped to create. Twentieth-century "humanists," for example, have ridiculed William Morris's Pre-Raphaelite *Odyssey* (1896) for its resort to an archaic English idiom when, in fact, it was the Renaissance humanists who had developed that King James idiom—and they had done so to the same end that Morris appropriated their invention: to represent the speech of an ancient Mediterranean people.

The complications and ironies are labyrinthine, but this fact, at least, seems sure: that the intricacies of the classicism controversy account for the failure of contemporary scholars to treat the problem of post-Renaissance classicism with the seriousness its solution requires. The complications introduced by the claims and terminology of romanticism, symbolism, and modernism have taxed the scholar's patience to an extreme, and as a consequence, the terms "classicist" and "classicism" have become increasingly disreputable for characterizing any writer or "school" of the years since 1800. Yet those writers made their claim as emphatically as any before 1800— the noun *classicisme*, in fact, is a nineteenth-century coinage. Each self-proclaimed classicism of the post-Renaissance period—including the romantic and post-romantic ones—has had its own claim to authenticity, based upon what its proponents knew or thought they knew about the classics. Have the neoclassicists a right to the totemic name of classicism that is any more self-evident than that of the romantics or the symbolists or the modernists?

A relatively controlled experiment: Let us, for a moment, limit our understanding of classicism to the classical tradition in literary theory. Let us, furthermore, limit our understanding of classicist literary theory to the Aristotelian tradition (and, after Nietzsche, this selection is by no means undisputed). Even with these limitations, there will not be agreement among intellectual historians on a definition of classicism. The Aristotelian critical terminology, while textually constant, will not mean anything like the same thing to a modern European as it did to Aristotle's students. The *Poetics* associates truth and beauty but, in the post-Newtonian Clock-maker's universe, truth more and more came to be conceived as physical or mechanical fact, and the world to be considered in terms of function. Truth is the standard of standards for art, at least implicitly, in all neo-Aristotelian, mimetic theories. But what neoclassical critics meant by truth was of necessity something new. As M. H. Abrams shows, in *The Mirror and the Lamp*, truth came to mean fidelity to Newtonian nature. Later, English Empiricist criticism held that the Ideals (*la belle nature*) which neoclassicists sought in their art were derived solely from sense experience (rather than from inspiration, divine or otherwise) and that an art work should therefore be judged according to its mimetic *accuracy*. Aristotle's words remain the same but their meaning could not be more different. Yet, who is to say that, had Aristotle known what Newton's contemporaries thought they knew, he would not have felt likewise? How, in other words, do we determine authenticity when we have a more or less fixed cultural foundation (or set of founding documents), while the condition of cultural life, especially in the technological West, is change? The term *mimesis* has a similar history. The romantic and post-romantic redefinition of *mimesis*—as the imitation by art of the *processes* of biological nature, rather than an illusionistic copy of nature's visible contours—is only the most recent in a long series of definitions, de-definitions, and redefinitions.

No truly useful history of the words "classic," "classical," and "classicism" exists, and it is easy to see why. *Le classicisme français* of Henri Peyre and E. R. Curtius' *European Literature and the Latin Middle Ages* make the valiant attempt, but the most we can glean from them is an enumeration of lexical categories: (1) the Latin, etymological use (*classici*), which pertains to the upper classes of Roman citizens (thus, classicism = classy-cism) and which came to mean, at an early date, the authors who are read in classrooms; (2) the use of the word "classics" in the sense of ancient literature; (3) the use of the word "classic" in the sense of "best" or "exemplary" or "permanent" ("Dickens is a classic writer"; "Here is a classic of the Orient"); (4) the use of the word "classical" in opposition to the word "popular" ("classical dance"); (5) the use of the word "classicist" to denote writers who imitate ancient authors or exemplary authors or the authors who are read in classrooms; (6) the use of the word "classicist" to denote an authority on ancient literature or history; (7) the use of the words "(neo)classic," "(neo)classical," and "(neo)classicist" to indicate writers in the French high style and their emulators elsewhere; and (8) the use of the words "classicist" or "classical" to label those who oppose the romantic and realist or, earlier, the Gothic and picaresque approaches to literature.

Then there is the bewildering array of eccentric, modernist definitions—Gide's ("I should take these two words to be synonyms: classic and French"), Pound's ("Anatole France is said to have spent a great deal of time searching for the least possible variant that would turn the most worn-out and commonest phrases of journalism into something distinguished. Such research is sometimes termed 'classicism' "), Stravinsky's ("submission to an established order"), Valéry's ("The essence of classicism is to come after. Order presupposes a certain disorder which it has just reduced"), Eliot's ("simply maturity"). There is also Charles Maurras' and T. E. Hulme's identification of classicism with the Catholic Church, or Julien Benda's (and, following him, Yvor Winters') identification of classicism with "the exactitude of the sciences in the portrayal of the moral world." In the first decades of this century, the battles among these competing definitions were fierce—many of them waged in the pages of *The Criterion* or in opposition to its editor (Eliot vs. Aldington, Pound and Benda vs. Eliot and Maurras, Yvor Winters vs. Eliot, Eliot vs. Middleton Murry, *an infinitum*). A good deal of the fighting also occurred in the countless, unsung journals which, like Winters' *Gyroscope*, were meant to be "an experiment toward, if not in, classicism."[18]

The multiplication of party platforms, and the dizzying progress of the classicism debate through five centuries of modern history, have led us to a salutary despair of definition. We must learn to define classicism generation by generation, just as we are learning to define "realism" dialectically. As realism has the Real to contend with and endlessly to redefine, so classicism has to deal with the Classics—with canon-making or unmaking, with fresh literary interpretations, with new insights into cultural context, with the discoveries of archeology and linguistics. It is in the critic's interest, if he hopes to evaluate modernism in the context of modernity, to transcend the dialectic of competing classicisms. Writers have been so busy making new definitions of the classical, and critics have been so busy debunking them, that no one has stopped to wonder at the extraordinary compulsion that has fueled this centuries-long pattern of definition/refutation/redefinition. The current trend in criticism looks, at first glance, like a departure from the pattern: contemporary critics have determined to dismiss the classicism issue altogether. But ignorance of a dialectic is not the same as transcendence, and our current understanding of modernism has suffered from the circumscription of our critical scope.

· · ·

THE MODERNISTS' insistence that modernism and classicism are one is our best window on the ideology of history that underwrote the modernist enterprise. In his most sustained exposition of that ideology, Eliot writes:

> . . . what I see, in the history of English poetry, is . . . the splitting up of personality. If we say that one of these partial personalities which may develop in a national mind is that which manifested itself in the period between Dryden and Johnson, then what we have to do is to reintegrate it: otherwise we are likely to get only successive alternations of personality.[19]

This statement represents a new historical perspective, for many earlier critics had attempted to wipe either neoclassicism or romanticism or (in the twentieth century) both off the cultural map. Eliot's place in the classicism debate is unique. He is not offering a new definition of the cultural personality and is therefore not a "humanist" as we have defined the term. He seems to address the humanists of his own day when he writes, in the same essay:

> . . . it is rather strong to suggest that the English mind has been deranged ever since the time of Shakespeare,

and that only recently have a few fitful rays of reason penetrated its darkness. If the malady is as chronic as that, it is pretty well beyond cure.[20]

Yet neither is Eliot's approach "ahistorical" and "evolutionist." His assumptions about deranged and partial cultural psyches imply the existence of a standard for health and wholeness, and the frequent references in his criticism to Aristotle and "the Greek ideal" indicate that Eliot, like most moderns, locates that standard in classical antiquity.

Eliot's implicit faith in the "chosenness" of his vantage point enabled him to come closer than anyone, before or since, to transcending the modern dialectic of rival classicisms. Much as the characters in Rousseau's *Julie* could perceive the circular pattern of their history only when it had been completed, so late moderns tend to believe that the late-modern vantage point makes visible, for the first time, the curve of modern history. This belief is best expressed by Paul Valéry in his 1944 essay on Mallarmé:

> In the poetry written up to his time he perceived the fragments of a universal work that had been magnificently adumbrated but not rendered explicit, since none of the great men had been able to conceive its whole or its guiding principle.[21]

What Valéry says of Mallarmé could also be said of Eliot, for Eliot seems to have believed that, as the historical ensemble neared completion, he had come to grasp the principles of its composition. Eliot's underlying presupposition is not unlike that in Pater's essay on Winckelmann. Eliot appears to be saying that the whole of modern literary theory and practice—Renaissance, neoclassical, romantic, symbolist—has been united in pursuit of one aim: the development of an authentic, latter-day version of ancient literary theory and practice. Eliot viewed the English (or European) mind as a fragmented consciousness. He saw neoclassicists and romantics, for instance, as representing different components of a single, though fragmented, tradition; and the reintegration of that (classical) tradition became early on the goal of Eliot's criticism.

In his pre-*Criterion* essays, Eliot's chief interest was in establishing the necessary components for a healthy mind of Europe. He writes forceful praise of the Stendhal/Flaubert/James tradition, of Donne and the Metaphysicals, of the *symbolistes*, of Jonson, of Marvell, and of *Noh* drama.[22] He writes scathing criticism of the Georgians, the Victorian novelists, Swinburne, Kipling, and the early romantics, of eighteenth-century shallowness, of Miltonic influence, and of certain aspects in the works of Yeats, Dryden, and even Shakespeare.[23] But in no instance is his praise unqualified or his condemnation complete (he insists, for example, that we disapprove of the Metaphysicals' occasionally tortuous metaphors rather than coddle them with "antiquarian affection"), for he is not so much interested in promoting or demoting any particular poet as he is in establishing criteria for excellence—for classical excellence. The criteria he enunciates in the late teens and twenties in fact comprise Eliot's explanation of what he meant by "classicism": craft and disinterested professionalism, the *transformation* of a mature and interesting personality into art,[24] originality which is aware of tradition, "a large and unique view of life," pureness and correctness of language, completeness and self-sufficiency, lucidity, and a refined nervous system.[25]

Of these criteria, oddly enough, the Impersonal Poet emphasizes those relating to the artist's personality, and this peculiarity is a key both to Eliot's critical principles and to his historical viewpoint. "A brilliant master of technique" is not necessarily, in the word's more profound sense, "an artist."[26] Eliot cannot fault Philip Massinger's language or technique, refuses to fault his difficult style; what makes him inferior, for Eliot, to Middleton or Webster is the inferiority and staleness of his feeling:

> Massinger is not simply a smaller personality: his personality hardly exists. He did not, out of his own personality, build a world of art, as Shakespeare and Marlowe and Jonson built. . . . The defect is precisely a defect of personality.[27]

Further, he dubs Milton and Dryden "two of the greatest masters of diction in our language," while deriding them for ignoring "the cerebral cortex, the nervous system, and the digestive tracts."[28] Nor will Eliot abide pretense. It is fine for Jonson's world to be superficial and solid, but hollowness (whether Beaumont and Fletcher's "clever appeal to emotions and associations which they have not themselves grasped," or Massinger's "social abstraction of emotions," or the romantics' "short cut to the strangeness without the reality") is intolerable.[29] Beneath its technically perfect surface, "deeper than style and the cause of style," great art must possess "a network of tentacular roots reaching down to the deepest terrors and desires."[30]

The operative word is "network." It is not enough for an artist to have journeyed deep into his personal underworld. The great poet's underworld—"simple, terrible, and unknown"—must, in addition, be as structured as the underworld of Dante's *Commedia*, in which the relation of each emotion to the others is precisely established.[31] "*Eriger en lois ses impressions personelles, c'est le grand effort d'un homme s'il est sincère*" (Remy de Gourmont, *Lettres à Amazone*) is the epigraph to the first essay in Eliot's first book of literary criticism. The truly profound artist will possess a "system of impressions" or, as it is described in the "Metaphysical Poets" essay, a "mechanism of sensibility," whereby the most obscure emotions and the most complex observations may associate to arrange themselves into an ordered structure:

> the ordinary man's experience is chaotic, irregular, fragmentary. . . . in the mind of the poet . . . experiences are always forming new wholes.[32]

(Similarly, the "mind of Europe" constantly changes as tradition and the "really new" continually combine to form new "compounds.") Anyone whose sensibility is not so ordered can, at best, create an art which is "well knit and . . . remote from unity."[33] In the closing essay of *The Sacred Wood*, the early Eliot remarks (with the Eliot of *For Lancelot Andrewes* already visible on the horizon) that the more "beautiful" the structure and the more completely absorbed it is in an accepted mythology, the more "successful" its artistic productions will be.[34]

From these observations it follows that there are two particularly unsatisfactory sorts of literary art. The first, Eliot defines with regard to Massinger but awards the distinction as well to Kipling, Swinburne, Tennyson, Dryden, and Sir Thomas Browne: "the highest degree of verbal excellence compatible with the most rudimentary development of the senses."[35] The second, unlike the first, includes writers who have journeyed to the underworld, but whose nervous system Eliot finds unsystematic (his complaint against Henry Adams) or structurally eccentric (essentially his judgment on Blake and, to a lesser extent, his pre-1922 evaluation of Yeats) or structurally ugly (his opinion of Milton).[36] Scarcely an English writer between the time of Marvell and that of Eliot escapes without being filed with one of these unsavory groupings. (The two main exceptions are Americans: Hawthorne and James.) For Eliot, especially at the beginning of his career, the English literary tradition reached its apogee with the Elizabethans and post-Elizabethans, and has been going wrong ever since. We are told that

> The seventeenth century sometimes seems for more than a moment to gather up and to digest into its art all the experience of the human mind which . . . the later centuries seem to have been partly engaged in repudiating[37]

—a sweeping statement written the same year as his comments on the "dissociation of sensibility."

We come closer to understanding Eliot's historical viewpoint in these two, related excerpts from *The Sacred Wood*:

> England . . . has produced a prodigious number of men of genius and comparatively few works of art. . . .[38]

and

> Dante is a classic, . . . Blake only a poet of genius. The fault is perhaps not with Blake himself but with the en-

vironment which failed to provide what such a poet needed.[39]

For Eliot, the difference between a classic artist and a "mere genius," all other things being equal, is the working material that each is given. Shakespeare and Donne inherited a satisfying Renaissance cosmology and the beautiful dogma of the Anglican Church; even Marvell was heir to the "French spirit of the age." But what did Wordsworth's age give to Wordsworth? A discontinuous tradition in mythology, a decadent morality, a licentious prudery, and Sir Isaac Newton: in short, a world order from which the life had passed away.[40] Eliot seems willing to forgive Blake and other visionaries (such as Shelley and Keats) for the eccentricity of their emotional systems, because they at least had real emotions which they attempted to structure—and "under conditions that seem[ed] unpropitious."[41] But Massinger's failure to develop a living emotional construct is unqualified, and Eliot formulates his criticism of Massinger as an assault upon the whole of the English neoclassical tradition from the eve of the Civil War to the romantic revolution:

> What may be considered corrupt or decadent in the morals of Massinger is not an alteration or diminution in morals; it is simply the disappearance of all the personal and real emotions which this morality supported and into which it introduced a kind of order. As soon as the emotions disappear the morality which ordered it appears hideous. . . . The Elizabethan morality was an important convention . . . because it provided a framework for emotions to which all classes could respond, and it hindered no feeling. . . . Fletcher and Massinger rendered it ridiculous; not by not believing it, but because they were men of great talents who could not vivify it. . . .[42]

In his *Sacred Wood* essay on Dante, Eliot states that one of the poet's prime functions is to "vivify" some important "philosophy" or moral system, to make it visible and viable to the reader. The artist's fresh, personal, contemporary understanding of a social abstraction—in Bradleyan terms, the artist's numerous, completely personal "finite-centers" uniting together to intend the same object as the artist's society intends—may be what Pound meant by the slogan "Make it new." It may even be what Rousseau, in *La Nouvelle Héloïse*, meant by *retour*. And it is this that the post-"dissociation" writers, like Massinger, were patently unable to accomplish. When the early Eliot writes about the English literature of the later seventeenth, eighteenth, and nineteenth centuries, a major assumption underlying his criticism is that The Tradition has been suspended. His almost political attitude closely parallels the conviction of Edmund Burke, after 1789, that "France is out of itself—the moral France is separated from the geographical." This comparison is not gratuitous, for the contrast between Burke's position and Eliot's provides a key to understanding precisely what Eliot hopes to accomplish by positing this split in the literary tradition.

When Burke decried the revolution as a schism in the French political tradition, he was referring to an order of things that had developed slowly, organically, for at least half a millennium. The literary tradition of England to which Eliot refers existed for perhaps a century and a half, from the time of Wyatt and Surrey to that of Marvell (Eliot does not refer to pre-Tudor writing in the early criticism), and was followed by a period of schism of approximately twice that length. Eliot manages to avoid facing this objection by an ingenious and revealing sleight-of-hand:

> The poets of the seventeenth century, the successors of the dramatists of the sixteenth . . . are simple, artificial, or fantastic, as their predecessors were; no less nor more than Dante, Guido Cavalcanti, Guinizelli, or Cino. In the seventeenth century a dissociation of sensibility set in. . . . What would have been the fate of the "Metaphysical" had the current of poetry descended in a direct line from them, as it descended in a direct line to them?[43]

He then proceeds to answer his own question in a discussion of the nineteenth-century attempt to restore that line of descent:

we get something which looks very much like the con-
ceit—we get, in fact, a method curiously similar to that
of the "metaphysical poets" . . . Jules Laforgue, and Tris-
tan Corbière in many of his poems, are nearer to the
"school of Donne" than any English poet. But poets more
classical than they have the same essential quality. . . .[44]

And out of Mr. Eliot's magic hat comes, not a magic rabbit,
but an opossum: a tradition of English literary classicism descending from Dante and Cavalcanti to Corbière and Laforgue.

What we have here is the delineation of an important Continental tradition in which English writers have occasionally
participated, though (except during the northern European
Renaissance) only by fits and starts. Eliot argues, however,
not only that England's "best verse is the product of European,
that is to say Latin, culture," but also that, although classicism
may not be naturally English, "The question is, . . . *not* what
comes natural . . . , but what is right?"[45] When English literature does not meet Continental, Latin standards, it cannot
be considered part of what Pound calls "the better tradition."
In this sense, the culprit dissociating the English artistic sensibility from the time of the Commonwealth to the reign of
George V was the English Channel. Throughout Eliot's critical
essays there is a ground bass muttering and mumbling about
English provinciality and, when the mumble grows loud enough
to hear, it has the virulence of a personal vendetta. (Even at
the end of the Great War, Eliot found it possible to view the
British intelligentsia "set down absurdly in a continent of
which they are unconscious.")[46]

What caused the widening of the Channel is a matter Eliot
could not solve when it most occupied his attention in 1920
("Blake") and 1921 ("The Metaphysical Poets"). In the former essay, he speculates "for amusement"

Whether it would not have been beneficial to . . . Britain
in particular to have had a more continuous religious
history . . . since [one] remarks about the Puritan mythology an historical thinness . . . a certain meanness of

culture ... the crankiness, the eccentricity,, which frequently affects writers outside of the Latin traditions.[47]

And, in the latter essay, he wants to blame dissociation and provinciality of viewpoint on the Civil War. In either case, the culpable party is an unbeautiful, low-church Protestantism.[48] Certain romantic visionaries in England attempted to create their own richer and more aesthetically satisfying mythologies along Catholic lines, but these poets erred in forgetting that the word "Catholic" implies universality. Blake, Keats, and Shelley are, however, "classicizers," sometimes more and sometimes less, for making the attempt to reassociate the English with the European mind. Labels aside, theirs are attempts to reach across the Schism to the metaphysical poets, just as Baudelaire and the *symbolistes* were attempting communication with Racine.

What remained for twentieth-century artists was to take the traditional bases of the European psyche, organize them into a beautiful mythological structure, and "make it new." Presumably this *retour* or reintegration would have been impossible at an earlier time, since

> Changes never come by a simple reinfusion into the form which the life has just left.[49]

To accomplish this feat it was necessary to formulate the "dissociation of sensibility" and to make three centuries of the English literary tradition seem somehow untraditional. Eliot could have followed Pound's example, largely ignoring his national literary tradition as though there were no literature but Western literature or even world literature. But Eliot wanted to divert the course of literature in his own language, to bring it into a thriving Continental (i.e., symbolist) tradition whose spirit, Eliot thought, came as close to the classical spirit as was conceivable in the modern world. In order to convince a highly provincial artistic/intellectual community to embrace this *symboliste* classicism (to say nothing of his own work), Eliot had to explain with authority that the classicist tradition of Renaissance England had been fragmented—its polish and urbanity taken over by so-called neoclassicists, its spiritual fire by so-called romantics—and that this divided tradition was in dire need of reunification.

The image, as Eliot said, is of "the splitting up of personality." The historical process of return, like those which pertain to the individual psyche, is one of growth, dislocation, and reintegration. The modernists who wrote in support of classicism were not antiquarians but psychologists of culture with a revolutionary perception: the history of Europe had been the unfolding of a self through time—a process of *égarement* and *retour* which, in the twentieth century, had come full circle.

• • •

ELIOT'S revisions of literary history were intentionally controversial, yet his maligned viewpoint is highly illuminating—and illuminating not only of modernism's artistic production, but even of modern culture as a whole. It is entirely possible to view the romantic rebellion in the way Eliot seems to have viewed it: as a self-conscious assault on neoclassicism for failure to achieve the classic ideal. Lessing's *Laokoön*, for instance, favors an autotelic art which eschews all the mannerisms of the neoclassical: its discursiveness and didacticism, its overreliance on description, its pictorialism and allegorical tendency, its ornamentation, and its limited subject matter. In fact, Lessing proposes an aesthetic very close to what later came to be called "romanticism"; the *Laokoön* lacks only romantic theories of imagination and irony for it to be a proto-romantic manifesto. But, as we already have observed, Lessing's assault on neoclassicism was performed in the name of a more authoritative classicism (Homer's and Sophocles'), and there is little doubt that Lessing thought his *Laokoön* a contribution to the line of neo-Aristotelian/neo-Longinian criticism of the Renaissance and post-Renaissance period. Under the influence of Winckelmann—and in the wake of epoch-making expeditions to Greece (the English explorers, Stuart and Revett, brought Western Europe its first accurate drawings of Athens since antiquity)—writers like Lessing in Germany or Collins in England undermined the academic aesthetic by redefining the nature of the classical.

This eighteenth-century redefinition of classicism passed into the mainstream of romantic aesthetics. Many of the major romantic literary tracts seem, like the *Laokoön*, to have been attempts to revise the neoclassical canon in accord with a fresh (post-Winckelmann) look at the classical. Harry Levin has called this phenomenon "Romantic Hellenism" because the new classical canon was, precisely, Hellenic. "We are all Greeks," Shelley writes in the preface to "Hellas," and he, together with most of his romantic predecessors (the chief exception being Wordsworth),[50] eliminated in wholesale fashion the entirety of Latin literature from their new canon. In *The Defence of Poetry*, Shelley excoriates Roman literature as the product of a "decadent" classicism—of a literature as frozen as (he makes the parallel quite explicitly in the *Defence*) that of eighteenth-century neoclassicism. What Shelley most objects to in these decadent classicisms is their insistence on extracting binding rules from the Greek classics—rules that must be applied to all literary effort. But he also dislikes the interpretation of classical literature on which those rules were based. In remaking the classical canon (with Homer, Aeschylus, and Sophocles in the premier positions), Shelley and his colleagues were mainly concerned to exalt the qualities that they valued in the earliest Greek literature: psychological penetration, titanic individualism, a passion for liberty (often combined with philhellenism), and an abundance of imagination. Their alteration of the neoclassical canon—which Shelley, typically, had mastered and rejected at Eton and Oxford—led to an aesthetic so very different from the neoclassicism it succeeded that romanticism came to be thought a rebellion against the classical per se.

Many post-romantic literary figures continued to see their own work as a modernized version of the authentic Hellenism which the romantics had unearthed. By Pater's time, in fact, it was commonplace to remark how Winckelmann and his spiritual heirs had supplanted a "flimsier, more artificial classical tradition" by "the clear ring, the eternal outline of the genuine antique."[51] Many other self-proclaimed classicists, however, found it necessary to reprove the romantic Hellenists, as the romantics in their turn had assaulted the neoclassicists. Matthew Arnold, the premier Hellenist of Victoria's Britain, did not develop a wholly new classical standard nor did he return to an earlier one (though his endorsement of an academy of letters for England, and his repudiation of the Homer-as-balladeer notion, indicate that he did have a "neoclassical" side).[52] Arnold did not so much deny the romantics' view of classicism as accuse them of not living up to it.

Their failure, Arnold speculated, was due to an uncritical veneration of Shakespeare, the one post-classical writer whom all romantics had included in their canon. As a consequence, he thought, romantic classicism was impure, marred by what he calls (in the 1853–54 prefaces to his collected poems) "eccentricity," "personal peculiarities," and "fancifulness." These qualities are at odds with those other qualities that romantics had claimed to admire in the Greeks: masculinity, nobility, ease, sweetness, rapid movement, idiomatic speech, and moderation. The love of Shakespeare led to an excessive emphasis on expression and an insufficient attention to construction (to what Goethe called *Architectonicé*). For Arnold, the classicist is interested in the whole, while the romantic is fixated on the parts. Worse yet, romanticism is attached to the very unclassical "dialogue of the mind with itself"—which, in Arnold's opinion, indicates the end, rather than the revival, of a classical epoch. The classical spirit, he says, demands that suffering and all things psychological find a vent in action—this was the basis of Arnold's objection to his own *Empedocles on Etna* and, as we shall see, it would become the basis of Eliot's objection to *Hamlet*, the work of Shakespeare that the romantics had adored most reverently.

The modernists' revision of romantic aesthetics is widely misconstrued and largely underrated; and it began at the meeting-place of classical and modern, of psychology and poetics, which Arnold had identified. It began, for Eliot, with Aristotle. Recognizing in the prevailing "organic theory" of Coleridge an affinity with Aristotle's psychological principle of "association"—an affinity which Coleridge had desired readers of his *Biographia* to observe[53]—Eliot felt comfortable with this romantic theorizing and was willing in some degree to affiliate himself with it. Moreover, "in the matter of mimesis," Eliot held that Wordsworth was "more deeply Aristotelian than some who have aimed at following Aristotle more closely."[54]

Eliot's focus was on an aspect of romantic ideology that is little discussed but demonstrably important: that many theorists of romanticism felt a strong affinity with the aesthetic and psychological texts of Aristotle. The Neoplatonism of the romantics has always been overdrawn: even Shelley had a career-long flirtation with Aristotelianism,[55] and romantic hostility was directed less toward Aristotle than toward his neoclassical interpreters. It is not that romantics desired to follow Aristotelian tenets but that some perceived a link between Aristotle and certain revolutionary developments of their own day. Lessing perhaps initiated this trend in his pairing of Aristotle with Shaftesbury and Locke; and, not long after, Aristotle would be thought to have his complement in Kantian idealism. As Hugh Lloyd-Jones notes, Johann Gottfried Hermann, one of Goethe's classical tutors, "was a close student of Kant, and interpreted Aristotle's *Poetics* in the light of Kantian aesthetics."[56] Eliot too, more than a century later, would find the idealist philosopher, F. H. Bradley, to be "like Aristotle" and close "to the Greek tradition"[57]—and Eliot, it seems, was given a thoroughly idealist (or "romantic") introduction to Aristotle at Oxford by Bradley's Merton College protégé, Harold Joachim.

No major theorist of romanticism, symbolism, or modernism left us with a comprehensive rereading of Aristotle, but it should not be difficult to piece together what modern aestheticians have found attractive or familiar in Aristotelian poetics. Perhaps the prime mover behind the *Poetics* is the idea, now labeled romantic, that a work of art is an inviolable "monument" or "monad"—that it is what Aristotle calls a "whole," a "unity," an "imitation of an action that is complete in itself." In order to make the work of art independent, Aristotle first of all liberates it from meaning: which is not to say that

Aristotelian art is without ideas (he calls poetry "philo-sophic"), but that the fable (or plot), rather than any "phi-losophising" by the characters, is the "end and purpose" of dramatic poetry.[58] Aristotle advises that art should not say but be, should not describe or ponder life but imitate or rep-resent it:

> All human happiness or misery takes the form of action; the end for which we live is a certain kind of activity, not a quality. . . . one may string together a series of characteristic speeches of the utmost finish as regards Diction and Thought, . . . but one will have much better success with a Plot, a combination of incidents. . . .[59]

Despite this injunction against rumination in poetry, the Aristotelian artist never could become a mere reporter, for Aristotle also has freed the work of art from dependence upon fact. Just as he takes pains to distinguish the poet from the rhetorician and the philosopher, so Aristotle carefully sepa-rates poetry from history:

> The distinction between historian and poet is not in the one writing prose and the other verse—you might put the work of Herodotus into verse, and it would still be a species of history; it consists really in this, that the one describes the thing that has been, and the other a kind of thing that might be. Hence poetry is something more philosophic and of graver import than history, since its statements are of the nature of universals, whereas those of history are singulars.[60]

A symbolist critic, reading these passages, might construe Aristotle to say that a poem means nothing besides itself, yet that poetry is both universal and timeless. And, in a more difficult and controversial passage, the symbolist reader might find in Aristotle congenial notions of the *poète maudit* and the anonymous artifact:

> Given the same natural qualifications, he who feels the emotions to be described will be the most convincing;

distress and anger, for instance, are portrayed most truthfully by one who is feeling them at the moment. Hence it is that poetry demands a man with a special gift for it, or else one with a touch of madness in him; the former can easily assume the required mood, and the latter may be actually beside himself with emotion.

His story, again, whether already or of his own making, he should first simplify and reduce to a universal form. . . .[61]

Once the artist has transformed his private emotional traumas into art, into a "universal form," his creation has no more to do with himself than with anyone else.

Hence, the *Poetics* could be taken to make the work of art independent of meaning, of fact, and even of the artist. The art work is, more or less, what Henry James calls a "thing." Yet it is not without purpose (trees provide shade) and the purpose to which Aristotle puts the most exalted work of art (tragedy) is catharsis: the emotional transfiguration of the audience. The specific purpose Aristotle assigns to any genre, however, is of less concern than his account of how an objective artifact, which makes no intellectual argument and deals with no real events or people, can cause a reaction of any sort—and this fact, too, was guaranteed to engage a symbolist's attention. It certainly engaged Eliot's: his Greek copy of *De anima*, in the John Hayward Bequest, is covered with marginalia, with notes taken during R. G. Collingwood's exposition of the text, and with excerpts, in Latin, from the commentary of Pacinus.[62]

As Eliot perceived, Aristotle's affectivist poetics are founded on his view of the psyche. In the *De anima*, Aristotle theorizes that the whole of a human being's physical, emotional, imaginative, and intellectual faculties comprises a unified *animus*— an associated sensibility—that carries on two fundamental types of activity: the physical ("local movement") and the nonphysical ("perception"). Local movement and perception, while distinguishable, are fused, just as the elements of perception (the senses, emotions, imagination, practical reason, and speculative intellect) are inseparable. We are told, for instance, that

> imagination . . . is not found without sensation, or judgement without it,

that

> when we think . . . , emotion is immediately produced,

and that

> Thinking . . . is held to be in part imagination, in part judgement. . . .[63]

Reason, imagination, and emotion are equally interdependent faculties; however, Aristotle emphasizes the relationship between imagination (defined as "that in virtue of which an image arises for us") and the speculative intellect. He repeats several times that to think of an abstraction is impossible, for we can think only of "sensible spatial magnitudes," and he states unequivocally that "when the mind is actively aware of anything it is necessarily aware of it along with an image."[64] Thus Aristotelian psychology brings us to the romantic image. Because the *animus* cannot truly know or believe anything that it has not seen with the mind's eye, the Aristotelian poet must eschew abstract discourse if he hopes to affect his reader. He must present a vivid image (an "action that is complete in itself") which will occasion a physical, emotional, and intellectual response in his reader's unified *animus*. The sense of *déjà vu* is intense, and one is tempted to assert that were Aristotle rewritten in modern terms, or were the symbolist critics translated into Aristotelian language, the *Poetics* and *De anima* might seem almost to comprise a romantic manifesto.

On the other hand, the difference between symbolist and Aristotelian terminology points to a basic disagreement about the nature of the image and of the imagination that produces it. Aristotle considers the external world to be objective—knowable through sense and intellect—and he sees the internal world as subjective and therefore unreliable. *De anima* assumes that

> sensations are always true, imaginations are for the most part false. . . . Neither is imagination *any* of the things that are never in error; e.g. knowledge or intelligence; for imagination may be false.[65]

Hence, if one's imaginings are proven true, it is either a matter of accident or a result of the imagination's intimate relationship with the perceptions of the senses and the musings of the intellect. The function of the Aristotelian imagination is to assist in the thought process by making abstract ideas concrete, and the literary image is nothing more than an artificial stimulant to active cognition. However, for many moderns, the literary image is "absolutely subjective" (Wilde) and has "nothing to do with memory" (Blake): it is the creation of the artist's unassisted imagination.

It is from the Aristotelian position that Eliot challenges the romantics' view of the imagination. Of the fancy/imagination distinction in Coleridge's *Biographia* (Book 13), Eliot writes:

> Fancy may be "no other than a mode of memory emancipated from the order of space and time"; but it seems unwise to talk of memory in connexion with fancy and omit it altogether from the account of imagination. . . . There is so much memory in imagination that if you are to distinguish between imagination and fancy in Coleridge's way you must define the difference between memory in imagination and memory in fancy.[66]

Aristotelian man—even the Aristotelian artist—can create nothing *ex nihilo*. The romantics rejected the central principle underlying the Aristotelian image: namely, that in the world external to the private mind are objective facts which, however ramified and complex, are knowable through sense and right reason. Repulsed by the external world, over which the Newtonians claimed dominion, the romantics internalized reality and glorified the imagination as a creative organ uniquely equipped to perceive truth.[67]

It is from the rejection of objectivity—Aristotelian or Newtonian—that many of romanticism's distinctive characteristics
and obsessions derive. And of all the enthusiasms arising from
the romantics' internalization of reality, the most enduring,
and the most significant for our purposes, was the obsession
with Shakespeare's persona Hamlet. *Hamlet* became the object of an almost religious veneration because romantics could
identify easily with its protagonist, whose predicament sym-
bolized a conviction near and dear to their hearts: that reality
transcends the evidence at hand and that one must pursue
truth wherever it leads, even if (or especially if) that means
appearing mad to the Philistines. The cultic adoration of *Hamlet* had been so universal since the time of Goethe and Coleridge that we may take 1919 as a turning point in aesthetic
history simply because during that year a cheeky London re-
viewer (T. S. Eliot) called *Hamlet* "an artistic failure."[68] We
can approach the romantic/modernist distinction most effec-
tively by comparing Coleridge's essay on *Hamlet* (1813) with
Eliot's of a hundred years later—Eliot's essay, in fact, is a
carefully contrived response to the various romantic *Hamlets*.
Coleridge is a temperate analyst, relative to other critics of
the play. He assumes that Shakespeare is presenting Hamlet
as an example of the "overbalance of the imaginative power"
and does not assume that Shakespeare finds this a praiseworthy thing. Yet Coleridge admires the play greatly for its
author's interest in "the world within" the protagonist, for
its author's understanding that "it is the nature of thought to
be indefinite," and, most importantly, for Shakespeare's understanding that "the sense of sublimity arises, not from the
sight of the outward object, but from the beholder's reflection
upon it;—not from the sensuous impression but from the
imaginative reflex."[69]

Eliot, with Aristotle standing behind him, denies this principle, and it is on the basis of that denial that Eliot finds
Hamlet "most certainly an artistic failure." In the *Poetics*, the
image which the artistic imagination produces is not something for contemplation and expansion by its audience, but a
specific kind of action, presented to the audience, which in all

normal cases results in certain predictable kinds of emotional and intellectual response in the observer. This is precisely what Eliot means by "objective correlative"—a term that he invented, it is too often forgotten, as a weapon against the romantic interpretation of a work that many romantics considered the greatest in world literature. Eliot objects to precisely that element in *Hamlet* which the romantic critics admire: the lack of a delineated correlation between the Prince's emotional condition and the external facts of the play. Which is to say that Eliot condemns both Hamlet the persona and *Hamlet* the play for their internalization of reality.

The objective correlative is not the romantic image remodeled, but an important part of Eliot's attempt to "tame" the image, to bring it back into the Aristotelian fold. Eliot's definition is carefully Aristotelian in its content and resoundingly Aristotelian in its language. Four years before he minted the term, Eliot was reading Aristotle with Joachim, and the famous passage from "Hamlet and His Problems" bears all the marks of having been written for a tutorial on the *Poetics*:

> The only way of expressing emotion in the form of art is by finding an "objective correlative"; in other words, a set of objects, a situation, a chain of events which shall be the formula of that *particular* emotion; such that when the external facts, which must terminate in sensory experience, are given, the emotion is immediately invoked.[70]

The brooding upon an image that Coleridge appreciates in *Hamlet* and that we are accustomed to find in the poems of Wordsworth (e.g., in "Tintern Abbey"), Eliot calls "a subject of study for pathologists" that "often occurs in adolescence." Coleridge writes that when Hartley differed from Aristotle, "he differed only to err";[71] Eliot would have said the same of Coleridge and of romantic poetics in general. But critics today have overlooked these distinctions in order to draw a symbolist, Coleridgean continuum in poetic theory from the late eighteenth century through the mid-twentieth, and they have travestied modernist aesthetics in the process.

Eliot was neither a romantic nor an anti-romantic but a

post-romantic with a talent for discrimination and a sense of history. As we have seen, Eliot found a derisible shallowness, anemia, and abstraction in the products of neoclassicism—found what he called "a dazzling disregard of the soul"—but he greatly admired the lucidity, correctness, anonymity of voice, and professional craftsmanship of neoclassical works. Yet if Eliot found neoclassicism wanting (and his great villain, until the 1947 retraction, was John Milton), neither was he satisfied with what supplanted it. Eliot derided the romantics' over-assertion of personality, "crankiness" of vision, and "short-cut to the strangeness without the reality," while applauding their imaginative power and the "simplicity" and "terrible-ness" of their "nervous systems."[72] After one hundred years of romantic/neoclassical dissonance, it had become evident that neither camp had a monopoly on artistic excellence and, further, that neither was any longer capable of greatness. The generation born toward the end of Victoria's reign thought it their task to salvage and reconcile what was still vital in two senile traditions:

> Surely the great poet is . . . one who not merely restores a tradition which has been in abeyance, but one who in his poetry re-twines as many straying strands of tradition as possible.[73]

Romanticism and neoclassicism, Eliot thought, could not be transcended until they were conjoined. In the late nineteenth century, their immiscibility had been assumed—but then, eminent Victorians had also assumed the antinomous distinctions of real vs. ideal, science vs. religion, body vs. mind, and sex vs. love.

The twentieth-century "school" that purported to be classicist found its solution to this artistic dilemma in 1911 when Georges Braque and Picasso invented collage. It is sometimes claimed that the purpose of collage was the mimesis of modern fragmentation and disorder, but the initiating impulse may have been virtually the reverse: to demonstrate that an authentic wholeness could be reconstructed, if only we would tear up and recompose the imposters which had usurped the place of more authentic symmetries and orders. Picasso's first collage was a *Still Life with Chair Caning*, a painted conglomeration of abstract geometric forms—each incomplete and overlapping with the others—all pressing heavily against an actual patch of chair caning glued in the foreground. By 1913, Picasso began to connect the carefully selected scraps with conciliating lines and shapes; in his *Violin* of that year, the newsprint and cardboard are parts of an overall form (the violin) created by chalk, ink, and paint lines surrounding, covering, and lightly shading the material fragments. Art historians Frank Elgar and Robert Maillard write of Picasso's collage technique that "as the fragments of alien material became increasingly important, the finished works became more compact and solid, finally acquiring an obvious and convincing harmony."[74] Which is to say that these odd-scrap compositions, made up of seemingly incomplete and unrelated images, developed into unified, monumental, even "classical" wholes. Eventually they metamorphosed into pure sculpture and pure painting, albeit executed with rough, carved bits of wood (e.g., *Mandoline*, 1914) or made up of sharp geometric facets. Picasso's art developed much as a blurred vision focuses: from collage diffusely formed of scraps whose relation is unsure, to collage in which the fragments unite into an overall form, to faceted cubism, to the work of his "neoclassical period" (1917–37). The development of collage parallels that of twentieth-century "classicism" as a whole: first, artists gleaned and juxtaposed what they saw as the classical elements of symbolism, romanticism, and neoclassicism; then, fit them together, as though in a jig-saw puzzle; and, finally, synthesized them into what they claimed was the most authentic classicism since antiquity—and also the apotheosis of what modernity had been struggling to become all along.

At about the time Picasso was painting analytical cubist canvases and Sergei Eisenstein was theorizing about film montage, T. S. Eliot was telling anyone interested that, in the twentieth century, the poet must "dislocate" language and ideas to fulfill the purpose of poetry. He then proceeded to paste together fragments of verse and song—connecting them with conciliating lines and shapes—to shore up the ruins of the Waste Land:

> London Bridge is falling down falling down falling down
> *Poi s'ascose nel foco che glia affina*
> *Quando fiam uti chelidon*—O swallow swallow
> *Le Prince d'Aquitaine à la tour abolie*
> These fragments I have shored against my ruins

And in *The Criterion*, Eliot's protégé, Fr. D'Arcy, insisted, somewhat bitterly, that even those who longed for a classical poet would not recognize him in our day, so radical was the surgery he would need to perform in order to reach the classic ideal. D'Arcy, no doubt, was alluding to Eliot. The article, written by a native speaker of English, concludes with an Old Possum subscription, set in capital letters: "Translated by T. S. ELIOT."

· · ·

THE COMBINATION of laughter and bitterness is not difficult to understand. Thirty years ago, Erich Auerbach called *Ulysses* a "mocking odi et amo hodgepodge" and critics today refer to Eliot as a symbolist romantic who was skillful in applying classical cosmetics to his work. Eliot's early works, for example, are often read as neoromantic poems that sympathetically present the dilemmas of a young romantic artist.[75] The same fate has befallen select works of other modernists. Until John Espey demonstrated the untenability of the interpretation, "Hugh Selwyn Mauberley" had been read as the unironic memoir of Ezra Pound the aesthete—and Stephen Dedalus' adolescent theorizing in *A Portrait of the Artist as a Young Man* is sometimes assumed to be nothing but the author's own point of view. But these works, along with Eliot's early poems, are declarations of independence from romantic aestheticism; all three writers had much to overcome and each succeeded in his own way and degree. The man who would later declare himself a European, a modernist, an Anglican, and a classicist was born near the Mississippi River in the nineteenth century to Unitarian parents who instilled in their son a love of Byronic verse. But—for example—Eliot's early monologues, "The Love Song of J. Alfred Prufrock" and "Portrait of a Lady," are intentionally romantic explorations of the romantic personality, and a poem that examines the phenomenon of romanticism in mock-romantic fashion is as distinct from a romantic poem as a wolf is from a sheep. Eliot thought that the "only cure for Romanticism is to analyse it" and he called his career a process of "escape from personality."[76] His early monologues, in fact, seem intended to laugh out of his system the romantic personality traits that his intellect rejected.

In "Prufrock" Eliot undermines—by developing to absurdity—Lord Tennyson's approved sonority (especially that of *Maud*), his hypnotic word repetition, minted phrases, and mesmerizing rhythm. Eliot's target in the "Portrait" is, probably, Matthew Arnold's "The Buried Life"—with its expressive posturing, its vague abstractions, and its metaphor of the river-of-life.[77] And just at Eliot's inflated versification satirizes literary romanticism, so his characterizations of Prufrock and the Lady are exposés of psychological romanticism. Portraits they are not. Eliot never was much interested in character analysis, individual psychologies, or even sociological typology. As Helen Gardner has written of "Sweeney Among the Nightingales":

> It is equally significant or insignificant whether it is Agamemnon who is betrayed or Sweeney. . . . we call one beautiful and the other ugly. . . . It is perhaps an illusion that we should think the death of Agamemnon important and the death of Sweeney sordid. The nightingales make no such distinction.[78]

Any apparent portrait in Eliot's poetry is subject to evaluation as a complex, speaking objective correlative. In fact, it is reasonable to view Prufrock and the Lady as the correlatives of two intimately related sorts of romanticism: the one, intellectual, internal, radical, and modern; and the other, emotional, external, Establishmentarian, and Victorian.

The first set of modifiers describes in abstract terms what

Eliot presents concretely, and somewhat startlingly, in the character of J. Alfred Prufrock. Beginning with Prufrock's jolting association of an "evening spread out against the sky" with a "patient etherised upon a table," the reader is aware that he has entered another world, an insular universe inside a mind that has no normal perception of reality. Prufrock manipulates objective reality in the way a sleeper sometimes can direct his dreams and tame his nightmares; he transforms the threatening yellow fog into an enormous cat, which he promptly domesticates and sends off to bed with a saucer of warm milk. The creations of his singular imagination are at least as real to him as reality—he wonders, seriously, whether the mermaids he has invented will sing to him. To state that Prufrock's mind is "a circle closed on the outside" is one way of putting it.[79] Another is to say that Prufrock is a victim of romantic solipsism.

Prufrock has doubts about the existence of an objective reality, yet he also believes that he alone knows the secrets of the universe. Like his spiritual descendants, Sweeney (Ago-nistes) and Harry Monchensey, Prufrock behaves as a man who has seen too much. He identifies with various prophets and insists he could (if ever he dared to) squeeze "the universe into a ball" and "tell you all." Prufrock's reliance on what Eliot derisively called the "inner voice" conforms to the def-inition that Saintsbury offered of the romantic's procedure for determining truth: "meeting by oneself in one's own house."[80] In any other epoch, Prufrock would have been winked at as an eccentric visionary, accepted as an authentic prophet, or beheaded. But in the romantic era, truth became a personal affair. Even as a young man, Eliot found this aspect of the romantic ethos unacceptable (his Ph.D. dissertation attempts to demonstrate the impossibility of private truths). Prufrock himself puts the question whether it is worthwhile to be a visionary in the age of sunsets and dooryards and novels, when even a newly risen Lazarus would be met with: "That is not what I meant at all."

It is no accident that just as Prufrock commiserates with himself over the dismissal of his vision, the poem collapses and he cries, "It is impossible to say just what I mean!"[81] Eliot is keenly aware that private truths render communication impossible. And although Prufrock immediately goes on trying ("But as if a magic lantern . . .") he is as distrustful of language and as incapable of human relationships as Dostoevsky's underground man. It is important to note that Prufrock fails to come up with an objective correlative to his meaning that satisfies him. He concludes that words are pointed instruments with which we force into formulae ideas and feelings that cannot be formulated; that human language can be dangerous ("we drown"); and, more radically, that he would be better off as an inanimate piece of flotsam (something that feels no need of communication) at the bottom of a silent sea. For this type of romantic, truth is ineffable, and words, since they can indicate only the simplest objects, are merely pretty, tinkling sounds—this was to be Eliot's prime objection to the verse of Swinburne.[82] His inability to establish a significant relationship with another creature leaves the solipsist to create a relationship among himself. Psychological bifurcation is manifest in Prufrock's ability to dissociate his private from his public self, and Eliot has no patience with Prufrock's nonstop self-consciousness. He neither agonizes over the condition nor celebrates it; Eliot simply condemns it as narcissism.[83] In each instance where Prufrock looks at Prufrock, it is through a portable mirror, darkly: all he observes are his thin limbs, natty clothing, and (slightly) balding head.

Flourishing in the same hedgerow with the kind of radical, inward-looking romanticism Prufrock represents is the Establishmentarian, outward-reaching romanticism of the Lady in Eliot's "Portrait." (It is appropriate that we see Prufrock through his own eyes and the Lady through someone else's.) In a sense, she is the face prepared "to meet the faces that you meet" in the "Love Song"—the cordial, but artificial, exterior that covers the romantic's inner anguish. She is also an emblem of the authorized romanticism that held sway in the English-speaking world from the accession of Victoria to the First World War, and that may be characterized (around the time Eliot wrote the poem) as stale, affected, emotion-centered, and solemn. The poem's narrator is perhaps the most Tom Eliot-like persona T. S. Eliot created (prior to Lord Claverton of *The Elder Statesman*): a sensitive, cultured, well-traveled young man, alternately self-questioning and self-possessed, who has an ironic wit and a talent for coining memorable phrases. He is a poet (this is *his* portrait of the Lady) and believes in something one might term an objective correlative (or, borrowing "every changing shape to find expression"). He likes, moreover, to quote from "The Love Song of J. Alfred Prufrock."[84] The "Portrait," then, may be evaluated as (among other things) a poem about a confrontation between the Georgian world and the author of "Prufrock," a confrontation that results in the new order's wondering whether it has been too cruel to that fading world and whether the modernists' twentieth century will be an improvement.

The Lady personifies Georgian culture. She takes herself seriously—an attitude which, like Prufrock's self-consciousness, implies a degree of narcissism—in the self-dramatizing fashion that Juliet displays in her graveyard suicide ("Portrait," line 6). In the Lady's Boston residence, laughter "falls heavily among the bric-a-brac." She has read the complete works of John Ruskin and believes life flows "too far, too darkly, too solemnly ever to smile." It is plain, in addition, that she has read the complete Pater, for she thinks life an art and arranges her days as Chopin arranges a rhapsody: with "attenuated tones and carefully caught regrets." Like Chopin, she leaves much "unsaid" and relies heavily on telepathy, though this limits her understanders to a small circle of tea-soaked friends. And when she does speak, it is in words of the highest abstraction or in the stalest of clichés ("Paris in the Spring"). From the narrator's point of view, her words are comparable to a "street piano, mechanical and tired," repeating a dated song to the accompaniment of hyacinths exuding flowery *eaux*.

The Tom Eliot persona finds it difficult either to like what the Lady stood for or to rejoice at her death. As he awaits her imminent passing through three seasons (in poetic terms, the Lady has overstayed her welcome—she should have died at the opening, when in the "very dead or winter"), he comes to realize that she is not unintelligent and is easily hurt. In the Marlovian epigraph, he recalls "in another country" that he once (to freshen Eliot's metaphor) "screwed over" a cultural phenomenon—one that was superior to his own at least in gentility and ease of expression. And perhaps he recognizes in the Lady something of himself: the need to escape from "the burnt out ends of smoky days" into a moving vision of "some infinitely gentle / Infinitely suffering thing." Such a sentimental vision, while tempting to his sensitive soul, is too maudlin for his anti-romantic intellect, which draws a hand across his mouth and induces laughter.[85] Prufrock, too, externalizes and objectifies aspects of the young poet's personality—his distrust of language, his Bradleyan doubts, his congenital shyness, his need to dissociate his private from his public self—and he is subject as well to Eliot's ambiguous ironic/sympathetic treatment.

As Flaubert in his examination of romanticism, *Madame Bovary*, so Eliot in his early monologues may be mocking romantic *moeurs* while enjoying their titillation. The important question, however, is not whether Eliot's was a romantic personality, but whether his monologues are neoromantic poems (they are decidedly mock-romantic) that approve of the romantic personality (their condemnation outweighs their sympathy).

• • •

FROM the early monologues forward, Eliot's creative labors can be viewed, from certain angles, as the record of his struggle to extract a recognizable version of classicism from the heritage of the nineteenth century. A voice in "Ash-Wednesday" bids the poet to restore "With a new verse the ancient rhyme," and it is a voice whose poignant timbre we heard before. Eliot had written that his appreciation of the classical elements in Dante (and, therefore, his composition of "Ash-Wednesday") had been "held up" for a long time by "what one hated in the nineteenth century."[86] The escape from personality—from the romanticism of his youth—consumed much of Eliot's energy for most of his productive years. It was not until *Four Quartets*, Eliot's summary statement, that the wider historical perspective and more profound cultural wisdom of his criticism came to be "affirmed in verse."[87] In the *Quartets* Eliot comes to terms with romanticism. Or rather, he makes his peace with the certainty of continuing warfare between romanticism and neoclassicism, romanticism and modernism—of warfare among the dissociated fragments of his culture's sensibility.

Romanticism and neoclassicism, sensation and reason, energy and style, spirit and letter, spirit and matter, the universal and particular, the abstract and the concrete, the poetic and the prosaic, the ultimate and the conventional, the fire and the rose are one. The distinction between fires and roses, like the battle between them, resulted from a mistake of perception. As Eliot writes in "Little Gidding," about more civil wars than the English one, the opposed forces are "United in the strife which divided them" and "are folded in a single party." Yet Eliot does not seem to regret this culture-wide series of civil wars, nor to resent the vast historical expanse to which the warring antinomies pertain; at least not late in his career. In the *Quartets*, Eliot takes each phenomenon of culture or psychology in its own historical context and allows each its own voice. Like the sea of "The Dry Salvages," the whole of the *Quartets* is composed of "many voices, many gods and many voices." Eliot always had been a master ventriloquist—in the early monologues, for instance, we hear several voices of romanticism—but in *Four Quartets* Eliot drops the parodistic intent. The attempt of the *Quartets* was to provide a sequence of contexts into which the voices of Eliot's own past, and of the Western tradition, could be ventriloquized and shown to have significance in a developing personality—an entelechy, both individual and cultural, which unfolds in time.

Eliot presents us with four such temporal contexts, to which he has appended spatial names: Burnt Norton, East Coker, the Dry Salvages, and Little Gidding. All four were places important to Eliot's emotional and intellectual life; in addition, each of the four represents a stage in the development of modernism, a stage in the development of post-Renaissance aesthetics, and a substantial period in the history of the post-Renaissance West. Thus, each quartet represents a mode, a season, of thought and sensibility, which repeats itself in the lives of nations, traditions, and individuals. The *Quartets* have long been known as Eliot's "complete consort," and Helen Gardner's painstaking work on the manuscripts has shown us the extent to which Eliot wanted his *Quartets* to allude, in carefully prepared contexts, to the most important of his earlier writings.[88] There are allusions to his poems, plays, and essays on virtually every page and, as Hugh Kenner has shown, the structure of each quartet is based on the form of *The Waste Land*. But the poem is not only a summary and critique of Eliot's life and career; it is also a summary and critique of modernist ideologies of history. Several readers of the *Quartets* have noted with something hardly less than alarm that "The Dry Salvages" seems a very nineteenth-century poem. Kenner has developed an outline for the poems in which the third element of all four-part propositions is a false synthesis of the first and second elements, thus preparing us for the true synthesis of the fourth—and Donald Davie, in extending Kenner's analysis, has wondered whether the third, "nineteenth-century" quartet might be a deliberate failure. Kenner's program is most suggestive and, with Davie, we must build upon it in a way that takes account of Eliot's strongly historical outlook. "The Dry Salvages" may in part be *about* the nineteenth century as an historical false synthesis, about what Eliot had termed "a period of apparent stabilisation which was shallow and premature."[89]

The poems in fact present fragments of thought from various periods of post-Renaissance history (and "Little Gidding," as Helen Gardner has demonstrated, shows how these fragments are united in, and transcended by, Eliot's understanding of Christianity). In *Four Quartets*, Eliot makes the "process of return" apply to modern history. The poem shows how each literary movement of the post-Renaissance period has possessed the same, largely unconscious aim, and how modernism finally attained that goal and revealed it for what it had been all along: a reconstitution of the classical tradition. Modernism had its most immediate beginnings in the French symbolist movement, and "Burnt Norton," to begin with, contains a symbolist poem (part II), based on Mallarmé's *"M'introduire dans ton histoire"* (*"Tonnerre et rubis aux moyeux"*: Thunder and rubies at the hubs). The magical garden and the couple in part I strongly resemble the gardens and couples in Mallarmé's poems, from *"L'après-midi d'un faune"* to *"Prose pour des Esseintes."* The aesthetic presented in part V is also symbolist in its preoccupations and its atmospheric accoutrements. The conclusion of "Burnt Norton" deals with the relation of music and poetry, and with the identity between the words of a poem and the "Word in the desert"—both obsessions of Mallarmé's linguistic metaphysics. There is even present a "disconsolate chimera," lifted from the dramatis personae of countless *symboliste* poems. However, the poetic of part V is not only symbolist but also in some sense classical. A poem is viewed there as a symbolist whole or *Gestalt*, but the terms in which that view is expressed are curiously Aristotelian: "the end and beginning were always there"; "itself unmoving, / Only the cause and end of movement."

The introductory poem of *Four Quartets* presents symbolism as a cold, clear, intellectualist version of classical principles, and the poet associates that aesthetic with his academically insulated youth. (The word *Erhebung* [I:74], for instance, alludes to a seminar Eliot taught while a graduate instructor in philosophy at Harvard.) "Shall we follow . . . ?" the narrator asks in part I of "Burnt Norton," and he says he is taking us back to "our first world." And here is the first world of modernism: a pristine, "timeless" realm in which the mover is as yet unmoved (V:159–68) and whose poetic is innocent of the disastrous history of the twentieth century. The symbolist or post-symbolist aesthetic of "Burnt Norton" is a classicism that has not yet been proved upon the pulses, and the *Quartets* will take us from an abstract, universalized consideration of time as a metaphysical category, to the consideration, in the final quartet, of history or experience—of the English Civil War and World War II. In the scheme of *Four Quartets*, both "Burnt Norton" and "Little Gidding" are poems of the twentieth century, but, after experiencing the "historical" poems ("East Coker" and "The Dry Salvages") which they frame, we return to our own era, at the end of the *Quartets*, and know the place for the first time. From "Burnt Norton" to "Little Gidding": from Time to History: from a dissociated sensibility that abstracts to a fully associated sensibility that contextualizes—this is a pattern of the *Quartets* and perhaps also of modern intellectual history, which moves, Eliot's poem would show us, from classicism to contextualism by way of historicism.

It is obvious that Eliot did not begin the *Quartets* with this pattern in mind as a controlling design—he did not even know that there would be more poems like "Burnt Norton"—but it is also clear that, by the time he commenced work on "East Coker," he had realized the possibilities of an historical patterning and determined to explore them. In a 1941 letter to Anne Ridler, Eliot writes of "East Coker":

> I am glad . . . that you like part IV, which is in a way the heart of the matter. My intention was . . . to do something in the style of Cleveland or Benlowes, only better; and I like the use of this so English XVII form. . . . But the poem as a whole—this five part form—is an attempt to weave several quite unrelated strands together in an emotional whole, so that really there isn't any heart of the matter.[90]

If there is a "heart of the matter" in "East Coker," Eliot says it is to be found in his selection of a second-rate seventeenth-century literary fashion as the vehicle of his expression. Herbert Howarth identifies part IV as an imitation of the English Petrarchans and calls it "a remarkable essay in neoclassicism."

The lyric of part IV ("The wounded surgeon") and the periphrastic poem of part II ("What is the late November doing") are examples of what presented itself as classicism during much of the seventeenth and eighteenth centuries; and part II, in particular, is accompanied by an examination of what Eliot thought was wrong with that style and its appellation:

> That was a way of putting it—not very satisfactory:
> A periphrastic study in a worn-out poetical fashion,
> Leaving one still with the intolerable wrestle
> With words and meanings. The poetry does not matter
>
> (II:68–71)

Making careful distinctions between the classical and unclassical elements of neoclassicist verse had been one of the prime tasks Eliot undertook in his early essays, and his prose critique of neoclassicism is strikingly similar to the judgment pronounced in "East Coker": "That was a way of putting it—not very satisfactory" (II:68). In his 1921 *Chapbook* essay, "Prose and Verse," Eliot draws a sharp distinction between verse and poetry—and, as we have seen, much of his early criticism was directed at the absence of poetry ("The poetry does not matter") in the verse of writers like Philip Massinger.[91]

"East Coker," then, brings us to the early days of the modernist movement, just as "Burnt Norton" explores modernism's symbolist origins. "East Coker" echoes the days when Eliot was simultaneously obsessed, as a critic, with the neoclassical style and conjoined in a poets' conspiracy (with Pound) to employ only the most formal of academic forms. It is the period of "The Hippopotamus" (1917) and "Ben Jonson" (1919). "East Coker" represents the ideology of return in its most deliberate and obvious—its most archaizing—aspect. (At the personal level, the poem visits, in part I, the home of Eliot's distinguished, but quaint, pre-Mayflower ancestry.) In the second quartet, we have left behind the pristine, insular world of the symbolists. Historical events have made quick work of aestheticism—these were "the years of *l'entre deux guerres*" (V:2)—and, hence, the aesthetic argument of part V is expressed in military images: "raid," "equipment," "squads," "venture," "fight," "conquer." Modernism was no longer so much about the "intense moment / Isolated, with no before and after" (V:192–93), because the pattern of existence had become "more complicated / Of dead and living" (V:191–92). "East Coker" shows us how Europe moved, under the pressure of events, from neoclassicism to romanticism, and from the modernism of the teens to the modernism of the twenties. By the close of the second quartet, "middle modernism" and neoclassicism each has progressed "Into another intensity" (V:205): "The Dry Salvages" will illustrate "a wholly new start, and a different kind of failure" (V:175).

As Donald Davie makes plain, the third quartet is dominated by images of the nineteenth century—of romanticism and Victorianism. This is the world of Eliot's childhood, and the poem is studded with quotations from his schoolboy reading. As Helen Gardner notes, the opening lines allude to Whitman's lilacs poem in the meter of Longfellow's "Evangeline," and the poem concludes with a sentiment out of Ruskin. "The Dry Salvages" is peopled by ghosts of the not-so-distant past: Wordsworth ("Tintern Abbey" and *The Prelude*),[92] Coleridge (the *Biographia*),[93] Shelley (the West Wind ode),[94] Tennyson ("Ulysses" and *In Memoriam*),[95] and Kipling (*Captains Courageous*).[96] The poem's evolutionist refrain is Darwinian, and one can hear echoes out of Spencer, the thinker who Eliot believed was the leading influence on Victorian culture.[97] The river that courses through the heart of the third quartet is both the river of progress (Eliot's characterization of Huck Finn's Mississippi)[98] and also the river of myth, which runs downstream into the heart of darkness. The nineteenth century followed the river in both its aspects and came to realize the complexities of that double commitment, both to progress and to myth.

The early modern centuries had held to the serene and rational belief that things change or even develop, and that the new succeeds the old:

> . . . In succession
> Houses rise and fall, crumble, are extended,
> Are removed, destroyed, restored, or in their place
> Is an open field, or a factory, or a by-pass.
>
> (I:1–4)

Yet even here, in "East Coker," Eliot's "neoclassical" quartet, we hear that man's world is full of "old stones that cannot be deciphered" (V:196), and a voice begins to wonder whether the optimistic calm of the seventeenth and eighteenth centuries was a mere self-deceit,

> The serenity only a deliberate hebetude,
> The wisdom only the knowledge of dead secrets
> Useless in the darkness into which they peered
> Or from which they turned their eyes
> (II:78–81)

That voice becomes a good deal more intense in the third quartet, as in fact the voice of questioning became in the nineteenth century. From the first line of "The Dry Salvages" ("I do not know much about gods"), linear progress and the optimism inherited from the eighteenth century—from the Enlightenment—are brought face to face with the obstacles posed by implacable deity. "The Dry Salvages" corrects the comfortable certainties of "East Coker" with a series of uncomfortable recognitions:

> Now, we come to discover that the moments of agony
> . . . are likewise permanent. . . .
> People change, and smile: but the agony abides.

> Time . . .
>   is what it always was. . . .
> And the way up is the way down, the way forward is the
>   way back.

> You cannot face it steadily, but this thing is sure,
> That time is no healer: the patient is no longer here.[99]

The willingness to face unpleasant facts, the sense of the strangeness of reality, is what Eliot admired most in romanticism:

> The strangeness . . . , the peculiarity is seen to be the
> peculiarity of all great poetry. . . . It is merely a peculiar
> honesty, which, is a world too frightened to be honest,
> is peculiarly terrifying. It is an honesty against which the

whole world conspires, because it is unpleasant. Blake's
poetry has the unpleasantness of great poetry.[100]

The nineteenth century's recognition of the gods, and its
readiness to peer into the abyss, make its poetry, for Eliot,
great poetry—but, in the third quartet, as in his criticism,
Eliot is put off by the romantics' mythological dilettantism.
Nature, the machine, and the "daemonic, chthonic / Powers"
have their aficionados, no less than Dionysus in part I, Death
in part II, Krishna in part III, the Virgin in part IV, or the
gods of psychology and superstition in part V. Eliot's objection
was not niggling: it had been the basis of his distinction between classic excellence and mere genius:

> The concentration resulting from a framework of my-
> thology and theology and philosophy is one of the reasons
> why Dante is a classic, and Blake only a poet of genius.[101]

Neoclassicism and early modernism had erred in the direction
of periphrasis and smug overcertainty; romanticism and the
"middle period" of modernism erred in the direction of self-
indulgence and an undisciplined lust for spirit.[102] "Ash-
Wednesday" and the "Ariel poems," the works of Eliot's
"middle period," are alluded to frequently in "The Dry Salvages,"[103] and one wonders in respectful silence at what comment Eliot might be making about the nature of his verse, and
even about the texture of his religious commitment, from his
conversion in 1927 through the decade of the thirties. On this
subject, Eliot made sobering remarks in private.[104]

The fourth quartet makes a radical departure from the state
of cultural mind embodied in the third. "Little Gidding" represents the break between the modernism of "Ash-Wednesday" and that of Four Quartets, as also between the nineteenth-century ethos and that of the twentieth century. Eliot
presents these breaks as an unexpected renaissance: "Mid-
winter spring is its own season. . . . the unimaginable / Zero
summer" (I:18–19). In the darkest hours of the Second World
War (to which Eliot alludes throughout "Little Gidding" and
during which three of the quartets were composed), the past

seems to find its explanation and fulfillment in the present. Eliot's colleague, Middleton Murry, refers to that war as "not just a war but the consummation of a civilization,"[105] and this "privileged" moment of history is what the speaker in "Burnt Norton" had seen as "both a new world / And the old made explicit, understood" (II:75–76). In part II of "Little Gidding," where the Eliot persona meets a ghost during a Nazi air raid on London, the dead masters of the first three quartets come to be resurrected as a *single figure* because, from the late-modern vantage point, the poet sees them "All touched by a common genius, / United in the strife which divided them" (III:173–74).

"The Dry Salvages" had already demonstrated how progressivist Victorians and anti-progressivist romantics were navigating a single river; in "Little Gidding," the poet attempts to show how the various insights of the various modern movements are reconciled and epiphanized in what has been called "high modernism" and in its ultimate document, *Four Quartets*. Eliot wrote, in a letter already quoted, that the *Quartets* were "an attempt to weave several quite unrelated strands into an emotional whole" and, in making this claim, Eliot points us toward the theory of personal identity he had offered decades earlier in his doctoral dissertation. In *Knowledge and Experience*, Eliot wrote that, in the Bradleyan philosophy, any individual consciousness is comprised of several points of view, which must be integrated and reconciled if the individual is to achieve maturity:

> we vary by passing from one point of view to another or as I have tried to suggest, by occupying more than one point of view at the same time, an attitude which gives us our assumptions, our half-objects, our figments of imagination; we vary by self-transcendence. The point of view (or finite centre) has for its object one consistent world and accordingly no finite centre can be self-sufficient, for the life of a soul does not consist in the contemplation of one consistent world but in the painful task of unifying . . . jarring and incompatible ones, and pass-

ing, when possible, from two or more discordant viewpoints to a higher one which shall somehow include and
transmute them.[106]

This passage is of capital importance to *Four Quartets*. The
cultural and aesthetic viewpoints of the first three poems are
reconciled by those of the fourth. The "indifference" of the
early modern centuries, and the dilettantism of the later modern ones, are overcome in "Little Gidding" in a demonstration
that the dichotomy has been based on a shallow interpretation
of events, a foregrounded picture of modern history:

> There are three conditions which often look alike
> Yet differ completely, flourish in the same hedgerow:
> Attachment to self and to things and to persons,
>   detachment
> From self and from things and from persons; and,
>   growing between them, indifference
> Which resembles the others as death resembles life,
> Being between two lives. . . .
>   (III:1–6)

Among the many things one can say about them, these three
conditions correspond to the three preceding quartets: "The
Dry Salvages" (attachment, or emotional intensity), "Burnt
Norton" (detachment, or intellectual abstraction), and, growing between them, "East Coker" (indifference). The opposing
qualities, like the corresponding quartets, are now "worlds
become much like each other" (II:122). And, as Rousseau
long before taught us, a different patterning of events can
renew or transfigure our history—indeed

>   This is the use of memory:
> For liberation . . .
> From the future as well as the past. . . .
>
>   . . . See, now they vanish,
> The faces and places, . . .
> To become renewed, transfigured, in another pattern.[107]

"Little Gidding" effects the union of romantic intensity and neoclassical discipline: "the fire and the rose are one." The poem passes, as Eliot describes the process in his dissertation, from "discordant viewpoints to a higher one."

Eliot had said, many years before he wrote the *Quartets*, that his "exasperated generation" had reviewed and, consequently, rejected both the Newton worship of the neoclassical centuries and the Darwin worship of the nineteenth century, and he wondered whether the twentieth century might come to "suspect that precision and profundity are not incompatible."[108] The union of discipline and intensity or "precision and profundity" is, for Eliot, a kind of *reunion*. The poet underscores this fact by including seventy lines of *terza rima* in his "complete consort," "intersection time" quartet—seventy lines, moreover, in which T. S. Eliot, elder statesman of European letters, is brought face to face with the whole Western tradition from, perhaps, Homer and Vergil to Dante and Milton and Yeats. In becoming the present, the past has come full circle with the future—this is the essence of the historical "process of return," of the historical outlook that Eliot associates with the word "classicism":

> We shall not cease from exploration
> And the end of all our exploring
> Will be to arrive where we started
> And know the place for the first time.
> Through the unknown, remembered gate
> When the last of earth left to discover
> Is that which was the beginning. . . .
> (LG V:239–45)

But the *Quartets* are not only a general presentation and analysis of the ideology of return, they also comprise the precise poetics of modernist classicism. We have noted how, in "Burnt Norton," part V, Eliot recognizes an analogy between the symbolist aesthetic and the Aristotelian principle of wholeness: ". . . the end precedes the beginning, / And the end and the beginning were always there / Before the beginning and after the end." In "East Coker," parts II and V, we find the neoclassical obsession with craft that appears in, for example, Horace—and, in part II especially, emphasis falls on the necessity to avoid the neoclassical pitfall of periphrasis. It is a necessity that Longinus, too, underscores: "periphrasis is a hazardous business. . . . it lapses quickly into insipidity, akin to empty chatter and dulness of wit."[109] The traditionalism of innovation is, thus, a leading theme of all the aesthetic discourses in the *Quartets*; but, in part V of "Little Gidding," Eliot for the first time sets forth his own poetic, and it reads almost as if it were a versification of Aristotle:

> . . . every phrase
> And sentence that is right (where every word is at home,
> Taking its place to support the others,
> The word neither diffident nor ostentatious,
> An easy commerce of the old and the new,
> The common word exact without vulgarity,
> The formal world precise but not pedantic,
> The complete consort dancing together). . . .
>   (V:216–23)

Eliot may have had in mind a passage like the following from the *Poetics*:

> a diction abounding in unfamiliar usages has a dignity. . . . However, the exclusive use of forms of this kind would result either in a riddle or in barbarism. . . . What is needed, then, is some mixture of these various elements. For the one kind will prevent the language from being mean and commonplace, that is, the unusual words, the metaphors, the ornamental terms, and the other figures I have described, while the everyday words give the necessary clarity.[110]

Taken in its broadest signification—that poetic excellence derives from the blending of opposed qualities—this passage from Aristotle is an explication of Eliot's formal procedure in the *Quartets*. Eliot's poem is a musical duel in which prosodic sections comment mordantly on imagist passages. Longinus, too, might have admired Eliot's procedure of composition, and, like Eliot, Longinus saw himself as a late representative of the classical tradition in aesthetics, as a Greek in a world of Romans: "Now Aristotle and Theophrastus declare that the following phrases have a softening effect on bold metaphors: 'as if,' and 'as it were,' and 'if one may put it like this,' and 'if one may venture the expression'; for qualifications, they say, mitigate the boldness."[111] The most amusing instances of the practice in *Four Quartets* are found in "East Coker," when the poet feels his imagism going too far:

> You say I am repeating
> Something I have said before
> (III:134–35)

and

> That was a way of putting it—not very satisfactory.
> (II:68)

At the formal level, Eliot is collapsing neoclassical discourse into the romantic image, an image whose ancestry he had traced earlier in his career to Aristotle. Thus, in the poem that is Eliot's consummate achievement, two "classical" traditions (neoclassical discourse and the romantic/Aristotelian image) eye each other suspiciously but, in the end, dance together. Eliot never denied that a classicism composed of harmonious fragments would be different from the classicism of fifteenth-century Florence, but then, Renaissance classicism diverges at least as widely from that of fifth-century Athens. Modernist classicism, if we concede the possibility of its existence, would necessarily be modern. In Eliot's words:

> It must not be forgotten that a poet in a romantic age cannot be a "classical" poet except in tendency. If he is sincere, he must express with individual differences the general state of mind—not as a duty, but simply because he cannot help participating in it.[112]

Yet we must qualify Eliot's self-conscious remark about Baudelaire, "the first counter-romantic in poetry." While "a poet in a romantic age cannot be a 'classical' poet except in tendency," it must not be forgotten that classicism itself is only a tendency and that, if an artist achieves the classic ideal, that ideal will be "altered in fulfillment" (LG I:34).

Ultimately, even Eliot may have conceived too large a gap between the romantic and the classic, between modernity and antiquity. To conceive a smaller one might be worth our while. That epistemic adventure could obviate some energy-consuming traumas: above all, the struggle to establish a continuity between romantics and modernists and a breach in our cultural history with the rise of romanticism. Our century's poet-critics—the modernists—placed a break, equally unhelpful, between the romantics and themselves; but later academic critics may have misplaced their talents in the attempt to undermine the modernists' understanding of their historical position. We might do well to imagine modernity as an uninterrupted, constructive development, and to imagine a break, if we must have one, at the classical revival of the Renaissance, with which the idea of modernity began.

PART TWO

The History of an Ideology: Case Studies

Tragedy

I should either have stuck closer to Aeschylus or else taken a great deal more liberty with his myth. One evidence of this is the appearance of those ill-fated figures, the Furies. . . . We put them on stage, and they looked like uninvited guests who had strayed in from a fancy dress ball. We concealed them behind gauze, and they suggested a still out of a Walt Disney film. We made them dimmer, and they looked like shrubbery just outside the window. . . . I have seen them signalling from across the garden, or swarming on to the stage like a football team, and they are never right. They never succeed in being either Greek goddesses or modern spooks. But their failure is merely a symptom of the failure to adjust the ancient with the modern.

T. S. Eliot, "Poetry and Drama"

A COMPELLING IDEA about history is not the same as historical destiny. As an historical principle, the "process of return" is lucid and eloquent but—as Jacob Burckhardt learned with bitterness—it is one thing to talk of an antique revival or to reformulate the canons of classicism, quite another to reinstate the cultural institutions of a distant past. For literary history, the rebirth of the classical world order necessarily would involve the revitalization of its fundamental genres: ritual tragedy, Homeric epic, and primitive myth. In the modernists' eyes, all three had been replaced by post-classical imposters: by naturalist drama, prose fiction, and the Christian *kerygma*. The most persistent of these frauds proved to be the realist theater, and, of all the "revivalist" efforts, the attempt to bring ritual tragedy onto a diffident bourgeois stage participated most in the "Burckhardtian" spirit. The tragic revival was

directed, in the most willful fashion, by an historical theory—
by the detestation of modernity for its refusal to produce,
spontaneously, a phenomenon that the ideology of return demanded.

This effort, and the belief in its apocalyptic significance,
began its most productive life in England during the early part
of the nineteenth century and had its most interesting embodiment in the modernist verse-plays of W. B. Yeats, but the
possibility of a tragic revival was raised first, perhaps, during
the period in Germany when dramatists and critics were determining the future direction of the young German national
theater. In his lectures on drama (published in 1809), August
Wilhelm Schlegel carefully considered the possibilities for a
revival of tragedy on the Aeschylus/Sophocles model, and he
found them more than somewhat unlikely. His assumption
throughout was that the modern stage and the ancient Greek
have so little in common that a single term could not encom-
pass both:

> When we hear the word "theatre," we naturally think of
> what with us bears the same name; and yet nothing can
> be more different from our theatre, in its entire structure,
> than that of the Greeks. If in reading the Grecian pieces
> we associate our own stage with them, the light in which
> we shall view them must be false in every respect.[1]

In the same lecture (the fourth), Schlegel emphasized that what
seem to moderns the most artificial elements of Greek tragedy—the chorus, the use of masks, and so forth—were not
peripheral, but central, to its meaning:

> Fidelity of representation was less their object than beauty;
> with us it is exactly the reverse. On this principle, the use
> of masks, which appears astonishing to us, was not only
> justifiable, but absolutely essential.[2]

The necessary artificiality of Greek verse-tragedy, and its
connection with religious ritual, were fairly recent discoveries
in Schlegel's time. Lessing, for example, had demonstrated in
1767–68 (in the *Hamburgische Dramaturgie*) how the French

classic dramatists had failed on this accont to understand the Greek tragedians—and Schlegel reiterated and expanded upon Lessing's criticism of the French, and of Aristotle, in lectures 17 and 18. Attic tragedy was thought to be a not-since-repeated form, distinct from any imitation or description, ancient or modern. Thus, in the fifth lecture of his series on drama, Schlegel predicted that the ritualistic tragedy of Athens would never be possible on the modern stage:

> The Greek tragedy, in its pure and unaltered state, will always for our theatres remain an exotic plant, which we can hardly hope to cultivate with any success, even in the hothouse of learned art and criticism. The Grecian mythology, which furnishes the materials of ancient tragedy, is as foreign to the minds and imaginations of most of the spectators, as its form and manner of representation. But to endeavour to force into that form materials of a wholly different nature . . . must always be a most unprofitable and hopeless attempt.[3]

And in concluding his lecture series, Schlegel reiterated his opinion, but on this occasion with a wistful air of regret:

> The genuine imitation of Greek Tragedy has far more affinity to our national ways of thinking; but it is beyond the comprehension of the multitude, and, like the contemplation of ancient statues, can never be more than an acquired artistic enjoyment for a few highly cultivated minds.[4]

This point of view, and the regretful tone in which Schlegel expressed it, have a long history in the aesthetic, and also in the sociological, thinking of the nineteenth and twentieth centuries. That history begins most conveniently in 1814, at a London production of *Hamlet*—a production known to posterity only because Percy Shelley, age twenty-two, made a premature exit from its audience. Shelley found the performance "disgusting," because, his wife recorded, this *Hamlet* was all wrong: overwrought, overgrand, overly mechanical, and utterly without nuance.[5] In walking out of the theater,

Shelley may have been protesting the nature of the building and of the audience as much as he was objecting to the nature of the production. Until as late as 1843, only two London theaters (Covent Garden and Drury Lane) had the right to legitimate play production, and these were the most bourgeois of British institutions. The theaters themselves were vast, cavernous structures, catering to the desire of middle-class audiences for bombastic acting and spectacular mechanical effects. The plays produced at the patent theaters, and in similar institutions on the Continent, were of a kind that, by the second quarter of the eighteenth century, had come to be called the *drame bourgeois*. From the first, these plays met the disapprobation of traditionalist critics. To describe and publicize his adaptation of Edward Moore's *The Gamester*, Bernard Joseph Saurin used the epithet "*tragédie bourgeoise*," and, in a letter of 1768, Friedrich Melchior von Grimm protested that that coinage was a contradiction in terms: "I disliked that advertisement at once. If *Béverly* is a tragedy, then why is it bourgeois?"[6]

To the traditionalist, the middle class was a subject fit only for comedy; a tragic bourgeois was as risible an impossibility as a *bourgeois gentilhomme*. The *drame bourgeois* was objectionably middle-class not only in its characters and its staging, but in its intentions as well. The bourgeois playwrights shifted the emphasis in tragedy writing from a mixture of aesthetic and moral considerations to an emphasis on morality—on middle-class morality—alone. As Joseph Mitchell wrote in his preface to *The Fatal Extravagance* (1726): "Everything in a tragedy which has not a direct and visible tendency to the moral it is writ for is superfluous and monstrous." The moral lessons taught, moreover, were of an entirely new and didactic kind. In his study, *The Early Middle Class Drama*, F. O. Nolte observes that while "Racine wrote for a mature audience that wanted to be reminded; Diderot [wrote] for an immature audience that needed to be initiated."[7] The new bourgeois tragedy was

strongly conditioned by social and economic changes, was distinctly popular in its appeal, and, to this end, was didactically rather than aesthetically inclined; it was given to propaganda and reform; its characteristic medium was prose. . . .[8]

This sort of didactic prose-drama possessed very little appeal for the romantic imagination, in general, or for Shelley, in particular. In the *Defence of Poetry*, published some six years after the *Hamlet* debacle, Shelley proposed that verse, music, and dancing be restored to a theater that, moreover, needed once again to establish "a relation between the drama and religion."[9] Shelley, in effect, was proposing to restore all those artificial elements of ritual tragedy which A. W. Schlegel had pronounced impossible for the modern, bourgeois stage. And, in the same essay, Shelley offered what is perhaps the earliest perception of the important place that a revival of ancient dramatic forms necessarily held for the ideologies of return:

> The connexion of poetry and social good is more observable in the drama than in whatever other form. And it is indisputable that the highest perfection of human society has ever corresponded with the highest dramatic excellence; and that the corruption or the extinction of the drama in a nation where it has once flourished, is a mark of corruption of manners, and an extinction of the energies which sustain the soul of social life. But . . . life may be preserved and renewed, if men should arise capable of bringing back the drama to its principles.[10]

Shelley turned the customarily accepted relation of art and history on its head: it was not that modern historical conditions would lead to a revival of ritual tragedy but that such a revival would significantly improve the complexion of modern history. As A. W. Schlegel had assumed, any attempt to resurrect the ritual drama of antiquity would itself be a tragic agon, undertaken in utter disregard of the natural conditions of modernity. Shelley's *Prometheus Unbound* is an unstageable play, antiqued with ritual gestures (Furies "tear the Veil" in act 1), paeans to Dionysus, and self-advertising verse ("To the Deep, to the Deep, down down!"). Its author's contempt for the modern theater was so extreme that, as M. H. Abrams has observed, he removed his "spirit drama" as far as possible from the real world of ordinary men and women, even from the ordinary world of the drama. There is, in the *Prometheus*, no interest in dramatic development, but only in the instants of turning that occupied the writers of romantic "crisis odes."[11] Shelley's *Prometheus* broke much ground and later dramatists have been indebted to it. When Robert Browning complained, in a letter to Elizabeth Barrett, that he had trouble writing for the stage since the only events that interested him were those in the characters' minds, the most important Victorian playwright was associating himself with a Shelleyan insight. The "follow follow" at the close of Eliot's *Family Reunion* is a quote from Shelley's revision of Aeschylus, and the whole "Circe" episode of *Ulysses* is a reverential travesty of *Prometheus Unbound*.[12]

Shelley was not the only English romantic whose dislike of contemporary theater brought him to write a new kind of drama. Lord Byron, Shelley's friend (and a governor of Drury Lane during 1814), insisted that he purposely wrote *Manfred* (1816–17) to be a drama "quite impossible for the stage, for which my intercourse with Drury Lane has given me the greatest contempt."[13] A much more accessible work than Shelley's *Prometheus*, though less influential, the *Manfred* of Byron is a better model of the new type of drama that emerged in the early nineteenth century. Byron's play bears at its head what might serve as epigraph for all the anti-theater drama that succeeds it: "There are more things in heaven and earth, Horatio, than are dreamt of in your philosophy." As in most subsequent plays of this kind, a character who lives at a very high altitude of reality (in this instance, the mountain climber Manfred) is played off against characters who (in the language of *Murder in the Cathedral*) live and partly live at a much lower level—the level we tend to associate with sensible, bourgeois existence. This second group of characters perceives the awakening that has come to the tragic hero as a form of madness—

CHAMOIS HUNTER. Alas! he's mad—but yet I must
    not leave him.
MANFRED. I would I were—for then the things I see
    Would be but a distempered dream.[14]

—and the two groups are utterly incapable of communication.
Byron goes so far as to make the disability physical: Manfred
cannot even hear the chamois hunter call to him as he stands
on the mountain's brink. More crucially, the higher level of
reality that Manfred—tragic hero—represents is associated
with classical antiquity. At the play's end, Manfred contemplates the ruins of antiquity and in them finds both "religion"
and a way of making beautiful an otherwise unlovely world.[15]

These attitudes were characteristic of several important
playwrights of the nineteenth century and of most of its distinguished failures. After the demise of his *Guy Domville*,
Henry James wrote in a letter, "I may have been meant for
the drama—God knows!—but I certainly wasn't meant for
the theatre." James's simultaneous love for the genre and contempt for its contemporary social expression is a good example of a distinction made by "art dramatists" in an age
when many playwrights felt it necessary to compose two versions of their works, one for the stage and one for publication.
All revivalist thinking about drama depends upon this bifurcated perception. The distinction that William Hazlitt makes,
in his *Lectures on the English Poets* (1818), between the bourgeois tragedy of sensibility and the "high tragedy" of the
passions partakes of it—as does the distinction Hegel makes,
in the lectures of 1826, between mere suffering and "truly
tragic suffering." So too, and more importantly, does Hegel's
opposition of the modern and the tragic world views:

The self-reliant solidity and totality of the heroic character does not wish to share the guilt and knows nothing
of this opposition of subjective intentions and objective
deeds and consequences, while the implications and ram-
ifications of modern actions are such that everybody tries
to push all guilt as far away from himself as possible.[16]

Hegel says he can make this claim because, in the ancient heroic age, "the individual was essentially one, and whatever was objective was and remained his, if it had issued from him." Tragedy is not merely a literary genre but the expression of an outlook diametrically opposed to, and vastly healthier than, that of modernity—all the revivalist dramaturges would subscribe to this assertion. The bourgeois ethic of modernity assumes that life is supposed to be made as easy and regular as possible, leading the collectivized man from a hygienic birth to an anesthetized death. The tragic world view is composed of oppositions (winter/spring, self/world, male/female, etc.) that drive the self-aware individual from a fatal confrontation to an agonistic rebirth. Schopenhauer would go so far as to represent tragedy as the opposite of life-as-the-mass-lives-it, almost as a turning away from life in general.

Although he formulated his theory of tragedy in opposition to Schopenhauer's, Nietzsche also participates in this bifurcated perception and in the assumption that the tragic and the modern are opposed states of consciousness. The most important theoretician of the new drama divides reality into a bourgeois, modern surface and a deeper level that he, like Hegel and Byron and Shelley, associates with things Greek. The one world is that of "mediocrity, democracy, and 'modern ideas' "; the other is a "new mode of existence"—a world he calls "tragic" in spirit—whose "precise nature we can divine only with the aid of Greek analogies." The former is "appearance"; the latter, "truly reality."[17] Each level possesses its peculiar form of drama. The terms Nietzsche chooses for discussing the theater of Euripides are revealing:

> From now on the stock phrases to represent everyday affairs were ready to hand. While hitherto the character of dramatic speech had been determined by the demigod in tragedy and the drunken satyr in comedy, that bourgeois mediocrity in which Euripides placed all his political hopes now came to the fore.[18]

The theater of the bourgeois *polis* is, according to Nietzsche, too militantly anti-mythical, too "Apollonian" and too "Socratic," too cheerily optimistic about the bond between knowledge and virtue. It is for him a kind of "genteel domestic drama" that spelled "the death of tragedy."[19] This naturalist drama aims at the suppression of all Dionysian energies, and Nietzsche describes that attempt in language that reflects the politics of a continent controlled by repressive bourgeois governments. "The only way I am able to view Doric art," he writes, ". . . is as a perpetual military encampment of the Apollonian forces," as an art that "could endure only in a continual state of resistance against the titanic and barbaric menace of Dionysos."[20] "Inarticulate naturalism" in the theater maintains this suppression by exalting the false god of realism—a realism based entirely on the topmost surface of "true reality."[21] This, Nietzsche calls "our idolatry of verisimilitude . . . the realm of the wax-works."[22]

In opposition to that sort of drama, Nietzsche proposes a return to the most "artificial" elements of Greek tragedy—to the chorus, the use of music, the poetic language, the close connection with religious ritual, and the grounding in myth.[23] Nietzsche's passionate attachment to artificial, classical verse-tragedy is, therefore, no mere aesthetic preference, and his assault on naturalist prose-drama is simultaneously an attack on an entire culture composed of "abstract man stripped of myth, abstract education, abstract mores, abstract law, abstract government."[24] The connection of sociological and formal questions concerning the drama is made with full consciousness of its philosophical and political implications. Nietzsche discusses, for example, why tragedy and what he calls the "tragic world view" have nothing in common with "constitutional democracy."[25] His hope that tragedy may be revived is not at all a prayer for better theater-going in Germany, but a wish that science—or the "theoretical" *Weltanschauung*—be "at last . . . pushed to its limits and, faced with those limits [be] forced to renounce its claim to universal validity."[26] In the new drama, science and symbolism will embrace with the fierceness of enemies who have fallen in love. Just as in Aeschylean Athens, the birth of tragedy (or the rebirth, in this case) will enact a rite of "glorious transfiguration" that seals the reconciliation of opponent world views.[27] Shelley had written that healthy societies will have healthy theatrical lives; Nietzsche writes that, when tragedy is born again, we will know that Western civilization has been reborn as well. And we will witness, Nietzsche says, an arcane form of drama in the act of consummating and celebrating that rebirth.

Nietzsche's youthful notions in *The Birth of Tragedy* suffer from the faults of overenthusiasm: as the author himself later recognized, they are embarrassingly naïve. A more hard-headed approach to modern tragedy begins—not surprisingly—with Karl Marx. A political theorist who, at one time, hoped to found a journal of drama criticism, Marx read Aeschylus every year in Greek and made very high claims for Greek tragedy—including that *Prometheus Bound* "mortally wounded" the "gods of Greece."[28] "Prometheus," Marx wrote in 1841, "is the foremost saint and martyr in the philosopher's calendar."[29] Furthermore, like those of Shelley, Byron, and Nietzsche, Marx's perception of the drama is bi-planar; he contrasts, unfavorably, "the narrow bourgeois form" with "the ancient conception" of art and life.[30] Yet despite his love of the classics, Marx's belief in social progress left him in what is, for us, an instructive bind:

> It is well known that Greek mythology is not only the arsenal of Greek art but also its foundation. Is the view of nature and of social relations which underlies the Greek imagination and also, therefore, Greek [mythology], possible with self-acting machines, railways, locomotives, and telegraphs? What chance has Vulcan against Roberts & Co., Jupiter against the lightning-conductor, and Hermes against the *crédit mobilier*? All mythology overcomes and dominates and shapes the forces of nature in the imagination and by the imagination: it therefore disappears when these have been truly mastered. . . . Looked at from another side: is Achilles possible with powder and lead? Or the *Iliad* with the printing-press, to say nothing of the printing machine? Do not song and saga and the Muse

necessarily come to an end with the printer's bar . . . ?
But the difficulty lies not in understanding that Greek art
[is] bound up with certain forms of social development.
The difficulty is that [it still affords] us artistic pleasure
and that in a certain respect [it] still counts as a norm
and as [an] unattainable model. A man cannot become
a child again, or he becomes childish. But does he not
find joy in the child's naivety, and must he not himself
strive to reproduce its truth at a higher stage? . . . [yet]
the immature social conditions under which it arose, and
under which alone it could arise, can never return.[31]

· · ·

FACED with this same dilemma, A. W. Schlegel sighed, and
Nietzsche could only hope for the arrival of social conditions
under which tragedy might again flourish. But for the pro-
spective playwright, a cosmic patience is no virtue. Playwrights must write plays, and so the modernists—who craved
to revive the "unattainable [Greek] model" which Marx and
Nietzsche loved, yet who also understood that any such reconstitution would be a sort of literary relic—were compelled
to make of their art a form and forum for sociological warfare.
In his note of 1923 on *The Only Jealousy of Emer*, W. B.
Yeats observes of his hieratic, anti-naturalist *Four Plays for
Dancers* that

> In writing these little plays I knew that I was creating
> something which could only fully succeed in a civilization
> very unlike ours. I think they should be written for some
> country where all clases share in a half-mythological,
> half-philosophical folk-belief which the writer and his
> small audience lift into a new subtlety. All my life I have
> longed for such a country, and always found it quite
> impossible to write without having as much belief in its
> real existence as a child has in that of the wooden birds,
> beasts, and persons of his toy Noah's ark.[32]

Yeats signals his assent to the Marxian proposition that
certain literary genres belong to certain types of society—the

realist prose-drama to commercial/progressive/science-oriented society, in this instance—but he makes it abundantly clear that he would prefer to write for a make-believe culture than to accept the artistic conventions that belong to his own. The modernists' attempt to write drama in arcane forms is a protest against the world outside the toy ark, and the theme of most ritual verse-drama in the modern era is summarized in a "Yeatsian" essay by Christopher Fry:

> what we *call* reality is a false god, the dull eye of custom. . . . And if you accept my proposition that reality is altogether different from our stale view of it, we can say that poetry is the language of reality.[33]

Yeats's toy ark, like its Biblical precursor, contains the last remnant of the *cognoscenti*: its make-believe world is not an invention—it is the only genuine reality. To E. E. Cummings and most other modern verse-dramatists, the world of realist prose-drama is "some unworld which would rather have its too than eat its cake."[34]

This modernist assault on the common culture poses large questions for the dramatist—the only writer, after all, who cannot pretend to ignore his audience. And it is the theatrical career of W. B. Yeats that represents the most honest and significant struggle with these sociological issues by a theorist of cultural *nostos*. Yeats came to deny that there was any longer a culture that "all classes share," but only the culture of a single class (of the bourgeoisie, as he states in several essays), which had been imposed on the whole civilization. Yeats decided, therefore—after several years of work for the commercial theater in Dublin—that he would write for "a small audience" of knowers who had acquired by intellectual effort the authentic, national culture that once all classes had shared as an unconscious heritage. He would not, however, relinquish his social and political themes, nor dissolve into an ineffectual aestheticism, for he had entered the theater, to begin with, in order to "plunge" art "back into social life." Even his later plays would be "only too powerful politically" and, in his voluminous theater notes, Yeats again and again connected his dramatic enterprise both with his commitment to the Irish Nationalist cause and with his hatred of the bourgeoisie.[35]

For, in fact, the three were one. Yeats's dislike of England was not so much an expression of his opposition to foreign rule as it was an expression of his hatred for the middle-class life of which Britain was then the chief exemplar. "It is easy," Yeats wrote in 1904,

> for us to hate England in this country, and we give that hatred something of nobility if we turn it now and again into hatred of the vulgarity of commercial syndicates, of all that commercial finish and pseudo-art she has done so much to cherish.[36]

Similarly, the Irish "folk" were praiseworthy because their delight in "bare facts" was at the polar extreme to the "sentimentality found among the middle classes."[37] The opposition between Ireland and England was for Yeats an opposition between two ways of life—ways he associated with different social classes—and he conjectured that the nationalist linguistic movements arose from a desire to restore what standardized and industrialized, busy bourgeois existence had stolen from European culture:

> a more picturesque way of life . . . in which the common man has some share in imaginative art. . . . A language enthusiast does not put it that way to himself; he says, rather, "If I can make the people talk Irish again they will be the less English"; but if you talk to him till you have hunted the words to their burrow, you will find that the word "Ireland" means to him a form of life delightful to his imagination, and that the word "England" suggests to him a cold, irreligious and ugly life.[38]

This was one of Yeats's favorite themes and it mutated little over the decades. In the *Wheels and Butterflies* collection of 1934, he still associated the "Irish spirit" with aristocracy, religion, "mythical thinking," and the Orient; and the English, with the middle classes, agnosticism or empty faith, abstract thought, and modern Western un-culture.[39]

"England" and "Ireland" sometimes seem hardly more than useful names for conditions or forces that just as easily could be named otherwise. In *The Countess Cathleen*, it really does not matter much whether the "Master of all merchants" who buys souls for gold is Imperial Britain or the Evil Principle or the upper bourgeoisie: they are perhaps the same thing in different guises:

> FIRST MERCHANT. There are some men who hold they
> have wolves' heads,
>   And say their limbs—dried by the infinite flame—
>   Have all the speed of storms; others, again,
>   Say they are gross and little; while a few
>   Will have it they seem much as mortals are,
>   But tall and brown and travelled—like us, lady—
>   Yet all agree there is a power in their looks
>   That makes all men bow, and flings a casting-net
>   About their souls.[40]

Yeats almost always employs the liveliest verse and highest drama in this (otherwise too Wagnerian) play when he satirizes the merchants ("Come, deal, deal, deal, deal, deal, deal"), but he saves his sharpest venom for the peasants who have succumbed so readily to the demons of materialism. In act 5, the merchants read auctioneers' descriptions of the spiritual merchandise for sale, and the country-folk come off poorly. The peasants who embrace their transformation into materialist proletarians "are not the true folk," Yeats asserts of the social type represented in his play by John Maher, Shemus, and Teigue.[41] And in the late plays he is equally unhappy with the noble classes for making a similar compromise:

> SECOND ATTENDANT. Why must these holy, haughty feet
> descend
>   From emblematic niches, and what hand
>   Ran that delicate raddle through their white?

My heart is broken, yet must understand.
What do they seek for? Why must they descend?
FIRST ATTENDANT. For desecration and the lover's night.[42]

If Yeats severely reprimands the upper classes and the "folk," it is only because he takes them seriously. He respects aristocracy in large part because art requires an audience that possesses its "traditional knowledge, a knowledge learned in leisure." He allies the "folk" with artists and with the righteous members of the nobility in *The King's Threshold, Deirdre,* and *The Herne's Egg,* for "simple people understand from sheer simplicity what we understand from scholarship and thought."[43] But for the middle class Yeats has no such respect. In his plays, Yeats never treats the merchant class with high seriousness, and the arrival of a bourgeois on the Yeatsian stage generally marks a transition to burlesque. We are not asked to take seriously such human clichés as Mrs. Mallet in *The Words Upon the Window Pane* (1934). We are meant to chuckle at a middle-class widow whose only question for her departed husband has to do with opening a teashop in Folkstone. On the other hand, Yeats would put up with no manner of giggle or titter when the Mary/Leda figure, Attracta, enters in scene 2 of his most "holy and queer" play, proclaiming: "There is no reality but the Great Herne," "there is no happiness but the Great Herne."[44]

The revivalists had no patience with the staleness of realist prose-drama; such art, Yeats says, "fills one's soul with a sense of commonness as with dust."[45] Yeats saw the bourgeoisie— the audience of naturalism—as

a class . . . already written of by so many dramatists that it is nearly impossible to see its dramatic situations with our own eyes, and those dramatic situations are perhaps exhausted. . . .[46]

Not only that, but a class for which material well-being is the primary concern had no right usurping the drama to begin with, for a play dealing with material principles "is essentially narrative and not dramatic." The characteristic bourgeois form is the novel, and the middle class should have confined itself to prose fiction.[47] Or as F. O. Nolte has written: "The middle class dramatists were victims of two more or less extensive fallacies. They confused the pattern of the drama with the pattern of the novel, and they confused the pattern of the drama with the pattern of reality itself."[48] Tragedy in particular, Yeats argued, cannot continue to exist "when the great are but the rich," for that arcane genre belongs to a society based upon privilege and the heroic, where the dominant class has its "peculiar capacity for adventure."[49]

Seen from this angle, Yeats's last play, *The Death of Cuchulain* (1939), enacts the impending death of tragedy. Aoife, mother of Cuchulain's only son, claims the sacred right to kill Cuchulain in vengeance for his accidental murder of their child. Cuchulain himself acknowledges her right and submits to it: any tragic hero will know the canons of his own genre. But, before Aoife lifts her sword, an old beggar (significantly blind) frustrates her rights, along with the play's tragic inevitability, and—in the language of the sociological critic— "does the job for cash (triumph of materialism)."[50] *The King's Threshold* (1922 version) develops a parallel theme: the poet's rights, "established at the establishment of the world," are uprooted by what today we would call the bureaucracy. As a result, Seanchan, the play's emblem for poetry, determines to starve to death, and he leaves his witnesses (the audience) with a sense of inevitable apocalypse:

> SEANCHAN. . . . I lie rolled up under the ragged thorns
> That are upon the edge of those great waters
> Where all things vanish away, and I have heard
> Murmurs that are the ending of all sound.[51]

The repudiation of ancient rights and artists' prerogatives— the substitution of material for spiritual values—Yeats understands to be the herald of a new, and repugnant, millennium.

> I am running to the world with the best news
> That has been brought it for a thousand years,[52]

pants Shemus in *The Countess Cathleen*—gold coins at hand— in annunciation of an epoch necessarily devoid of beauty, poetry, and tragedy.

Rather than participate in hastening the inevitable, Yeats gathered up his wooden birds, beasts, and persons, and climbed aboard the toy ark. Nor was this a late decision, though we could be misled into thinking so by the overloud fanfare with which Yeats proclaimed the departure of his *Four Plays for Dancers*. He had written as early as 1902 that drama could be saved only through a change in its audience:

> Plays about drawing-rooms are written for the middle classes of great cities, for the classes who live in drawing-rooms, but if you would ennoble the man of the roads you must write about the roads, or about the people of romance, or about great historical people. . . . If . . . we busy ourselves with poetry and the countryman, two things which have always mixed with one another in life as on the stage, we may yet recover, in the course of years, a lost art. . . .[53]

But Yeats did not content himself with whistling romantic tunes while the rain fell; he was already building the boat:

> I . . . asked a dramatic company to let me rehearse them in barrels that they might forget gesture and have their minds free to think of speech. . . . The barrels, I thought, might be on castors, so that I could shove them about with a pole when the action required it. . . . I would like to see poetical drama, which tried to keep at a distance from daily life that it may keep its emotion untroubled, staged with about two or three colours.[54]

In pursuing this hieratic formalism, Yeats was making a sociological statement as well as an aesthetic one. His hatred of large-scale, broad-gestured prose-drama is a hatred that takes us back to that evening in 1814 when Percy Shelley preferred the brisk night air to a humid and histrionic *Hamlet*. Yeats's loathing of modern theatricalities, like Shelley's, is intimately related to his belief that the overelaboration of the theater had been undertaken "in the interests of a class . . . , doing whatever is easiest rather than what is most noble."[55] The result of Yeats's conviction that "the theatre must be reformed in its plays, its speaking, its acting, and its scenery" was the development of what he dubbed "the theatre's anti-self"—and his motto in that counter-naturalist rebellion was to become: "that all may be as artificial as possible."[56] The stage directions to the *Four Plays for Dancers* and those to the plays of the 1930s, are indicative of the extent to which Yeats, like Shelley and Byron before him, had determined to shake up the commercial, London-centered theater. In each of the *Four Plays*, characters are masked in *Noh* fashion and a change of mask (in *The Only Jealousy of Emer*, for instance) is intended to denote a change of personality. In *At the Hawk's Well*, the stylized movements center-stage are described by stageside musicians, much as in Stravinsky's counter-operatic *Renard* of the same period. In *The King of the Great Clock Tower* and *A Full Moon in March*, we are treated to song and dance for Severed Head and, in *The Death of Cuchulain*, "a very old man looking like something out of mythology" spits three times (in the poet's behalf) on middle-class audiences and the stage conventions with which they feel at home.

The ultimate purpose of verse in such a theater is "to keep us in that state of perhaps real trance, in which the mind liberated from the pressure of the will is unfolded in symbols."[57] But a more immediate justification for the verse is that it is not prose. Some of the early plays in early versions commingle verse and prose (as do most of Auden's plays)—and Denis Donoghue has shown with finesse how verse is used to dramatize the "mental unfolding," and prose, to emphasize the quotidian surface of things.[58] Yeats's craftiest use of prose in the effort to undermine middle-class English naturalism came in 1934 when he wrote *Words Upon the Window Pane*. This play's opening is so urbanely bourgeois that we wonder, as the scene begins, whether it might not be a late and contrite attempt to reach the audience Yeats had expelled from his theater. However, while *Words* opens with all the trite cordialities of witty, naturalist drama, it moves rapidly into the séance-within-a-play, whose grand emotion and poetic prose reduce the naturalist frame-play to rubble. The bourgeois players become the audience for this Yeatsian spirit-drama, and their critical judgment upon it is expressed by Mrs. Mallet: "some kind of horrible play."[59] (Only John Corbet, the graduate student in English literature, dissents from this judgment, but then he has a professional interest.) The frame-play and the spirit-drama are brought to a close simultaneously. The medium, Mrs. Henderson, speaking alternately from the two dimensions of reality, wanders out-of-control across the stage— shattering in the process the saucer of her mislaid teacup, the nerves of everyone in the theater, and, by strong implication, the theatrical world of saucers, teacups, and tea-caddies.

Yet the almost palpable tension in *Words Upon the Window Pane* is not merely that between the bourgeois and the aristocratic—though the tension between Swift's ghost and "the ruin to come, Democracy, Rousseau, the French Revolution" certainly derives from the more basic one and serves to reinforce it. Nor is the most fundamental tension that between the naturalistic drama of the drawing room and the spirit-drama Yeats ventriloquizes into its midst. As Conor Cruise O'Brien suggests, we must think of Yeats's specific social concerns "as cognate expressions . . . , anterior to both politics and poetry."[60] What actually underlies the social tensions of Yeatsian drama is clearer in some of the early plays that lack overt sociological themes, for the pattern they set is the basis of much later development. We know what to expect from *The Land of Heart's Desire* as soon as we have read its opening stage directions:

> A room with a hearth on the floor. . . . There are benches in the alcove and a table; and a crucifix on the wall. . . . Through the door one can see the forest. It is night, but the moon of a late sunset glimmers through the trees and carries the eye far off into a vague, mysterious world. . . . Mary Bruin stands by the door reading a book. If she looks up she can see through the door into the wood.[61]

This play (written in 1894 but the first to be produced) is drama on the *symboliste* model. Yeats wrote an admiring review of Villiers de l'Isle Adam's *Axël* ("a sacred book") in the same year that he wrote *Heart's Desire*,[62] and the contrast that the symbolist theater inevitably posits—between the everyday world and a world beyond—Yeats has built into his physical set as a kind of subjective correlative. Indoors, there is the cozy room, complete with hearth, furniture, and traditional religious image. Outside are the moon, the forest (the *forêt de symboles*, perhaps?), and a "mysterious world" (species: "vague"). Between these two dimensions, our gaze is fixed on a young, romantic bride, standing beside (*de rigueur*) an open door.

The tension that develops in this play is that between wholesome, safe, collective, responsible family life and the carefree life of vision. As in Rousseau's *Julie*, the central tension is that between Real and Ideal. *Father* Hart and the Faery *Child* pose the new bride's choice:

> FATHER HART. Think of this house and your duties in it.
> CHILD. . . . if you hear him you grow like the rest;
>   Bear children, cook and bend over the churn. . . .
> FATHER HART. Daughter, I point you out the way to
>   Heaven.
> CHILD. But I can lead you, newly-married bride,
>   Where nobody gets old and crafty and wise, . . .
>   For we are but obedient to the thoughts
>   That drift into the mind at the wink of an eye.[63]

Father Hart can see the Land of Heart's Desire as only

> the Waste beyond His peace,
> . . . maddening freedom and bewildering light.[64]

The Faery Child can see nothing in the crucifix but an "ugly thing on the black cross."[65] Mary's alternatives are mutually exclusive: sacramental, social life, or the independent, visionary life. There can be no compromise, no synthesis, no transcendence of the dialectic. In Villiers' play, Axël and Sara commit suicide rather than desert the visionary way for the life of society.

The primary theme of twentieth-century ritual drama derives from that of the nineteenth: baptize the alternatives of

Heart's Desire and you have Eliot's basic scheme for *The Cocktail Party*. Yeats's next major variation on this theme is of the twentieth century, but only just. *On Baile's Strand* (written in 1902) no longer poses the opposition of *Heart's Desire* in such black and white terms, but the outcome of the tension is no less tragic. *Baile*'s hearth-and-marriage world is embodied in the Agamemnon-figure, Conchubar, and in his pithless sons; the world of "freedom" and "light" is represented by the son-less (or so we think) hero Cuchulain, a figure based in part of Achilles.[66] To ensure the safety of the state, High King Conchubar attempts to domesticate the unpredictable Cuchulain by making him swear fealty to the crown. After some arguing, Cuchulain submits and takes the oath; immediately Conlaoch, Cuchulain's only son, enters and Cuchulain is commanded to do battle with him. (The play's second major version, of 1905, makes the son's entry even more·precipitate, presumably to emphasize the cause and effect.)

The Ideal and the heroic, when left to their own devices, are, paradoxically, part of the wider social order: the high king admits that his wisdom is incomplete without Cuchulain's strength, and the hero in fact has a son—Yeats's habitual symbol in the plays for social responsibility.[67] The alternatives presented by *Heart's Desire* are no longer mutually exclusive: the opposed worlds are now delicately interrelated. But the instant the hero (the Ideal) is divested of his freedom and forced to enter into a defined relationship with the social order (the Real), disaster follows automatically. Conchubar forfeits his wisdom and Cuchulain's fire is extinguished in the tide. For one who perceived this tension as a controlling design of life, it would not be unnatural to dislike the middle classes, for it is easy to regard the bourgeoisie as a monopolistic phenomenon that threatens to bring every aspect of Western culture to its service. The middle class, like Conchubar, may mean well, but Cuchulain and his modern-world counterparts (any heroic anachronism: artists, the aristocracy) cannot survive assimilation.

If Yeats's anti-bourgeois vituperations seem to exceed their object, we should recall that there is no emotion so powerful as one born of an internal paradigm projected onto an external circumstance. That Yeats impressed this pattern on a series of ritualist stage tragedies is entirely appropriate, for the revival of that genre in the modern period is itself an expression of the *Heart's Desire* tension. Ritual tragedy is, in relation to modern life, what Yeats believed it to be: a kind of toy ark—quaint and nostalgic, but probably not quite seaworthy. Still, as Yeats acknowledged, the struggle to write for the theater—for a medium based upon interaction between writer and audience, between character and character—necessarily alters one's perception of the Real/Ideal tension:

> when one constructs, bringing one's characters into complicated relations with one another, something comes into the story. Society, fate, "tendency", something not quite human, begins to arrange the characters.[68]

When ritual and the revivalist mentality meet naturalist stage conventions and audience suppositions, a movement toward accommodation is probably inevitable. Yeats's modification of the *Heart's Desire* opposition in *On Baile's Strand* was one step in that process. And the movement toward reconciliation of the heroic/Ideal with the bourgeois/Real is often more interesting than the plays themselves. There is, however, one sublime exception.

Purgatory (1939) is the most accessible of Yeats's mature tragedies—the one that can transfix almost any audience—and in it his accommodation of the symbolist spirit-drama to the modern stage is complete. He has developed a kind of "common idiom" plainsong in speech, based loosely on iambic tetrameter, and has forfeited chorus, masks, and poetic ornament to achieve this final fusion of stylization and naturalism.[69] In 1906, in *On Baile's Strand*, the father who kills his son is a mythological hero, attended in his grief by two masked figures of ritual, and the grieving requires twenty-two lines of highflying poetry:

> Where? where? where? My sword against the thunder!
> But not, for they have always been my friends;

And though they love to blow a smoking coal
Till it's all flame, the wars they blow aflame
Are full of glory, and heart-uplifting pride,
And not like this. The wars they love awaken
Old fingers and the sleepy strings of harps.[70]

But, in 1939, the father figure is a "wretched foul old man," alone, with but five lines of bare-bone verse to absorb the murder—three of which seem to disavow the literary ("in a book") quality of Yeats's earlier dramatic verse:

"Hush-a-bye baby, thy father's a knight,
Thy mother's a lady, lovely and bright."
No, that is something that I read in a book,
And if I sing it must be to my mother,
And I lack rhyme.[71]

The synthesis is so successful in these technical matters that we naturally expect time will have mellowed the *Heart's Desire* tension as well—but it is, in fact, even more pressingly present at the end of Yeats's career than at the beginning. "To me all things are made of the conflict of two states of consciousness," Yeats wrote in a letter of 1938, and *Purgatory* is an embodiment of that visionary conviction.[72] As in *A Full Moon in March*, the realm of the Ideal has descended from its emblematic niche to experience "desecration and the lover's night." And, as in "The Black Tower," the heroic world has been leveled—its only remnant, a murderous old peddler (he knew some Latin once) whose mind is the sole surviving battleground for the now-homogenized states of consciousness. There is, therefore, no longer any productive tension between those states, and the realm of the Real is no longer a sacramental alternative but a bestial temptation.

Purgatory is probably the most "sociological" of Yeats's plays: it was published in his political book, *On the Boiler*, and the states of consciousness in the play are viewed in an historical perspective. The play is, on one level at least, an allegory of modern European cultural history. The Old Man, a representative of Yeats's own generation, suffers from cultural aphasia but is old enough to remember that once there were

> old books and books made fine
> By eighteenth-century French binding, books
> Modern and ancient, books by the ton.[73]

The Boy portrays the remainder of the century as Yeats thought it would look—absolutely cut off from the past ("Books, library, all were burnt"), thoroughly materialist and mercenary:

> What's right and wrong?
> My grand-dad got the girl and the money.[74]

The Old Man retains some culture and some sense of morality because his mother was of a great house—one of those great houses Yeats magnifies in *On the Boiler*:

> Great people lived and died in this house;
> Magistrates, colonels, members of Parliament,
> Captains and Governors, and long ago
> Men that fought at Aughrim and the Boyne.[75]

The Old Man's murderous aspect is the only inheritance left him by his drunkard father—a man Yeats associates so closely with the horses he groomed as to make him seem almost a centaur; his son calls him "that beast there." The Old Man has killed off the heroic, gracious life represented by his mother (she dies in giving birth to him); the bestial life represented by his father ("I stuck him with a knife"); and finally, foreseeing a degrading future, he kills his son as well.

Yeats's prophecy concerning the future of Europe was realized within a matter of months; almost a whole generation would die in combat. Had it not been for historical developments, Yeats might have been inclined to accommodate his theater's central theme to modern social realities in the same way that he brought its technique to conform with the requirements of the modern stage. Writing when he did, Yeats could not make that accommodation: Europe in 1939 needed to be told the undiluted truth. The basic ordering myth behind *Purgatory* (as behind the totalitarian movements of the thirties, for some of which Yeats felt considerable sympathy) is that of "annual renewal." Fifty years before, at age sixteen, the Old Man killed his father with the knife that cuts his meat; now *his* son is sixteen, and the scene moves inexorably toward a Zeus/Kronos type of confrontation and the new world order that would result from it:

> BOY. What if I killed you? You killed my grand-dad,
> Because you were young and he was old.
> Now I am young and you are old.[76]

But Yeats frustrates our expectation—the father kills the son—and, instead of ringing in the New Year, however horrible, Yeats ushers back the old to be repeated "not once but many times." This purgatory is an eternal present that knows no past and expects no future because it has killed them both: Yeats's generation was to be "Twice a murderer and all for nothing."[77]

In its skeletal use of poetry, deflation of myth, and expectation of a New Year that never comes, *Purgatory* looks forward to one current in the drama of our own day. The drama is bound inextricably to its social context, and the theater of Return commenced to play Endgames even before the nations could draw up the rules.

· · ·

IF MODERNITY was the climactic episode of Western history, and if modernism was to be its apotheosis, then—*après moi, le déluge*. That was the attitude of modernism's most radical believer in the ideology of return, and with Hitler's troops poised on the Polish border, Yeats appeared to have history on his side. But modernism was not one of the war's conspicuous victors: if anything, the war demonstrated more conclusively than ever the strength and resilience of bourgeois modernity. From the first, drama had been the main theater-of-operations in the struggle of modernism against modernity. When that battle seemed finally lost, there commenced in response a revelatory epilogue to the entire curious history of revivalist drama. T. S. Eliot's incursion into the London theater was determined, to a great extent, by the work, theoretical and theatrical, of revivalist dramaturges from the early romantics down to Eliot's own mentor and antagonist, W. B. Yeats.[78] Eliot's affinities with this tradition of anti-bourgeois, anti-naturalist drama are easily documented. Like Yeats—and also like Marx, Nietzsche, Byron, and Shelley—Eliot felt contempt for the bourgeois tendency to fold all social classes at the middle. Of bourgeois foibles, it was the love of standardization that Eliot most disliked:

> Both middle class and lower class are finding safety in Regular Hours, Regular Pensions, and Regular Ideas. In other words, there will soon be only one class and the second flood is here.[79]

Eliot contended that, when the uniqueness of individual things is too far devalued, the "tragic spirit" (as Nietzsche had called it) necessarily will wane:

> With the decline of orthodox theology and its admirable theory of the soul, the unique importance of events has vanished. A man is important only as he is classed. Hence, there is no tragedy, or no appreciation of tragedy, which is the same thing.[80]

Moreover, as is evident in both *Sweeney Agonistes* and the later plays, Eliot's dramatic work is based upon an anti-naturalist vision of the theater. "Is not every dramatic representation artificial?" he asked his readers in the twenties. "And are we not merely deceiving ourselves when we aim at greater and greater realism? Are we not contenting ourselves with appearances, instead of insisting upon fundamentals?"[81] Eliot's work for the stage, until the last plays of the fifties, is dominated by the same theme that dominates the plays of Byron and Yeats: the great divide between minds at different levels of understanding. The assassins of Thomas Becket and the siblings of Amy Monchensey form a community of misunderstanding unrivaled by anything outside the London gentlemen's clubs T. S. Eliot frequented.

But the distinctions between Eliot and the earlier "revivers" of tragic norms are sharp ones and need emphasizing. Strangely enough, this arch-conservative's dramatic theory is perhaps closer to Karl Marx's than to that of any other predecessor. Like Marx and unlike Yeats, Eliot insisted that an art form be at all times closely in touch with the demands and conventions of its age. In an essay written some five years before his earliest attempt at drama, Eliot wrote that "a dramatic poet needs to have some *kind* of dramatic form given to him as the condition of his time. . . ."[82] For *The Rock* (1934) and *Murder in the Cathedral* (1935)—both written to order for Anglican Church groups—Eliot chose the Mass as the given form of his time (and of his limited, Christian audience). Like Yeats, Nietzsche, and Shelley, Eliot believed that "drama springs from religious liturgy, and . . . it cannot afford to depart far from religious liturgy."[83] But unlike those earlier theorists, Eliot chose the liturgy of his own time and place, even when, as in *The Cocktail Party*, he integrates the Christian liturgy into an ancient-Greek framework. Eliot asserted that the Mass was "the perfect and ideal drama" and referred to stage plays as a "liturgy less divine . . . the human drama, related to the divine drama, but not the same." This attitude, too, distinguishes Eliot from Nietzsche and the others, who wrote of tragedy and the tragic vision as a sort of Antichrist that possessed "an exalted notion of active sin as the properly Promethean virtue."[84]

Nietzscheans would use a revival of tragedy to undermine the status quo; Eliot uses the norms of ritual tragedy to transform the status quo into something subversive. *Murder in the Cathedral* (as also *The Cocktail Party* after and *Sweeney Agonistes* before it) is intended as a stage version of the Mass, but it is also a primitivization of the current liturgy. *Murder* is so constructed to remind us that the Mass is a dramatization of the crucifixion, which itself is a re-enactment of still older rituals. "And the world must be cleansed in the winter," the chorus intones, "or we shall have only / A sour spring, a parched summer, an empty harvest." The sacrifice of a societal leader of behalf of communal fertility—this rite is perhaps as ancient as the first primate community. In succeeding civilizations, the basic impulse is further and further refined until, eventually, the impulse becomes an intellectual abstraction. The eighteenth century called this Enlightenment; the nineteenth and twentieth have branded it a calamity. Nietzsche mourned that Greek tragedy, which began with the ritual dismemberment of Dionysus, should end with the Socratic dramas of Euripides. Eliot found both the drama and the Mass in a state of advanced Enlightenment, and he sought to reinvigorate both with what he described (in his 1923 essay, "The Beating of a Drum") as a "shot in the arm" of the "crude fore-runner."

Until 1939, Eliot wrote for a Christian audience, for an audience in touch with a ritual *langage* if not necessarily with the ritual *langue*. In *The Family Reunion*, Eliot for the first time accepted the secular culture's dramatic mode—the London West End's "Drawing Room, After Tea"[85]—and sought to make of this unlikely material a modernist version of ritual drama. Into the bourgeois naturalism of *The Family Reunion*, Eliot injected a Christianized version of pre-classical energies (the Furies become "bright angels"), and he did so according to a procedure he had outlined in an article some twenty years before:

> The phantom psychology of Orestes and Macbeth is as good as that of the Awoi; but the method of making the ghost real is different. In the former case the ghost is given in the mind of the possessed, in the latter case the mind of the sufferer is inferred from the reality of the ghosts. . . . In fact, it is only the ghosts that are actual; the world of the active passions is observed through the veil of another world.[86]

In writing this review, Eliot may have been remembering a familiar passage in *The Birth of Tragedy*:

> our everyday reality . . . is an illusion, hiding another, totally different kind of reality. It was Schopenhauer who considered the ability to view at certain times all men and things as mere phantoms . . . to be the true mark of philosophic talent.[87]

Even a Christian can quote Nietzsche to his purpose. As Frazer led Eliot to baptism, so the Nietzscheans may have led him to holy communion.

But to make Yeatsian drama work in the West End—that, it seems, was a feat beyond even Eliot's talents. Yeats, however, had considered the possibility himself as early as 1906:

> the romantic work and the poetic work reasonably good, we can take up the life of our drawing-rooms, and see if there is something characteristic there.[88]

While Yeats might have been prepared to attend a performance of *The Confidential Clerk*, he was not about to write it himself. That sort of play, Yeats thought, was produced by

> the insincerities of subjectives, who being very able men have learned to hold an audience that is not their natural audience. To be intelligible they are compelled to harden, to externalize and deform.[89]

Yeats's own *Words upon the Window Pane* was not a prototype for the theater of T. S. Eliot, but rather its prophetic condemnation. Yeats's formal accommodation to the modern stage altered, perhaps permanently, the modern stage. *Waiting for Godot* was brought to us courtesy of *Purgatory*. Yeatsian drama, even if it helped to readjust the bourgeois eye, made absolutely no accommodation to what Yeats saw as the bourgeois range of spiritual possibilities. Eliot, however, even moved toward a thematic accommodation after the war, exchanging his John of the Cross (*via negativa*) ideal of the prewar plays for a Dantean (*via media*) ideal in the postwar period. What Eliot did not do—despite appearances to the contrary—was to alter significantly the presuppositions of the revivalist drama.

From its inception, the revival movement was based upon what may have been a serious misconception about the ancient drama, the new drama's ultimate model. The modernists' bifurcated, Idealist perception—their perception of the bourgeois stage as the realm of the contemptibly Real, and of Greek tragedy as the realm of the life-giving, Real-contemning Ideal—affected every major revivalist dramaturge from Shelley to

Yeats to Eliot. Yet it is probable that this perceived relation between sordid, mercantile mundanity and the glory-that-was-Greece may have been largely specious. It is very unlikely that the daily life of Athens at the time when tragedy was born would have been much more congenial to Yeats than turn-of-the-century life in London. According to George Thomson (*Aeschylus in Athens*), by the time the first tragedies were produced the middle class had more or less won its struggle for effective control of Athens and had instituted what, despite aristocratic remnants, might be called a bourgeois democracy. Athens was a mercantile society, and we owe to it not only the birth of tragedy but the birth of science as well. Not only was Aeschylean Greece the home of Dionysus and the Orphics and Eleusis (where Aeschylus is thought to have been brought up), but also home to the court of the Areopagus, to the development of money and the overseas merchant-trade, to belief in the march of progress, and to a middle-man/profiteer economy. Aeschylus, a democrat and (according to tradition) a Pythagorean, must have felt very much at home in this burgeoning mercantile state, and his gift to Athens was to make its new institutions feel ancient and sacred.

In a sense, the *Oresteia* requires to be read backwards. If we begin with the image of the Areopagus which concludes *The Eumenides*, we approach more closely the effect the plays might have had on a fifth-century audience. One has to imagine the Areopagus as a place somewhat like the Supreme Court building in Washington, D. C.: an aging mass of columns, taken very much for granted as a part of quotidian reality. But the *Oresteia* allows us to take nothing for granted. The establishment of this court has been costly: a royal house slaughtered, Hesiod's *Theogony* turned upsidedown (chthonic gods rising, sky deities tumbling), matricide, regicide, insanity, prophetic frenzy, hierophanies galore. The contemporary, the democratic, the mercantile, the day-to-day are "epiphanized" and now seen to possess an ancient religious meaning. Moreover, if, as most historians agree, the Greeks until the fifth century perceived form and content, Ideal and Real, spirit and letter as one—then the numinous could not have found expression except through the quotidian. A perfect emblem for this characteristically Greek kind of wholeness was the law in Athens that wealthy persons were required, as a sort of tax, to finance the Dionysian liturgies ("holy doings"), which today we know as tragedies. Thus, the Mercantile underwrote the Awesome—and then merchants submitted themselves as audience to artistic presentations of the Awful. Renato Poggioli has made a similar evaluation of the bourgeois' role in advancing the modernist avant-garde.[90]

While Eliot acknowledged the extent to which his mythico-contemporary drama had failed—"failure" was *his* word—he never acknowledged its instructive cause. He understood (1951) that "the deepest flaw of all, was in a failure of adjustment between the Greek story and the modern situation," but he did not, at least publicly, recognize the ultimate reason for his Eumenides seeming "uninvited guests who had strayed in from a fancy dress ball."[91] Problems arose because Eliot, like all the revivalist theorists who preceded him, thought that

> what distinguishes poetic drama from prosaic drama is a kind of doubleness in the action, as if it took place on two planes at once. . . . In poetic drama a certain apparent irrelevance may be the symptom of doubleness; or the drama has an under-pattern less manifest than the theatrical one . . . the kind of pattern which we perceive in our own lives only at rare moments of inattention and detachment, drowsing in sunlight.[92]

For Eliot, as for Yeats and for all the major revivalist playwrights, the modern and the tragic—the Real and the Ideal—do not mix. Eliot forced sudden Greek infusions into modern dramatic situations in order to subvert the modern world and to impose upon it a shape and significance from outside. Who can and cannot see his Furies is the test that separates Eliot's Manfreds from his chamois hunters.

This technique was a conflation of the avant-garde's old *épater-le-bourgeois* approach and its mythical method. Eliot's difficulties with play-writing, in fact, may have commenced with his discovery of the mythical method of *Ulysses*. Eliot's

1923 review of Joyce's novel embodies a fatal misreading of the method by which *Ulysses* was constructed. The mythical method of *Ulysses*—"using the myth, . . . manipulating a continuous parallel between contemporaneity and antiquity"— was deployed, Eliot said, to control, order, and give shape "to the immense panorama of futility and anarchy which is contemporary history."[93] Eliot believed, then, that Joyce's technique implied a negative judgment on modernity. It is more likely that the opposite is the case, for that method dignifies a modernity that Joyce, at any rate, saw as affirmable, and not the less stately for being a little plump. Joyce's approach lends to modernity the dignity he thought that, even without his novel, it already possessed. The mythical method of Joyce has more in common with that of the *Oresteia* than with that of *The Family Reunion*.

From this angle, modernism would appear to come in two basic kinds: one that contemns bourgeois modernity and one that (by and large) affirms it, one that radically divides the modern from the ancient, or the conventional from the ultimate, and one that declines to do so. The former is "Burckhardtian" in spirit, the latter "Paterian"; and virtually the whole revivalist current in the drama flowed into that Burckhardtian kind of modernism which was at war with modernity. But this model is relatively crude and Eliot's case is extraordinarily subtle. Eliot's mythical method—in the plays, though not, interestingly, in his major poems—was an expression of the missionary spirit. Eliot had his reservations about modernity, but he thought modern audiences might be amenable to conversion if, as he wrote to Pound, the "monkey tricks" he played on stage would have their desired effect. In Christianizing Nietzsche and in Nietzscheizing Christianity, in archaizing realism and in making a quasi-naturalist theater out of Yeatsian spirit-drama, Eliot tried to unite bourgeois modernity with symbolist modernism, its great adversary. The Greek tragedians had no need to bring together the quotidian and the sacramental because they despised neither and saw no essential contradiction between them. But revivalist playwrights viewed them as estranged partners and even stranger bedfellows. The marriage Eliot patched up turned out to be an uneasy reunion, like the one his Heracles figure arranges, in *The Cocktail Party*, between unloving Edward and unlovable Lavinia.

After a century and a half of recrimination over custody of the theater, the drama would hardly be the most conducive forum in which to bring together a legitimate past and a questionable present—in which to unite modernism and modernity. Eliot's effort in this direction was Promethean, but fully successful drama it did not make. With very few exceptions (*Murder in the Cathedral*, Yeats's later plays, a few pieces of Cocteau's, the Beckettian inheritance), as much may be said, in general, of the tragic revival. Yet Wallace Stevens' judgment on that movement ("The poetic drama needs a terrible genius before it is anything more than a literary relic") was too harsh.[94] The revival can boast more than one "terrible genius" whose very conception of the enterprise made him a martyr to misprision. The effort to revive the poetic and ritual elements in drama is among the most complex chapters in the modernists' progress. But it is to another, less strained chapter that we must turn if we hope to contemplate the structures of success.

Novel and Epic: Reading
Backwards from *Ulysses*

Certainly all that is best in modern poetry tends toward antiquity in spirit and even in kind, as if there
were to be a return to it. Just as our literature began
with the novel, so the Greek began with the epic and
dissolved in it.

Friedrich Schlegel, "Letter About the Novel"

UNLIKE MODERN WRITERS of ritual tragedy, the pioneers of
the novel did not set out to revive a form that was thought
to run counter to modern cultural conditions. Much cogent
criticism has been devoted to showing that virtually all novels
have been written by, about, and for the middle classes—and
most sociological theorists of the novel believe that the conception of the novel as a modern incarnation of epic "may be
regarded as presenting something of a challenge to the basic
argument" that the novel is a "new form" which resulted
from "social change."[1] Ian Watt holds that, for example,
"Fielding's celebrated formula of 'the comic epic in prose'
undoubtedly lends some authority to the view that, far from
being the unique literary expression of modern society, the
novel is essentially a continuation of a very old and honoured
narrative tradition."[2] Accordingly, Watt finds it necessary to
discredit Fielding's sense of his own project and to make *Joseph Andrews* and *Tom Jones* seem anomalous events in the
history of the novel. But the sociological theory of the novel
and the epic theory are not mutually exclusive: they are, oddly
enough, complementary. Individually, neither theory can make
adequate sense of the facts. The novel was a native product
of bourgeois modernity, born during the Renaissance—but,
at the same time, several of the novel's most important prac-

titioners and theorists, in each stage of its development, were believers in the humanist *nostos*, believers in the novel as a reincarnation of Greco-Roman epic.

The dialectic of these tendencies—the intuition of a return to basics and sources, the glorying in modern novelties—is a keynote in the genre's history. The publication of *Ulysses* marks but the climax of what Hegel dubbed the "bourgeois epic"; behind Joyce's full-blown reconstruction of Homer lies a long and venerable tradition which descends, ultimately, from the genre's origins in the Renaissance. Since the Renaissance, the novel has sought to define itself in relation to the epic. As Watt has shown, novelists often have regarded their genre as the modern world's replacement for epic, as a sign of modernity's rejection of the ancient narrative forms and of the values they embody. Many novels have been written in conscientious opposition to epic conventions: some have adopted a mock-heroic stance, for instance—and the whole picaresque mode is essentially an inversion of epic's teleological, theodicean, historical, and heroic tendencies. But many important novels exhibit a much more ambiguous and suggestive relation to epic. Some have been misconstrued as parodies of epic conventions and values when they could be characterized more accurately as parodies of the epic's post-classical offshoots. To negate what one views as the decadent forms of a genre may be a type of affirmation. *Don Quixote*, the first novel of Europe, is a point-by-point parody of chivalric romance and, far from rejecting heroism, the book is a bittersweet search for the hero's place in a new, seemingly unheroic age.

The distinction between ancient warrior epic and the chivalric romance is clear-cut, and attention to it makes more accessible the aims of Cervantes and the originating impetus of the novel. The distinction is well illustrated by the difference between Homer's *Odyssey* and Charles Lamb's recasting of that epic amidst what he called an "air of romance." (A comparison of Homer with a writer of medieval romance would yield fewer useful parallels.) In *The Adventures of Ulysses* (1827), Ulysses' moly becomes a "wondrous girdle" or "charm" that guarantees his safe return to Ithaca; and Lamb's Ulysses possesses a personal virtue and an invincibility which, like his magical enchantments, pertain more to Sir Gawain than they could to any Greek hero. Romance elements dissolve the wedge that Homer installed between the *telos* of his poem and the hero's attainment of it. Even the divine interventions of the *Odyssey* lack the magical quality of Lamb's "Homeric" romance—they offer no automatic solutions to the hero's dilemmas and they work no psychological transformations. The Odysseus of Homer fulfills his destiny through a combination of hand-soiling, bloodcurdling activity and the plainest sort of horse sense. The hero is fallible, his progress uncharmed, and, above all, his *nostos* is earned. Odysseus takes nothing for granted, not even the value of his hard-won return. In disguise, he re-examines every crag of life on Ithaca before he is willing to commit himself to it. The world of the epic hugs closer to the facts of life than does the world of romance. The normative existence of the *Odyssey* is family life, its superior acts of heroism are enacted literally at hearthside, its supreme human virtues are cussedness and lovability, and its highest value is an easygoing intercourse between men and gods.

By the waning of the Middle Ages, the romance spirit was ascendant, and so it became necessary to negate the chivalric romance and its world in order to affirm the epic and the world of epic. *Don Quixote* reaches back behind the world of romance to the world of epic that the chivalric romances had magnified and thereby diminished. The novel absorbs much of the dignity and scope of the epic, and it bestows on modernity the attribute of the quixotic and a proud shimmer that modernity otherwise might lack. Cervantes himself was very much a participant in the humanist era's pursuit of antiquity and of ancient values—his *Persiles y Sigismunda* is a "classicist" novel, based on Renaissance conceptions of certain Greek poems—and the influence of Europe's first great novelist on the genre's subsequent development can scarcely be overestimated.

The novel/epic theory per se probably begins, as Watt indicates, with Henry Fielding, Cervantes' English disciple. Like

Don Quixote, which it forthrightly imitates, *Joseph Andrews* wants to become a kind of epic by assaulting the epic's degenerate, post-classical forms, and by pointing to an earlier, simpler, and more legitimate world order for modernity to regenerate. *Joseph Andrews* begins by stripping the epic genre of its most objectionable, post-Homeric accretions: the fancifulness of medieval romance, the pedantry of Renaissance and post-Renaissance humanism, the pomposity of the heroic-gallant novel, the rhetorical flourishes of rococo neoclassicism. Fielding's novel exposes what masquerade as heroism and epic style in order to extol and embody a more authentic classicism and a less idealized, more Homeric human race. Fielding also hoped to expose, in the service of real virtue and true faith, what posed as Christianity. His first novel attempts to defeat the bloodless, prissy Christianity of Pamela Andrews (and of the enormous audience of Richardson's *Pamela*), both through ridicule and by championing instead the muscular, lusty Christianity of Adams, Fanny, and especially Joseph—a religious ethos that Fielding, in various essays, associates with the vigorous and pure Christianity of the early church.[3] *Joseph Andrews* represents Fielding's attempt to overturn—on behalf of an original, ancestral order—all debased, conventional versions of that order, both formal and moral.

The terms best suited to define the nature of Fielding's venture are those of Matthew Arnold, a later English moralist and man of letters. Fielding hoped, like a good Protestant humanist, that Europe would return to the practice of authentic Hellenism in the arts and primitive Hebraism in religion. In *Joseph Andrews* he was trying to demonstrate that the Cervantean comic novel was an appropriate genre in which to enact that return. Don Quixote is a man struggling to convince an aging society that it can, like its literature, become young again; and Fielding evidently read Cervantes' tale of Quixote and Sancho as an exercise in fusing the modern extremes of idealism and realism, sanctimony and licentiousness, into a blend of traits that Fielding seems to have taken as simultaneously Homeric and Biblical. The obstacles to cultural regeneration in *Joseph Andrews*, as in its model, *Don*

Quixote, are characters and institutions that represent either degraded or overrefined versions of the human virtues which comprise original Hebraism and original Hellenism. The simple truth has come to be seen as simple-minded and the protagonists of Cervantes' and Fielding's novels engage in an epic battle to liberate truth from triteness, virtue from prudery, love from lubriciousness, intelligence from pedantry, and strength from brutality. The battle between ancient values and their modern distortions is one that doubtless raged in these authors' minds, and out of that warfare emerged a new kind of character for fiction: a thoroughly modern man who embodies, juggles, and redefines the characteristics of Biblical heroism and Homeric virtue. And the exigencies of narrating that battle developed, in the hands of Cervantes and Fielding, a genre that appears to be both epic and scripture but, at the same time, seems so very modern that it has come to be called, simply, *novel*.

Joyce left a paucity of critical writings but *Ulysses*, beginning with its extraordinary title, implies a history or theory of the novel. As Hugh Kenner writes, Joyce's Homeric scoffold

> implies that the *Odyssey* is Western man's pioneer novel, so in rewriting it *sub specie* MCMIV, Joyce undertook to take stock of what the art of narrative had been up to during twenty-seven intervening centuries. He concluded that it had done little more than contrive variations on Homer; thus *The Count of Monte Cristo* . . . is unquestionably an *Odyssey* for adolescents. . . . *Hamlet* fits neatly into the pattern, an *Odyssey* told from the viewpoint of the son. . . . *Don Giovanni* is an *Odyssey* too, told from the viewpoint of the usurper. . . . Sancho Panza, it turns out, was all the time Ulysses in a clown's mask.[4]

The struggle of certain early novels to be latter-day epics must have interested Joyce, but this subject has been treated elsewhere and the purpose of this case study is to deal with the relation of novel and epic in the more immediate ancestors of *Ulysses*.[5] The battle metaphor of *Don Quixote* and *Joseph Andrews* underwent major changes in the nineteenth-century novel and it was in its more recent form that the figure became what Richard Ellmann has chronicled as "the battle for Dublin."[6] The plot-level action of *Ulysses* is a war against modern Europe's ossified, false oppositions (church vs. state, Ireland vs. Britain, soul vs. body—in other words, the Ideal-vs.-Real opposition that dominates the history of the novel from *Don Quixote* forward)—a war fought in order to reach back to the oneness of truth.

Stephen Dedalus, at the outset, declares war on what masquerades as home. He already has refused to submit to Dublin's Italian church when the book opens and, in the first episode, he takes his leave of Martello Tower—the false home he shares with Ireland's "gay betrayer" Buck Mulligan, and with Mulligan's English companion Haines, the representative of an empire in its dotage. London, Rome, and Dublin are at odds only on the slippery surface of things; they are very much in league, and their common enemy is the simple truth. Stephen's battle against falsehood is literary as well as political and philosophic. Halfway through his day (in "Scylla and Charybdis"), Stephen will oppose both the idealist (or "romantic") and naturalist theories of art forwarded, respectively, by George Russell and Buck Mulligan—following which, it seems, these two supposed antagonists will get together over tea at Russell's residence, while Stephen goes off to battle more Britons and Jesuits and Dublin betrayers. Leopold Bloom, too, has volunteered for armed service in this campaign. In fact, he nearly becomes a battle casualty when he decides to take on the "Cyclops": a Dublin super-patriot who buys the land of fellow Irishmen evicted by British landlords, a devoted Christian who hurls his biscuit-tin at a Jew who "loves to love love." The modern Cyclops has two eyes but, as Ellmann observes, he chooses to look now with one, now with the other. The battle for Dublin is an attempt to expose dichotomy as duplicity.

In *Joseph Andrews*, the combat has been largely internecine—as Marianne Moore has observed, "there never was a war that was not inward." But, in the following centuries, the battle was undertaken by novelists raised on the frontiers of

Europe—in Russia, America, Ireland—where oral literature still flourished in the not yet demythologized regions of the West, and where the ancestral claims of Western civilization were taken both more and less seriously than in France or England. By the mid-nineteenth century, France and England had led all of Western Europe's advanced nations into self-conciousness, doubt, materialist values, and the supposedly exclusive ideologies of rationalism and anti-rationalism, neo-classicism and romanticism. Even *Salammbô*—perhaps the most conscientious attempt by a Frenchman to write epic/novel—is not an instrument of return to first principles, but a final interment of them in stale exoticism annd overrefinement:

> "Never! . . . the hermaphrodite Baals do not reveal them-
> selves except for us alone. . . . Your desire is a sacrilege;
> be satisfied with the knowledge which you possess!"
> She fell on her knees, placing two fingers in her ears
> as a sign of repentance; and she sobbed, crushed by the
> priest's words, and filled at the same time with anger
> against him, with terror and humiliation. . . . Already the
> birds were singing, a cold wind was blowing, little clouds
> ran across the pale sky.
> Suddenly there appeared on the horizon beyond Tunis,
> like gentle fogs which obstruct the sun, a great curtain
> of gray powder . . . dromedaries, spears. . . . It was the
> army of the Barbarians advancing on Carthage.[7]

Despite the rosy-fingered *accoutrements*, this novel is far removed from the spirit of classical epic. In a letter to Turgenev, Flaubert wrote that he felt like a fourth-century Roman waiting for an inevitable collapse,[8] and his reasons for writing *Salammbô* may have been more akin to Nero's for fiddling than to Vergil's for battling home. The author of *Salammbô* obviously suffered from an acute case of cultural nostalgia: Flaubert read the *Aeneid* after years of living with Emma Bovary and felt an itch for epic ("*des prurits d'épopée*").[9] But his attempt at epic/novel enacts no Return. A citizen of nine-teenth-century Paris could appreciate neither the quiet, domestic heroisms that impressed Homer, nor the reconstructive, theodicean urge that animated the great epic poems. Domesticity was, to the French, bourgeois—unheroic by definition; and any attempt at theodicy in the Parisian *ambience* surely would have withered away in irony. The narrative flow of Stendhal's *Chartreuse de Parme* is emblematic of the historical dilemma. The novel moves, as if inevitably, from the wobbly last stand of heroism (martial and moral, perhaps even metaphysical) at Waterloo, into the trivialized, bureaucratized, Council of Vienna-ized world of Ranuce-Enest IV and his *commedia dell'arte* way of life. Europe's was no longer (in Stendhal's words) "the life of the forum" but "the life of the salon,"[10] and the perception of this contrast resulted in a series of tragic comedies, extending from *Rouge et Noir* to *Madame Bovary* to *Middlemarch*.

By mid-century, war seemed a solution to *ennui*, since warfare could make the trivial—at least momentarily—monumental, and might give some purpose to living. "Better barbarism than boredom!" was Gautier's *Salammbô*-like battle cry. And the symbolic speaker of Tennyson's *Maud* mourns for his symbolic father ("Did he fling himself down? who knows? for a vast speculation had fail'd"), then urges his countrymen to launch into symbolic battle:

My life has crept so long on a broken wing
Thro' cells of madness, haunts of horror and fear,
That I come to be grateful at last for a little thing.
. . . a hope for the world in the coming wars—

. . . the peace, that I deem'd no peace, is over and done,
And now by the side of the Black and the Baltic deep,
And deathful-grinning mouths of the fortress, flames
The blood-red blossom of war with a heart of fire.

Let it flame or fade, and the war roll down like a wind,
We have proved we have hearts in a cause, we are noble
still. . . .[11]

• • •

TENNYSON'S symbolic battle was fought with real soldiers in the Crimea from 1854–56. The Western powers (primarily France and Britain) represented the war as a struggle between civilization and barbarism. The forces of the Christian tsar, doubtless, felt much the same thing as they took up arms against the iconoclastic West. At least one Russian soldier, however, came to interpret the Crimean War as a struggle of all Europe to recover its soul and its God. As that soldier's account of that war, the *Sebastopol* tales of Tolstoy comprise an immediate ancestor of "the battle for Dublin." The most accessible avenue into this aspect of Tolstoy's fiction is the "literary" one which Boris Eikhenbaum takes. In his essay, "The Struggle with Romanticism," Eikhenbaum argues that Tolstoy's "choice of battle material is itself prompted mainly by a desire to liquidate the romantic stereotypes."[12] This is to read both too much Joyce into Tolstoy, and too little. It is clear that Tolstoy was primarily anxious to record his impressions of a battle in which he, after all, was personally engaged—that his opposition to the French was something more than a literary grudge. It is clear, too, that, at the literary level, the battle is not merely against romanticism but also for some modern sort of Homeric narration.

Tolstoy contrasts the "snobbery and vanity" of modern literature with the more powerful emotions of earlier writers, including Homer (p. 45).[13] The opening lines of *Sebastopol*—

> Dawn tinges the horizon above Mount Sapouné; the shadows of the night have left the surface of the sea . . . a cold wind blows from the fog-enveloped bay. . . . The quiet of the morning is disturbed only by the incessant murmuring of the waves, and is broken at long intervals by the dull roar of cannon. (p. 3)

—are as Iliadic as Tolstoy could make them:

> . . . The north and west winds
> issued with a wondrous cry, both driving
> cloud before them. . . .

Now when the star of morning eastward rose
to herald daylight on the earth, and Dawn
came after, yellow-robed, above the sea,
the pyre died down, the flame sank, and the winds
departed, veering homeward once again
by sea for Thrace, as the ground swell heaved and foamed.[14]

But Eikhenbaum is surely correct, given these necessary reservations, to assert the *Sebastopol* was intended to be a literary manifesto. It is, in fact, a kind of manifesto-on-wheels, for we are addressed in the second person by an unnamed guide who tours us through this war and points up its literary moral: "You will see war without the brilliant and accurate alignment of troops, without music" (p. 15). When our guide insists that we climb down the "black space, all muddy" (p. 21) out of the realm of red banners and majestic cannon-thunder into the fourth bastion, he is inviting readers to climb down out of the French neoclassical and French romantic conceptions of warfare into a conception that is truer and nobler but, at the same time, lower.

In his introductory story, the young soldier-poet tries to reconcile the first exhilaration of combat and natural Russian patriotism with an enthusiasm for both Stendhalian and classical battle-scene techniques. The result is an ungainly mixture of Homeric ticktack ("The rising sun gives a rosy tinge, upon the hostile fleet": p. 5), Vergilian candor ("A nauseating, corpse-like odor rises to your nostrils": p. 12), and heroic-gallant platitude ("you can only bow in silence before this unconscious grandeur": p. 13)—together with some undigested bits of *Chartreuse de Parme* ("heaps of things give you the impression of a strange and aimless disorder": p. 23). The soldiers in "December, 1854" are meant to seem far more heroic than the neoclassical and romantic soldiers of Western Europe, for their suffering is infinitely more random and hideous—yet they are heroic in the conventional sense: they show bravery in the face of death. But early on in *Sebastopol*, this in itself is enough to invite ecstatic celebration. War has brought "interesting sensations" (p. 27) of extreme service:

At the instant the projectile reaches you, you invariably think it will kill you. . . . So when it has passed without grazing you, you live again. . . . The hissing, the blow, the explosion are repeated, but this time accompanied by a human groan. You go up to the wounded man. . . . Part of his chest has been carried away. . . . an exalted expression, elevated by restrained thoughts enliven his features. (pp 27–28)

This is the flip side—the Russian side—of *Maud*'s coin, and these soldiers attain what Tennyson craved most: "much simplicity" with "little effort" (p. 30). War is a saving shortcut to heroic living.

"May, 1855," however, commences with another sort of vision. Bombs have "ploughed up the soil," human beings are motivated by "self-love," men and bullets are quantified in "thousands" and "millions." Each detail seems calculated to contradict the principal images of the first story. Realism is compromised by mythologizing: "the angel of death had constantly hovered over them" (p. 35). No longer is combat waged for the experience of extreme sensations or for escape from *ennui*. This skirmish has become, involuntarily, a world war, fought on the field of a question whose answer is not in human hands:

A crowd composed of heterogeneous races, moved by quite different desires, converged from all parts of the world towards this fatal spot. Powder and blood had not succeeded in solving the question which diplomats could not settle. (p. 36)

The changes in tone, atmosphere, and attitude posited in this short introductory section become even sharper when, immediately after it, the narration returns precisely to the final paragraph of the first *Sebastopol* story—to the regimental band music, to the "just and joyous" sunlight. Tolstoy takes drastic measures to emphasize the importance of this contrast: he even satirizes his own earlier representation of war's natural beauty:

the two officers, leaning on the window, watched the lines of fire which the shells traced crossing each other in the air, the white powder-smoke, the flashes which preceded each report and illuminated for a second the blue-black sky; they listened to the roar of the cannonade, which increased in violence.

"What a charming panorama!" said Kalouguine, attracting his guest's attention to the truly beautiful spectacle. "Do you know that sometimes one can't tell a star from a bomb-shell?" (p. 60)

He likewise exposes the sort of heroism put on display in "December, 1854" as but one more literary falsehood. The retelling of those heroic deeds in the military gazette provides a novelistic titillation for the Emma Bovarys of Petersburg:

"When they bring us the *Invalide*, Poupka . . . rushes into the antechamber, seizes the paper, and throws herself upon the sofa in the arbor. . . . You can't imagine the enthusiasm with which she reads the story of your heroic exploits! . . . (p. 38)

Even inside the bastion there is literary activity. Prince Galtzine already is reading a book when Kalouguine arrives to relate the day's events—in effect, to create a war romance: "These incidents naturally arranged themselves so as to make it appear how he, Kalouguine, was a brave and capable officer" (p. 89). Worse still, Praskoukine hopes that, if the stray shell lying near Mikhailoff and himself detonates, it will kill his comrade-in-arms rather than himself (so much for heroic self-sacrifice), and he muses on the time when he might, like a romantic novelist, "tell how we were close together and how I was covered in his blood" (p. 91).

"Sebastopol in May, 1855" comes near to undermining the very idea of heroism. Heroism is a means of promotion in the army (pp. 40–41) or of attaining personal glory, and it usually is bound closely to the most trivial forms of vanity. (Tolstoy lavishes an unconscionable amount of attention on his officers' clothing—though the countless pairs of white gloves in this story no longer seem so irreproachably white as they appeared in December.)[15] The narrator goes so far as to claim that there can be no heroes among men, for "all are good and all are bad" (p. 109). Yet even in this second tale, heroism is not entirely dissolved; it is being melted down and reshaped. As in *Don Quixote* and *Joseph Andrews*, negation is a creative act. Probably the bravest man in the "May, 1855" story is the naval captain who visits Kalouguine's command, and he is "indifferent" to "courageous deeds": "he did not thoughtlessly risk his life, and limited himself to fulfilling strictly his duty" (p. 78). He is crafty, like Odysseus, and takes no chances with human life. There is no longer a delight in danger; it has been replaced by a yearning for the quiet, domestic life that once seemed less worthy than war of the heart's devotion. In a time of siege, Mikhailoff comes to cherish quiet memories of laughter shared with his wife and friends:

> All these pictures in their familiar frames arose in his imagination with marvellous softness. He saw them in a rosy atmosphere, and, smiling at them, he handled affectionately the letters in the bottom of his pocket.
> These memories brought the captain involuntarily back to his hopes, to his dreams. (p. 40)

Tolstoy's fullest redefinition of heroism—a redefinition not unlike that found in *Joseph Andrews* or *Don Quixote*—is embodied in the "August, 1855" story of young Volodia. With his head full of literary expectations, Volodia arrives at Sebastopol and discovers (like Fabrice at Waterloo) that the heroism of romances and novels has no counterpart in reality. Unlike Fabrice, however, Volodia also discovers that, if it did exist, martial heroism alone would be unsatisfying. Volodia imagines a romantic scene in which he and his brother die together in combat, but he feels real emotion only when he deals honestly with his brother and their shared situation:

> "Are you angry with me, Micha?" he asked, after a few moments.
> "Why?"

"Because—nothing. I thought there had been between us—"

"Not at all," rejoined the elder, turning towards him and giving him a friendly tap on the knee.

"I ask pardon, Micha, if I have offended you," said the younger, turning aside to hide the tears which filled his eyes. (p. 141)

The real war is against oneself: to become "quite undeceived" (p. 163) by oneself about oneself. And true heroism resides in simple, honest acts of brother-love. These are Volodia's discoveries and it is they, more than any of his acts of martial bravery, that define what makes him "a real hero" (p. 211). Humility is the ultimate heroism in *Sebastopol*, and humility stems from the creaturely admission that no abstraction of self (e.g., "honor") is more important than actuality (e.g., "food") (p. 148). This is an Homeric attitude: Achilles, greatest of all Greek war heroes, tells Odysseus in Hades that it is "Better to break sod as a farm hand" on earth than to have honor and power "among the dead men's shades."[16] Yet shortly before his death, Volodia takes what appears to be the same stance of romantic heroism which, earlier in this work, Tolstoy had seemed to condemn. We should not be surprised: the man of domestic virtue is most heroic in giving up his home to fight on home's behalf. After the "Baptism of fire" (p. 196) that Volodia has undergone—after all that Tolstoy's reader has undergone—a scene of conventional heroics has the feel of earned authenticity.

Romanticism and realism, in such cases, become one:

As to Volodia . . . Being even a little vain of his bravery, he got up on the *banquette*, unbuttoning his coat so as to be well observed. The commander of the bastion, in going his rounds, although he had been accustomed during eight months to courage in all its forms, could not help admiring this fine-looking boy with animated face and eyes, his unbuttoned coat exposing a red shirt, which confined a white and delicate neck, clapping his hands, and crying in a voice of command, "First! second!" and

jumping gayly on the rampart to see where his shell had
fallen. (pp. 211-12)

If Tolstoy has brought our conception of heroism full circle,
we should recall that there are some circles that really do get
somewhere. This return has been earned, transfigured by what
Volodia and we have learned about the heroisms of the soul.

The spiral effect—the dialectical progression—appears to
be a loose organizing principle of *Sebastopol*, just as it is of
Ulysses. This principle applies as much to the book's literary
nostos as to its ideological one. The Hellenic posturing of
"December, 1854" is meant to seem too easy:

> it is now only that the anecdote of Korniloff, that hero
> worthy of antique Greece, who said to his troops, "Chil-
> dren, we will die, but we will not surrender Sebastopol,"
> and the reply of our brave soldiers, incapable of using
> set speeches, "We will die, hurrah!"—it is now only that
> these stories have ceased to be to you beautiful historical
> legends, since they have become truth, facts. (p. 31)

In "August, 1855," however, the "Homerisms" no longer are
obtrusive and self-advertising, but integral and decorous. The
siege of Sebastopol becomes a living version of the siege of
Troy:

> As on the preceding evening, the lights of the hostile fleet
> sparkled afar on the sea, calm and insolent. The masts
> of our scuttled vessels, slowly settling into the depths of
> the water, contrasted sharply against the red glow of the
> fires. . . . Now and then, in the midst of the regular chop-
> ping of the waves struck by the wheels, and the hissing
> of escaping steam, could be heard the snorting of horses,
> . . . the dolorous groaning of the wounded. Vlang, who
> had not eaten since the day before, drew a crust of bread
> from his pocket and gnawed it, but at the thought of
> Volodia he broke out sobbing so violently that the sol-
> diers were surprised at it.
>   "Look! our Vlang is eating bread and weeping," said
> Vassina. . . .

"See! they have burned our barracks!" he continued, sighing. "How many of our fellows are dead, and dead to no purpose, for the French have got possession!" . . . "It's all the same. It is maddening!" "Why? Do you think they will lead a happy life there?" (p. 113–25, excerpts)

One could analyze this moving passage in the terms of the nineteenth-century critical debate. The sentiment and poeticism could be called "romantic," the conviction of futility and the tragi-comic dialogue are "Stendhalian," some of the description is "realist," the crust of bread is a typically Tolstoyan domestic detail. Yet these elements have fused completely in the mind of a novelist who was a devoted reader of Homer and who felt a kinship between his "primitive" European country and the Greek poet's. The way back, however, was not through self-conscious archaism; the way forward was the way back. Tolstoy began not with Homer, but with Lermontov and Stendhal.[17] *Sebastopol* follows that "way to unity" which Rachel Bespaloff calls "the flux of Becoming that undoes and remakes."[18] Bespaloff refers here both to Tolstoy and to Homer, his teacher, and she refers not only to aesthetic concerns but to religious ones as well. *Sebastopol*, like the *Iliad* and the *Odyssey*, battles after truth of an ultimate kind, though this aspect of Tolstoy's Crimean War emerges only after the combat of the French and Russians begins to seem "fatal"—larger than itself—in the second story (p. 36). France, besides being, and remaining, a physically present enemy nation, becomes a kind of cipher for all the elements of modern culture Tolstoy detests; "France" comes to fulfill a function in *Sebastopol* like that of "England" in Yeats's early plays. The officers—as Russian noblemen, post-Peter the Great—often speak in French and they are very often presented as if characters in some trivial French society-novel.[19]

But alien notions have penetrated not merely the Russian aristocracy: that observation would be a mere commonplace. In an authorial interpolation, Tolstoy complains (for instance) that

The word *aristocrat*, taken in the sense of a particular group, selected with great care, belonging to every class of society, has lately gained a great popularity among us in Russia—where it never ought to have taken root. (p. 43)

French (read: decadent) influence is seen to have penetrated every nationality and every social class, and the book moves slowly toward the blurring of national distinctions. Blacks, Cossacks, Jews, and Russians fight together, just as Eastern and Western Europeans die together: "On the earth, torn up by a recent explosion, were lying, here and there, broken beams, crushed bodies of Russians and French . . ." (p. 226). Curiously affecting images lead us to believe in an intercontinental but unicultural West. Rumors spread that the American fleet is on its way to aid the tsar at Sebastopol (p. 205), and, even more suggestively, "a curly-haired Jewish infantryman" (p. 206) crafts a cross out of a bullet and bestows it upon a "brother" soldier (p. 210) as a medal for bravery. The embattled nations share more than just a war, though that is a great deal to share. Warfare brings them to understand that they share as well as common culture and a common humanity, based upon a common faith. The proximity to death during war leads men to yearn "unconsciously" for "new, broad, and luminous regions" (p. 170)—regions which, really, are not all that new: Volodia's experience of them "aroused in him a feeling of infinite, long-forgotten calm" (p. 169). To borrow terms from contemporary theology, the mind is brought face to face with a mystery which, for long years, the mind had known only through its own concepts. This too, then, is a kind of return.

Tolstoy concludes "May, 1855" with the famous statement that the hero of his book is Truth and, in the "August" story, the author addresses his Protagonist directly:

Lord, Thou alone hast heard, Thou alone knowest the simple but ardent and despairing prayers of ignorance, the confused repentance asking for the cure of the body and the purification of the soul—the prayers which rise

to Thee from these places where death resides ...
(p. 170)

Like its Homeric Hellenism, the Hebraism (or Christianity)
of *Sebastopol* is reduced to its bare skeleton. "Christian art,"
Tolstoy writes in "What is Art?" (1898), "is of a kind that
... can unite men with God and with one another"—it need
not be conspicuously Christian. The faith of *Sebastopol*, precisely like that of *Joseph Andrews* and *Don Quixote* (or, for
that matter, of *Julie*), requires but love and honesty. It is the
nondogmatic religion Tolstoy writes about in his Crimean
War diary (March 5, 1855):

> A conversation about Divinity and Faith has suggested
> to me a great, stupendous idea, to the realization of which
> I feel capable of devoting my life. That idea is the found-
> ing of a new religion corresponding to the present state
> of mankind: the religion of Christ purged of dogmas and
> mysticism—a practical religion, not promising future bliss
> but giving bliss on earth.

This faith is more or less congruent with the humble, loving
heroism of Volodia—who, seen from this angle, becomes the
first martyr for Tolstoy's new/old religion, just as he is the
first representative of Tolstoyan/Homeric *virtu*. Saintliness and
heroism necessarily go together in Tolstoy's "new man." The
simple truth—the spirit of the Hebrew prophets behind Christian dogma, the spirit of Homer behind "realism" and "romanticism"—can be regained only by battling home. As much
blood is spilt in the *Odyssey* as in the *Iliad*, and the dedication
of a prodigal on his way back determines the extent to which
the place reached will be home.

• • •

IT IS, perhaps, because Tolstoy embodied these insights in his
fiction more than half a century before *Ulysses* was conceived
that Joyce thought Tolstoy "a magnificent writer ... head and
shoulders above the others." Yet *Sebastopol* and *Ulysses* seem
worlds apart on a first reading and, in fact, there is a great

gap between them. Henry James—another Western novelist born outside the Paris/London axis—stands in the breach between Tolstoy and Joyce. James admired Tolstoy's "epic genius" and the "truth" expressed in his fiction, but he objected to the insufficiently "rounded" form of Tolstoy's works.[20] James's theme in *The Ambassadors* is much the same as Tolstoy's in *Sebastopol*: the battle with Paris. His chief innovations—the ones which make his novel seem such an unlikely complement to Tolstoy's—have to do with his approach to the common material. James attempted, in *The Ambassadors*, to cultivate a formal geometry that would precisely represent his subject matter. So also, Joyce. Strether and Bloom each makes an odyssey that can be traced as a perfect circle on a map, and it was James's circular composition that Joyce most admired. Joyce also was impressed by James's wit, and the difference in tone between Tolstoy and his American and Irish colleagues is immediately obvious.[21] The near-comic tone *cum* deadly-serious intent of *The Ambassadors* is the direct result of another innovation: the battle has penetrated the modern drawing room. This technique, which James called "adventure transposed,"[22] translates all the heroism of warfare directly into the most chic parlors of Paris. Of course, this process is already operative in *Sebastopol*, where heroism is made to some degree a homely virtue. And already in *Sebastopol* the language of warfare is used to describe the psychological states of fictional characters ("His young and impressionable soul was . . . wounded by his isolation": p. 159), but it is *The Ambassadors* that moves first to obliterate Stendhal's distinction between the "*beau idéal antique*" and the "*beau idéal moderne.*" In *The Ambassadors*, the life of the salon becomes a new forum for the heroic life.[23]

Combat terminology dominates the metaphorical language of *The Ambassadors*—critics have made this observation before.[24] Ambassador Strether is dispatched on a mission whose goal is to rescue a kind of male Helen of Troy from the iniquitous arms of a city named Paris. When the home front perceives that Strether has had second thoughts about this engagement, an exchange of ambassadors is arranged (Book

7) and, from that point on, the military images fly fast and furious. At Mrs. Pocock's arrival, "Madame de Vionnet was already on the field" (p. 217), and James's delectable sentences are full of invaders (p. 221); acts of "valour" (p. 247); shipwrecks (p. 251); fights, triumphs, and "spoils of conquest" (p. 264); "forces" (p. 271); "daily cables, questions, answers, signals" (p. 272); and demands for unconditional surrender (p. 275). Strether feels an almost Iliadic sense of two great powers, for "three years glowering" at each other "across the sea" (p. 278), and, when he learns that Sarah Pocock plans to approach his Parisian encampment, he comprehends the military resonances of that intelligence. "What is she coming *for*," Strether asks Sarah's messenger, "—to kill me?" (p. 270). Strether finds Mrs. Pocock's Iliadic solemnity "funny enough" when Waymarsh announces her imminent descent, and James is as jaunty as can be in his use of martial metaphor. Mock-epic is the only attitude James could take in introducing heroism to bourgeois domestic life—the "battles" of Don Quixote, Joseph Andrews, and Stephen Dedalus are likewise outrageously funny—yet James, as Joyce after him and as Fielding and Cervantes before, takes responsibility for the grave implications of the metaphor.

Strether soon learns that, while Mrs. Pocock will shoot no arrow through his intestines, neither will she hesitate to employ social and financial weapons powerful enough to bring his life, as he has known it, to an abrupt end:

> Her departure had been for some minutes marked as imminent, and she was already at the door that stood open to the court, from the threshold of which she delivered herself of this judgement. It rang out so loud as to produce for the first time the hush of everything else. Strether quite, as an effect of it, breathed less bravely; he could acknowledge it, but simply enough. "Oh if you think *that*—!"
>
> "Then all's at an end? So much the better. I do think that!" . . . She made for it with decision, and the manner of her break, the sharp shaft of her rejoinder, had an

intensity by which Strether was at first kept in arrest. She had let fly at him as from a stretched cord, and it took him a minute to recover from the sense of being pierced. It was not the penetration of surprise; it was that, much more, of certainty; his case being put for him as he had as yet only put it to himself. . . . It probably *was* all at an end. (p. 280)

"A whole moral and intellectual being" is threatened in this scene "at the point of a bayonet" (p. 298). To stand up to this show of (American) force is plainly an act of heroism, just as it is heroic of Strether to stand up for moral *gaucheries* in a (European) community that possesses but a "sufficiency" (p. 126) of moral fiber. In either case, Strether acts without self-interest. His "only logic," he says, is "not . . . to have got anything" for himself (p. 344). Strether's imaginative objectivity and his commitment to being "right" (p. 344) are ultimately what make him "the hero" (p. 265) of a book in which heroism is redefined for modern circumstances—and, while Strether's heroism is often a comic spectacle (the weapons used against him are so very bourgeois), it can be a most somber one as well. When Miss Gostrey finally sighs this book away on our behalf, it is "all comically, all tragically" (p. 345).

The comic skirmishes in *The Ambassadors* are part of an all-out, tragic war of persons, families, corporate interests, social classes, and even nations—a war that threatens lives and livelihoods. So far as we can tell, this war has left Strether "dished," and both Mme. de Vionnet and Miss Gostrey "unmanned." It has resulted in what looks like a total victory for the American forces: despite Strether's admonition, we fully expect that Chad will show up one day in Woollett as master ad-man for his family's manufacturing concern. But this war, like the siege of Sebastopol, is also an "inward exercise" (p. 303) and, at that level, it is not so clear which side may claim victory. Chad makes his "definite surrender" to Strether in Book 7 (p. 184), almost exactly halfway through the novel—and, when Strether decides against returning home with Chad

(" 'Let the Pococks come!' Strether repeated," with all the relish of a James character who knows he has stunned the reader),[25] we are signaled that Strether's consciousness has been the most important battlefield all along. Europe is a part of Strether's "inward picture" (p. 24) as much as it is an actual place. And this psychological battle is not a mere case of attack-and-resistance; Strether's history does not partake of "the dreadful little old tradition" that Americans change under the influence of Paris.[26] Europe does indeed require him to abandon "his odious suspicion of any form of beauty" (p. 118) and to make a great many other adjustments, all of which leave him "changed . . . somewhere deep down" (p. 209). But the forceful reintroduction of American influence, which Strether himself summons to Paris in the person of Sarah Pocock, makes this psychological process a genuine tug of war. Sarah's shocking opinion that Chad has changed for the worst, and her view that Strether has been sacrificing "mothers and sisters" to a strange and indecent goddess (p. 277), leaves Strether floundering between two cogent ways of seeing.

"Ways of seeing" are what Paris and Boston/Woollett come to represent for Strether, just as they did for James himself. In his "Preface" to *The Ambassadors*, James calls Paris "a mere symbol for more things than had been dreamt of in the philosophy of Woollett."[27] For James, neither city's point of view is satisfactory on its own. Henry James is the amphibolous American artist: a creature content neither on land nor in water. Paris—the Old World—is both "exciting and depressing" for him[28] and, in a letter of July 4, 1876 (America's centennial), he wrote home that "The longer I live in France the better I like the French personally, but the more convinced I am of their bottomless superficiality."[29] What James means by "superficiality" is made clearer in his 1874 review of the *Tentation de St. Antoine*, where he insists that Flaubert's novel contains nothing but acute, microscopic description. (Miss Barrace, too, says that Parisians "run too much to mere eye": p. 126.) Flaubert, James believes, "proceeds upon the assumption that these innumerable marvels of observation will hold together without the underlying moral unity of what is called a 'purpose,' " and he goes on to expand his critique of the *Tentation* into a polemical analysis of French literary culture:

> It seems to us to throw a tolerably vivid light on the present condition of the French literary intellect. M. Flaubert and his contemporaries have pushed so far the education of the senses . . . that it has left them morally stranded and helpless. . . . Behind M. Flaubert stands a whole society of aesthetic *raffinés*. . . . The human mind, even in indifferent health, does after all need to be *nourished*, and thrives but scantily on a regimen of pigments and sauces.[30]

In an article of 1876 on the Goncourts, James makes the same observations in almost identical words:

> They are the most Parisian thing I know. . . . a culture sensibly limited, but very exquisite in its kind; an imagination in the highest degree *raffiné*—fed upon made dishes. Their inspiration is altogether artistic.[31]

Which is to say that Paris feeds off itself culturally—feeds only off culture. Because of its unbalanced diet, France's "spiritual sense" is dying, "the moral side . . . is dry and thin." The view of Paris James presents in these essays is precisely the view he offers in *The Ambassadors*. Strether's first impression of the city is that "the air had a taste as of something mixed with art, something that presented nature as a white-capped master-chef" (p. 59). Strether even applies this culinary/artistic metaphor to the changes that Paris has made in Chad:

> Was all the difference therefore that he was actually smooth? Possibly; for that he *was* smooth was as marked as in the taste of a sauce. . . . it had retouched his features, drawn them with a cleaner line. . . . it had given him a form and a surface, almost a design. . . . (p. 97)

In their combination of love for the city's exquisite charm and revulsion at its "Gallic lightness of soil in the moral region,"[32] the markings of James on Paris read like those of

Matthew Arnold on the beauty and decadence of classical Athens or of Renaissance Rome. James was an early convert to Arnoldian culture and it appears that James had Arnold in mind when he arrived at his "symbols of an opposition" (p. 210): Paris and Woollett, Mme. de Vionnet and Mrs. Newsome, Jeanne and Mamie. The novel's first scenes draw this opposition in Arnoldian terms, for, when Strether arrives in Europe, he has left the American "plane" of "morals" (p. 23) to enter into a very different kind of world, in which "sin" is an alien concept. In an early scene, Maria Gostrey puzzles over Strether's sense of guilt:

> "It's she who hasn't sinned," Strether replied. "I've sinned the most."
> "Ah," Miss Gostrey cynically laughed, "what a picture of *her*! Have you robbed the widow and the orphan?"
> "I've sinned enough," said Strether.
> "Enough for whom? Enough for what?"
> "Well, to be where I am."
> "Thank you!" (p. 52)

Related to this genius for locating guilt is the Woollett craving for simple good/bad distinctions. A fortnight after his arrival at Chester, what Strether "wanted most was some idea that would simplify" (p. 61) the enormous complexity of "relations" in Paris—for the city is to him a "vast bright Babylon . . . a jewel brilliant and hard, in which parts were not to be discriminated nor differences comfortably marked" (p. 64). Again, the *ficelle*, Miss Gostrey, is our gauge of Woollett's temperament. Strether speaks to her of "people who are *not* nice," and Miss Gostrey replies: "I delight . . . in your classifications" (p. 107).

James seems to have lifted Woollett straight out of the pages of *Culture and Anarchy*. "From Maine to Florida, and back again," Arnold opines, "all America Hebraises."[33] The term "sacred rage" which Strether coins (pp. 41, 158) is almost a quote from Arnold's analysis of Hebraism, and Miss Barrace associates Waymarsh—Massachusetts' ultimate representative in Paris—with Old Testament figures: "Oh your friend's a type," she points out for our edification. "The grand old American—what shall one call it? The Hebrew prophet, Ezekiel, Jeremiah" (p. 177). James describes Waymarsh as a Hebrew Patriarch as well: having "always more or less the air sitting at the door of his tent" (p. 183). Arnoldian Hebraism is precisely what Mrs. Newsome and the Pococks are about. They care only for standards of behavior, which they apply in mechanical fashion. On the other hand—and as Arnold defines the term—we easily can associate the Parisians of James's novel with Hellenism. Unlike the Americans, their concern is not with a settled standard of behavior, but with the relativity of relationships: "the quality produced by measure and balance, the fine relation of part to part and space to space" (p. 69). Thus, Paris is both "classic and casual" (p. 67), and James describes this nineteenth-century holy city as the modern world's Athens: "the background of fiction, the medium of art, the nursery of letters; practically as distant as Greece but practically also well-nigh as consecrated" (p. 301). James dwells on Mme. de Vionnet's "antique" aspect:

> Her head, extremely fair and exquisitely festal, was like a happy fancy, a notion of the antique . . . while her slim lightness and brightness, her gaiety, her expression, her decision, contributed to an effect that might have been felt by a poet as half mythological and half conventional. He could have compared her to a goddess. . . . (p. 160)

Similarly, Maria Gostrey's home is, for Strether, "a haunt of ancient peace" (p. 341), while Chad is "a happy young Pagan, handsome but oddly indulgent" (p. 141).

James obviously has taken great pains to make these distinctions compelling.[34] When Strether first hits upon this "young Pagan"/"sacred rage" terminology, James looks out, over the top of the book jacket, straight into his reader's eyes, and remarks, "the idea was a clue" (p. 99).[35] The Hebraism/Hellenism distinction was attractive to James—he had used it before in works of fiction (in *Roderick Hudson* and "The Last of the Valerii")—and what he found most "inexpressibly disagreeable" about the *Tentation* was Flaubert's failure to exploit that favored theme: "When the author has a really beautiful point to treat—as the assembly of the Greek deities fading and paling away in the light of Christianity—he becomes singularly commonplace and ineffective."[36] However engaging he found Arnold's dichotomy, though, James's Paris/Woollett opposition is a more intricate affair. In James' novel, there is cleavage not only between Hebraism and Hellenism but also between fact and relation (pp. 150–51), Protestant and Catholic,[37] eighteenth century and nineteenth century,[38] Reformation and Renaissance,[39] bourgeois progressivism and aristocratic traditionalism,[40] the future and the past.[41] Even this list is far from exhaustive, for, like Tolstoy and Arnold before him (and like Joyce and Eliot after), James is attempting to delineate an enormously complicated "dissociation of sensibility" in the Western mind.

For James, this dissociation is not merely an unfortunate condition but a psychosis requiring emergency treatment. The Hebraism of Waymarsh is no longer the vibrant faith of Moses. It is, in little Bilham's words, the distorted Hebraism of a "Moses, on the ceiling, brought down to the floor; overwhelming, colossal, but somehow portable" (p. 125).[42] Moreover, "Mr. Waymarsh was for *his* part joyless"—a devastating comment on a figure who represents a religion which (according to Arnold) existed precisely to bring mankind "joy."[43] And despite her great beauty of appearance and manner, Mme. de Vionnet is without sublimity. She recognizes with remorse that Strether finds the dishonesty in her relationship with Chad both "vulgar" and "ugly":

> ". . . ugly or beautiful—it doesn't matter what we call them . . . we're detestable. We bore you. . . . And I who should have liked to seem to you—well, sublime! . . . I'm old and abject and hideous. . . . It's a doom—I know it. (p. 324)

Mme. de Vionnet is not the only aging person in this novel, though she is one of those static characters for whom old age will be a doom. Mrs. Newsome is a middle-aged invalid and Chad, her youthful son, has graying hair. Strether and Miss

Gostrey can see each other only through two pair of glasses (p. 25). Waymarsh's face tells us that he has "at the end of years, barely escaped, by flight of time, a general nervous collapse" (p. 30). When Miss Gostrey tells Strether, "Your failure's general," she might as well be addressing the whole of Jamesian Woollett and Jamesian Paris: all of America and Europe, both Hebraism and Hellenism.

The dissociation had reached a stage so critical that it was imperative for salvageable Americans (artists, editors of literary periodicals) to be "made over" in Paris, where that sort of operation was a "specialty" (p. 96). Strether is Paris' most "wonderful" masterpiece, presumably because, from the start, he wanted to be "put through the whole thing" (p. 336). He is pronounced "complete" near the end of Book 12 (p. 330), for he has come to combine Woollett's moral way of seeing with Paris' aesthetic one. James calls the resulting combination "moral glamour" (p. 64), and Strether makes that combination work, gives it life, with a third important quality: the "blest imagination."[44] Chad has had the same opportunities as Strether to achieve this reassociation of sensibility, but he had failed because, as Strether tells him, he has "no imagination . . . at all" (p. 290). Strether will return to America for reasons diametrically opposed to Chad's and, while both men will return changed, their new personalities could hardly differ more. Chad will return as a mere statistic, as but one more American in the "dreadful little old tradition" of Americans who sow wild oats in Paris and acquire polish. He will return out of boredom, and for money. Strether will return for reasons we can only call religious. He feels he must always "give" (the quintessence of Jamesian Hebraism) but never take (pp. 321–22), and to stay in Paris would mean "taking" either Maria Gostrey or Mme. de Vionnet. His decision to return will "put on record, somehow, my own fidelity—fundamentally unchanged after all" to the God of Woollett.

In His name, Strether rejects the actual Paris in favor of a virtuous Paris that has existed all along only in his imagination. Strether arranges, like his pioneering ancestors, for a New Paris to be built in the New World. He encourages little

Bilham to marry Mamie Pocock—for, in this way, two young, Paris-exposed Americans of great potential (he is "the best," she is "splendid") might come to follow Strether's example. In any case, Bilham will inherit all Strether has to bequeath him (p. 257). We assume he will put his spiritual inheritance, at least, to good use, for John Little Bilham is the closest thing in *The Ambassadors* to Fielding's Joseph, Tolstoy's Volodia, and Joyce's "Blephen." He is potentially the "new man" who will emerge someday from this book's warfare of false oppositions; he may turn out to be the end product of its dialectic. Strether is already too old to be the New Adam ("I'm old. . . . It's too late," he tells Bilham) and, at any rate, the two men share many characteristics: "admirable innocence," "intensity," appreciation for the "mystery" of Paris, a dedication to the "aesthetic lyre" (pp. 83–85). Bilham undertook the battle with Paris before Strether had contemplated a visit, and Miss Barrace recalls how Bilham had, like Strether, "come over to convert the savages" (p. 125). Bilham's sense of things is fine and prescient: long before Strether arrives at his final conclusion about the Chad/Mme. de Vionnet liaison—that the relation is virtuous despite the technical adultery and that, therefore, it should be maintained permanently—little Bilham has come to the same opinion. It is the opinion of an associated sensibility, one which is "Jewgreek" in its thought processes: Bilham is both "more American than anybody" (p. 83) and, as he himself acknowledges, "eaten" alive by Paris. Strether is more noble, more self-sacrificing—he is the novel's "hero"— but little Bilham seems to be the one who will take what Strether has found good in the Old World and who will give it renewed life in the New World. He is James's representative of "artist-man" (p. 83)—a kind of new/old breed of *homo sapiens*—and, it seems, the future's best hope.

In a similar way—in a way probably intended to be precisely parallel—James's novel itself (like Cervantes' and Fielding's and Tolstoy's) is a new sort of fiction, based upon old forms. *The Ambassadors* (again, like *Don Quixote, Joseph Andrews*, and *Sebastopol*) is among the most self-consciously literary of fictions: Strether's Christian name is Lewis Lambert, Chad lives in the rue Scribe, and James's characters make reference to—often pronounce opinions on—the novels of Hugo, Goldsmith, Mürger, Thackeray, and Balzac. Each of James's major characters is plotting a text: Strether "was of course always writing" to Mrs. Newsome (p. 194) and he wonders, for instance, how Chad's friends will "suit his book" (p. 107). Miss Gostrey's "book" is suited by Jim Pocock (p. 245), Sarah speaks "by book" (p. 278), and Mme. de Vionnet is called Chad's "editor" (p. 112). Strether and Miss Gostrey usually are aware of the literariness of their situation, and sometimes they discuss it. In their first encounter, Maria says, "you've recognized me—which *is* rather beautiful and rare" (p. 25). Even more than in *Sebastopol*, where officers and their ladies-left-behind continually create new fictions, the battling after truth in *The Ambassadors* is a literary affair. There is a supreme fiction somewhere, but Strether can find it only by wading through a library full of personal fictions. The universe of the novel sometimes is seen as a literary text by the characters who live within it. On Strether's fateful country trip, there was "not a breath of the cooler evening that wasn't somehow a syllable of the text" (p. 306). It is a text with whose structure and symmetry Strether is much concerned (p. 291), for in his interpretation of the Book being written he wants to "be right" (p. 344).

Strether leaves America thinking he is about to live through a kind of *Iliad* and ends by realizing that his story has been an *Odyssey* all along: a drama of return. When he discerns, at the last, what Ezra Pound calls the "moral geometry" underlying all of this book's fictions, he immediately determines to affirm it in action. He decides to complete the circle by returning home. Yet his view of Paris has not "swung back" (p. 328) to that of Mrs. Newsome, for here is yet another circle that goes somewhere. He is spiraling home to "a great difference" (p. 344). As in the most perfect epic poems—the *Odyssey*, or Dante's *Commedia* for instance—the form of this book emits the same moral vibrations as its content. Even the most self-conscious of art-novelists—even Flaubert—does not make his narratives into poetry to this extraordinary degree.

But perhaps the epic and poetic qualities of James's novel are qualities we can see only in reading forward from Cervantes, Fielding, and Tolstoy, or in reading backwards from *Ulysses*. All the possible references to Homer or Vergil in this book are at most comic quasi-references: the martial imagery and pagan imagery, the rituals of strange gods, the return across a western sea, the redemption of heroism, Chad's capture, Mme. de Vionnet's Calypso-like portrayal (cf. p. 324), James's insistence (in correspondence with his publishers) upon the novel's division into twelve books.

It is impossible to say how much, or even whether, all of this was part of a grand, epic plan for *The Ambassadors*. However, it is clear that James did realize (as Tolstoy and many other writers realized) that the opposing literary currents of his time were too constrictive and needed transcending. Accordingly, *The Ambassadors* was made to be "full of mystery, yet full of reality" (p. 282), to be made "lurid but clear" (p. 244), to contain events and persons that are "true but . . . incredible" (p. 286). Like Tolstoy, James may have understood that his reconciliation of realism and typological romanticism was a return to something far older than either. James seems aware of the search to find "romance . . . on classic ground" (p. 242), of his own need to reaffirm "the oddity, the originality, the poetry" of the "pseudo-classic" (p. 236), in order to make it truly classic once more. He accomplishes this feat in the same stroke that unites Hebraism and Hellenism, America and the Old World—since his novel combines New World/Christian typology and moral concern with Old World/classical form and style.

• • •

CRITICS have given much attention to the way in which a number of nineteenth- and twentieth-century novels combine and transcend the two main literary currents of the modern period. Much, for example, has been made of *Ulysses'* peculiar blend of extreme realism ("He tore away half the prize story sharply and wiped himself with it") and extreme symbolism ("The heaventree of stars hung with humid nightblue fruit").

Donald Fanger calls this phenomenon "romantic realism" or "fantastic fidelity." Joyce preferred to call it, simply, "Homer"—and when T. S. Eliot called it "classicism" in a famous article, the author of *Ulysses* expressed approval.[45] Fanger concludes his study, *Dostoevsky and Romantic Realism*, with lines relevant to the present discussion: "By the early twentieth century," he writes, "these currents of symbolism and naturalism were meeting again. . . . Joyce in this way immortalized Dublin in *Ulysses*. . . . But that is all another story."[46] Joyce saw his own story, and the one Fanger details, as a continuum. The whole history of the European novel, from Cervantes to Fielding to Tolstoy to James, can be read as one long story about the dialectical battle between various kinds of realism and various kinds of idealization.[47] Many of the greatest novels have been those that have found a way of blending or reconciling the two tendencies—often with a disciple's eye on the ancient epics—and it is the history of these novels for which *Ulysses* was meant to stand as the modernist apotheosis or epiphany. We are so accustomed by now to the book's title that we have become immune to the daring of its implications. As Ellmann observes, in *The Consciousness of Joyce*, for a novelist to title his work *Ulysses* took hardly less conviction of purpose than for him to have called it *The Bible*. Like *Don Quixote, Joseph Andrews, Sebastopol*, and *The Ambassadors*, *Ulysses* is an epic/novel based upon the Odyssean metaphor— the return, or, more accurately, the battling home—and, as in those earlier works, both the homeland, and the obstacles met along the way, are phenomena of culture.

The battles of Cervantes, Fielding, Tolstoy, James, and Joyce have a good deal in common, but we also should acknowledge the important qualitative distinctions among them. For one thing, the adversary in each case is distinct (for Fielding, it is the rococo; for Tolstoy, it is romanticism and realism) and the ancestral past for which each novelist marches off to war is not necessarily the same past, though each falls under Arnold's useful rubric: Hebraism and Hellenism. Both Tolstoy and Joyce would have claimed, at least semiseriously, that their narrative styles were Homeric in the modern context.

Yet the plain style of *Sebastopol* and *Ulysses'* mannerist macaronics have little more in common than intentionality. Both Tolstoy and James would assert that the heroism of their protagonists was of epic proportions, yet the still martial heroics of *Sebastopol* are comparable to those of *The Ambassadors* only with an act of the imagination. On the other hand, those novelists were one in their ultimate pursuit, if not in their understanding of its end-point or the details of its execution. Each one effects, by liquidating all obstacles, a return to basics—religious, sexual, cultural, literary—and embodies that return in a form which reflects it. And each writer seems convinced that the novel was born to the tasks which, in ages past, had been the glory of epic poetry. By the twentieth century, this intuition of the novel's epic mission had grown so strong—become so commonplace—that no one was shocked when Samuel Butler and then T. E. Lawrence asserted its inverse corollary: that the *Odyssey* was the first novel of Europe.

Nor was anyone shocked by the Homeric chapter titles of *Ulysses* when Joyce chose to reveal them. In fact, as A. Walton Litz has shown, some of the novel's most enthusiastic readers, like T. S. Eliot, were relieved to learn of the Homeric scaffolding.[48] But the epic analogue serves as far more than scaffolding for the construction of *Ulysses*. We do not judge a building by its scaffold, though if the platform is left permanently in place, it can make an otherwise unapproachable monument appear somewhat insecure and therefore comic. Homeric parallelism and Homeric ticktack may have been necessities of composition for Joyce, as they were for Vergil, but these are less relevant to the novel's reader than to its author. *Ulysses* makes our century the Ithaca of history; the epic/novel epiphanizes the modern as the return to an ancient world. As such, *Ulysses* is our ultimate statement on the ideologies of return, and the epic/novel genre is their most cogent witness. Joyce even saw the past in the terms of the present: Frank Budgen reports that, during the First World War, Joyce was pleased to consider Odysseus as Europe's first draft dodger. In no other genre was such an easy concourse between antiquity and modernity achieved. (It is an achievement that Joyce's tragedian colleagues did not even recognize as plausible or worthy.) And among novels, *Ulysses* arrives at that concourse with the most astonishing blend of affability and integrity, of modernity and modernism.

Yet Joyce's novel does not—could not possibly—stand alone. Behind it stands a history of the novel, a long tradition of novel/epics which *Ulysses* was intended to culminate: which *Ulysses* may have invented by culminating. To debate the merits of the novel/epic theory is probably less fruitful than to apply it—to read backwards from *Ulysses*. We are not dealing with matters of truth and falsehood but with a question of historical explanation, and *Ulysses* is most productively read in the context of the history it implies. In any case, it is possible that we have no choice, or so Eliot seems to have thought. It was very likely with *Ulysses* in mind that Eliot formulated the modernist theory of tradition and history:

> what happens when a new work of art is created is something that happens simultaneously to all the works of art which preceded it. The existing monuments form an ideal order among themselves, which is modified by the introduction of the new (the really new) work of art among them. The existing order is complete before the new work arrives; for order to persist after the supervention of novelty, the *whole* existing order must be, if ever so slightly, altered; and so the relations, proportions, values of each work of art toward the whole are readjusted; and this is conformity between the old and the new. Whoever has approved this idea of order, of the form of European, of English, literature, will not find it preposterous that the past should be altered by the present as much as the present is directed by the past. And the poet who is aware of this will be aware of great difficulties and responsibilities.[49]

Always searching for new difficulties and new responsibilities, Joyce might well have subtitled *Ulysses*: Tradition and the Individual Talent.

· VI ·

Novel and Epic:
The Ithaca of History

> . . . the first thing was this: you had six centuries that
> hadn't been packaged. It was a question of dealing
> with material that wasn't in the *Divina Commedia*.
> . . . The problem was to build up a circle of refer-
> ence—taking the modern mind to be the mediaeval
> mind with wash after wash of classical culture poured
> over it since the Renaissance. That was the psyche,
> if you like.
>
> Ezra Pound, *Paris Review* interview

WHATEVER Joyce's intentions, reading backwards from *Ulys-*
ses probably tells us less about the history of the novel than
about modern presuppositions regarding epic. *Joseph An-*
drews, Sebastopol, and even *The Ambassadors* aspire to epic
stature and all three novels are embroiled—as is virtually every
modern attempt at epic poetry, from *Paradise Lost* to *The*
Prelude, and beyond—in the controversy that Heine and Arnold labeled "Hebraism and Hellenism." This fact is extraordinary, and it is extraordinarily eloquent about the demands
we make of epic. The writer of epic is expected to comprehend
and justify his civilization, its history, and his own era—he is
asked, in the loosest sense, to justify the ways of God to man—
and he is to do so in relation to the theodicean statements of
earlier writers in the epic tradition. In every age that produced
a great epic, this was an improbable undertaking, but in the
modern period it was plainly impossible. Vergil had concerned
himself with the transition from the swashbuckling cosmos
of Homer to the reticent, duty-bound, disciplined, and public
Empire of Rome; and he used the Homeric scheme to grace,
with an Odyssean glow of homely destination, the Augustan

sense of historical destiny. Vergil had to deal with two epics (the *Iliad* and the *Odyssey*) and two epochs (the archaic and the classical), but the Christian poets had to contend with two sets of primary epics (the Homeric-Vergilian epic and the Hebrew/Greek Bible) and with the two "theogonies" underlying them (Hesiod's and the Book of Genesis), and it took a millennium to produce Dante's *Commedia*.

With Dante, the problem of Hebraism and Hellenism enters the epic tradition as a theme, for the *Commedia* is a self-conscious embodiment of the "Christian synthesis," which St. Paul, as a Jewish-Christian, had catalyzed with his symbolic pilgrimage to the Areopagus of Athens. But almost as soon as the Christian synthesis was achieved in poetry, it began to disintegrate, for Dante had arrived not so much at a synthesis of Israel and Greece as a subordination of both. Ulysses may be found in the eighth circle of *Inferno*; Homer would have worshipped, under more archaic names, deities scattered throughout Dante's hell; and the children of Israel in *Paradiso* qualify for bliss only as proto-Christians. In the terms of medieval exegesis, this process is known as "plundering the Egyptians"—taking from antiquity (from one's own past) what is workable (Isaiah, Plato, Vergil) and relegating to the unconscious underworld all that is not.

Yet, as Freud was to tell Europe, subconscious contents have a way of surfacing—like Roman manuscripts and Greek statuary. By Milton's time, it was already necessary to reopen the double theogony that underlay the Christian synthesis and to reconcile what already had been reconciled in philosophical terms (by Aquinas and others) on the level of irreconcilable mythologies. The resulting compromise is disconcerting to say the least, and even twentieth-century readers can be taken aback when the rebel angels of *Paradise Lost* look upon Christ as the Titans might have looked upon some Olympian upstart, or when the Father calls His fallen servants "gods."[1] In the centuries following Milton's, the absolute sway of Christianity waned and the Christian synthesis decomposed slowly into its original elements. The development of Hellenism, as a phenomenon independent of Christianity, has already been traced in some detail (chapter three). To do the same for Hebraism would take a chapter of equal length and is a question more immediately relevant to Jewish studies, except as its progress touches the composition of *Ulysses*.

Joyce's approach to Hebraism was relatively new. When Arnold used the term Hebraism, he meant Christianity: the celebrated essay in *Culture and Anarchy* was primarily a polemic against the lower Protestant churches, which were then opposing the traditional, classical education of Britain and asserting that the Bible was the one needful study. But for Joyce, the Hebraism of the Hebraism-and-Hellenism formulation was not Christianity but Judaism or, more accurately, "Jewishness." Joyce's guide through Homer's Mediterranean, Victor Bérard, had written in *Les Phéniciens et l'Odyssée* that "It is, in fact, a Semitic voyage which must be supposed as the original source of the *Nostos*"—and Joyce took Bérard at his word.[2] The Jewish nation antedated not only Christendom but even Homeric civilization and, more interesting for Joyce's purposes, the Jews seemed to be surviving the Christian era and making plans for a modern *nostos* of more than provincial significance.

Joyce did some reading in Zionist literature (witness the *Agendath Netaim* pamphlets in *Ulysses* and the presence of Herzl's *Judenstaat* in his library)[3] and the following passages from Moses Hess's influential book, *Rome and Jerusalem* (1862), may give us some notion of the Zionist ideas Joyce was assimilating:

> It is certain . . . that our [the Jews'] present yearning is for a Redemption of far broader outline than any that Christianity ever imagined, or could ever have imagined. Christianity was a star in the darkness, which provided consolation and hope for the peoples after the sun of ancient culture had set; it shed its light over the graves of the nations of antiquity. Since it is a religion of death, its mission is ended the moment the nations reawaken into life. The history of the nations of Europe in the last three hundred years amply illustrates the truth of this

assertion. . . . Judaism is not threatened, like Christianity,
with danger from the nationalistic and humanistic aspirations of our time, for, in reality, the spirit of the age is
approaching ever closer to the essential Jewish emphasis
on real life. . . . Do you not believe that in [the] opening
words of the prophecies of Second Isaiah, as well as in
the closing verse of the book of Obadiah (1:21), the conditions of our day are depicted?[4]

In such Zionist tracts, Joyce might have found congenial the
definition of Christianity as a "religion of death" and the
supposition that the modern world, since the sixteenth century, had been disengaging slowly from Christianity. Joyce
may have been impressed, too, by the notion that modernity's
un-Christian, "humanistic aspirations" were "approaching ever
closer to the essential Jewish emphasis on real life"—that
"post-Christian" might, in some sense, mean Jewish.

In making his Odysseus figure Jewish, Joyce may have wanted
to indicate a parallel between the *Odyssey* and the Hebrew
Bible, and thereby to locate a "Jewgreek"—a culturally sanc-
tioned—basis for his own, modern convictions and obsessions. To state what Joyce might have found to connect in
these books is impure, but remunerative, speculation: *Ulysses*,
the *Odyssey*, and the Hebrew Scriptures are all *nostos*-cen-
tered texts and focus on what to St. Paul would seem hope-
lessly petty details of social rituals and religious practices, and
on the minutiae of human commercial, political, and biological relations. Furthermore, the authors of all three works
would want to dispute the Pauline distinction between letter
and spirit, and to agree with Flaubert that "God is in the
detail." Moses had no more interest in Another World than
did Homer or Joyce—of the three, only Joyce had heard of
metaphysics—and each found in this world, and especially in
its domestic and aesthetic details, a sacred quality reserved in
many cultures for a divine realm. In Homer, as in Joyce, the
division of *psyche* and *soma* is vague and, in Biblical Hebrew,
there is only one word (*nefesh*) for soul and appetite—much
as the Homeric epics and the Pentateuch share with *Ulysses'*

"Hades" episode a reticence about the afterlife. (Hades and Sheol seem to be the same type of place—a place where, to use the idiom of Genesis, one sleeps with one's fathers.) Richard Ellmann has traced the large importance of Aristotle for *Ulysses*,[5] and Joyce's appreciation of Aristotle was doubtless due to the indifference to the transcendent which that philosopher shares with the authors of the Pentateuch and the *Odyssey*. But Aristotle is a *theorist* of immanence where the Hebrew Bible and the *Odyssey* are its personable embodiments, and it is their "personality" above all that seems to have impressed Joyce in the ancient Mediterranean epics.

In fact, the personality characteristics glorified in those texts can seem, from certain angles, to be oddly similar. In Book 13 of the *Odyssey*, Athena, after telling Odysseus a cock-and-bull story and receiving one in return, calls him and herself "two of a kind" and goes on to appreciate his detachment, cool-headedness, quickness of mind, eloquence, stubbornness, and cheek. In Genesis 18 the God of Israel seemingly picks an argument with Abraham by telling him about the coming destruction of the Plain ("Shall I hide from Abraham that which I am doing . . . ?"), and the patriarch bargains with God on behalf of fifty, forty-five, forty, thirty, twenty, and finally ten possible righteous men—for, as he asks, in a question more provocative than any Odysseus ever puts to Athena, "Shall not the Judge of all the earth do justly?" The central figures of Genesis and the *Odyssey* are obstinate, skeptical, argumentative, imaginative, well-spoken and outspoken—like the characters in *Ulysses*—and, in summary, the worlds of all three "epics" adhere at least as closely to what Moses Hess calls "real life" as real life ever does.

Joyce was not the first to bring together these two eastern Mediterranean epics—in 1685, Zachary Bogan, an Oxford scholar, published a book entitled, *Homerus Hebraizon*—but Joyce was the first writer in the epic tradition to determine that a Jew could serve as symbol for both Hebraism and Hellenism. Beyond this signal honor, Leopold Bloom may be said to represent in *Ulysses* the daily life of the twentieth century; and Joyce, by this vortex of emblems, may be making a gesture like that of Freud's *Totem and Taboo*, a book that explicates modern life in terms of archaic cultures (especially the Greek) and that whispers, in the preface to the Hebrew translation, that "the new Jewry" and the new science are not strangers. (The Nazis agreed and forbade the teaching of "Jewish science" in German universities.) In Bloom—in *Ulysses*—modernity meets antiquity, Hebraism meets Hellenism, and "real life" meets the new science of Einstein and Freud. We could rephrase the famous line from *Finnegans Wake* and say, "Here comes everything," except that, in the stew-like symbiosis of *Ulysses*, the dominating ingredient of Western culture—Christianity—is not a part of the recipe. As a self-proclaimed epic poet, Joyce had to face and defeat the same difficulties that had plagued the Christian poets, Dante and Milton, but, in one aspect at least, his task was easier than theirs. In the twentieth century, Joyce could view the multiple foundations of Western culture through a new—a post-Christian—lens.

Christianity and *Ulysses* are parallel but incompatible amalgams. Both match the past with the present, the Hebraic with the Hellenic; but for Joyce that past was Old-Testament and Homeric, rather than New-Testament and Platonic—and, in *Ulysses*, the present is an "immanentist" reaction against Christian transcendence. Joycean Hebraism and Joycean Hellenism are pre-spiritual, just as Joycean modernity is post-spiritual. Yet, while exorcising Christianity, *Ulysses* reasserts the Greco-Jewish structure of the Christian synthesis and, like a proper epic, it attaches contemporary culture to the roots of civilization. It is precisely the idea of return—of a modern return to something behind Christian transcendence—that makes this post-Christian epic possible and its Odyssean, *nostos*-centered framework necessary. If the modern dispensation—Einstein, Freud, bourgeois urban life—has for its precedents the culture's two founding epics (the Hebrew Bible and Homer), then modernity could itself be the subject of epic, and even of theodicy. The *Aeneid*, in some respects the closest parallel to *Ulysses* in the epic canon, is also a nonspiritual theodicy: the apotheosis of a divinized world view, the epiphany of a way of life.

• • •

BUT any approach to *Ulysses* must begin with caveats. This novel, like the world, seems constructed to resist every scheme that arises from the contemplation of its design. It does not appear extravagant to claim that a book with such a title—a book in which the main actor leaves his home at the outset and comes back at the conclusion—has to do with some kind of return. "What parallel courses did Bloom and Stephen follow returning?"—in a novel based on Homer's *Odyssey*, this leading question is placed strategically as the opening line, of the center episode, in what are known as the "*nostos* chapters." The question is loaded, and the narrating voice of "Ithaca" has a resonant response: our heroes start "united"; they quickly separate, reducing pace; and (disparately, eventually) they reach the same point at the same time.

The urge to allegory is irresistible. By the time a reader gets to this question and answer, he already has ingenious notions about who Bloom and Stephen *really* are, and the author has fed his ingenuity. Though both men have been baptized (Bloom three times), Stephen bears the name of the Greeks' "fabulous artificer" and Bloom—we are reminded in almost every episode—was born to a Jewish father. From *Ulysses'* first page, Hebraism and Hellenism are at issue: Mulligan comments on Dedalus' "absurd name, an ancient Greek" and mis-muses that his own Hebrew name, Malachi, "has a Hellenic ring." In their first triads of episodes, Stephen is bid to "Hellenise" Ireland and to read Greek literature "in the original," while Bloom, at the same hours of the day, exchanges meaningful glances with his Zionist pork-butcher and engages in reveries about the promised return to the Promised Land. In "Eolus," Stephen thinks about the Greeks' wars for independence (p. 133) while Bloom meditates on the Jews' festival of freedom (p. 122).[6] Western history, we allegorize from the itinerary given in "Ithaca," began with an act of dissociation and (since the falls of Jerusalem, Athens, and Rome) its two main components—the Judaic and the Hellenic—have pursued distinct but parallel fates in a northern exile, erring and learning, "passing from land to land, among peoples, amid events." In the end, the process will come full circle: "Somewhere imperceptibly he would hear and somehow reluctantly, suncompelled, obey the summons of recall . . . after incalculable eons of peregrination return . . ." (p. 728).

However (and there is always, with *Ulysses*, a "however"), the whole idea of return—Biblical, Homeric, and modern—is dismissed, elsewhere in "Ithaca," as self-evidently out of the question:

> What would render such return irrational?
> An unsatisfactory equation between an exodus and return in time through reversible space and an exodus and return in space through irreversible time. (p. 728)

It is, doubtless, an intended irony that the *nostos* chapters are filled with such disclaimers. In "Eumaeus," we read that "a return" is usually "highly inadvisable, all things considered" (p. 649) and that "the coming back was the worst thing you ever did because it went without saying you would feel out of place as things always moved with the times" (p. 651). The narrative voices of *Ulysses'* final chapters state baldly what many ideologists of return have labored hard to obscure: that a literal return to any past life is impossible. On the other hand, it is doubtful that we are meant to resist the allegorical urge—the urge that would make of *Ulysses* the epic of a civilization's process of return. Joyce has set in our path too many temptations and, as Michael Seidel writes, it is not Joyce's "way to structure a narrative joke for nearly eight hundred pages without letting the joke itself assume a sustaining energy."[7] As the modern world's great theoretician of *felix culpa*, Joyce probably hoped we would give in to temptation and, facing such retributions as "irreversible time," re-educate our conceptions of historical return. *Ulysses* is not, like Pound's *Cantos*, an imaginative projection onto modernity of the nostos myth, but rather, like *Four Quartets*, a discriminating critique of that myth and its projections. In the *nostos* chap-

ters, Joyce tried to make his return in three different ways—
one too trite and easy, one too pat and perfect, one just right—
before he was satisfied.

In *Ulysses*, some *nostoi* are clearly better than others. The
book purges, by comic catharsis, the apocalyptics that often
accompany historical return theories. Elijah and his crumpled
throwaway in "Wandering Rocks" and "Lestrygonians," the
apotheosis of Ben-Bloom Elijah in "Cyclops," the humorous
invocation of Joachim of Fiore (in "Proteus" and "Wandering
Rocks"), and the Armageddon of "Circe" ridicule into obliv-
ion our sense of an ending. The various nationalisms, mas-
querading as *nostoi*, also represent a silly version of history:

> A most interesting discussion took place in the ancient
> hall of *Brian O'Ciarnain's* in *Sraid na Bretaine Bheag*,
> under the auspices of *Sluagh na h-Eirann*, on the revival
> of ancient Gaelic sports and the importance of physical
> culture, as understood in ancient Greece and ancient Rome
> and ancient Ireland. . . . a most interesting and instructive
> discussion of the usual high standard of excellence ensued
> as to the desirability of the revivability of the ancient
> games and sports of our ancient panceltic forefathers.
> (pp. 316–17)

The Zionist movement comes off somewhat better than the
Irish Nationalist, though the two usually are considered in
tandem. The "restoration in Chanan David of Zion and the
possibility of Irish political autonomy" (p. 689) are equated
and, despite the indulgent recurrence of excerpts from Zionist
literature and strains from *Hatikvah*, Joyce seems to view the
demise of Israel much as he viewed the death of Paddy Dignam—as something quite permanent:

> They fade, sad phantoms: all is gone. Agendath is a waste
> land, a home of screech-owls and the sandblind upupa.
> Netaim, the golden, is no more. (p. 414)

However much sympathy Joyce may have had for the wandering Jew, however much he may have sought to identify
him with his hero Odysseus, *Ulysses* presents both the Hebraic

and the Hellenic as cultures that have passed into European civilization and that no longer have an independent existence of dynamic, international significance.[8]

"Classicism" is yet another phenomenon of "return" that *Ulysses* prods and questions. It is clear, from "Telemachus" onward, that *Ulysses* is, among countless other things, an exploration of what classicism might mean in the modern world. But we begin in a world where the relation of classical and modern is made too easily. Most of the relevant statements in "Telemachus" are placed in the mouth of Buck Mulligan, denier and usurper. He calls Martello Tower the *omphalos*, spouts neo-Homeric epithets ("The snotgreen sea. The scrotumtightening sea. *Epi oinopa ponton. . . . Thalatta! Thalatta!*"), suggests a jaunt to Athens, and, in general, is proposing what "fearful jesuit" Stephen Dedalus analyzes as a "new paganism" (p.7). Mulligan even plays at being a Nietzschean: he cries, "I'm the *Uebermensch*" (p. 22) and, after torturing a Biblical verse, proclaims, "Thus spake Zarathustra" (p. 23). In the midst of this Hellenizing there appears, with an air of irrelevance, "A deaf gardener, aproned, masked with Matthew Arnold's face" (p. 7); and in "Circe," Philip Drunk, likewise disguised as Arnold, spouts a line of Greek (pp. 518–19). Mr. Deasy, in "Nestor," is an insatiable misreader of Greek poetry—his classical learning provides him with tags for his reactionary opinions:

> That doctrine of *laissez faire* which so often in our history. Our cattle trade. The way of all our old industries. Liverpool ring which jockeyed the Galway harbour scheme. European conflagration. Grain supplies through the narrow waters of the channel. The pluterperfect imperturbability of the department of agriculture. Pardoned a classical allusion. Cassandra. (p. 33)

> A woman brought sin into the world. For a woman who was no better than she should be, Helen, the runaway wife of Menelaus, ten years the Greeks made war on Troy. A faithless wife first brought the strangers to our shore here. . . . (pp. 34–35)

The Hellenism of Victorians and schoolmasters, of Decadents and Nietzschean *poseurs* are, for Joyce, trivial varieties of classicism.[9]

Joyce gives the older forms of Hellenism a more serious hearing but, in the end, seems to reject them, too. Stephen's approach to the classics is markedly neoclassical, even (in the medieval sense) scholastic. Trained by Jesuits to become a Jesuit, Stephen views all matters of culture and intellect through Aristotle's spectacles, much as Chistendom had done for centuries. In "Proteus," for example, Stephen's attempt to reconcile Berkeley with the Greeks' *maestro di color che sanno*, the solipsist with the political animal, is as scholastic—as Thomist—as can be. The philosophical Hellenism, the categorical logic, of "Proteus" is especially apposite because, on both the Gilbert and Linati schemas, Joyce paralleled this "monologue: male" with Penelope/Molly's "monologue: female." The contrast between the two episodes is devastating and instructive. Molly reduces the pretensions of Stephen's scholasticism: the first grammatical unit of her soliloquy is almost as elementary a thought presentation as is possible in English: the basic affirmative word ("Yes") followed by the most common conjunction of explanation ("because"), then one of the two most elementary personal pronouns ("he"), the firmest word of negation ("never"), one of the simplest verbs in the simple past tense ("did"), the most basic direct object preceded by the least specific article ("a thing"), and the simplest possible referent ("that"). In contrast to the sky-scraping, Hellenic abstractions of "Proteus" ("Ineluctable modality of the visible"), the "Penelope" episode represents a *reductio ad elementum*. The single time Molly reflects on a question of philosophy, she recalls sitting in a "swamp" of menstrual blood at the opera while some "gentleman of fashion" discoursed about Spinoza (p. 769).

Yet despite her lack of what Stephen might think of as classical discipline, the spontaneous poetry of Molly's soliloquy is of a beauty beyond anything he could hope to compose:

easy God I remember one time I could scout it out straight
whistling like a man almost easy O Lord how noisy I
hope theyre bubbles on it for a wad of money from some
fellow Ill have to perfume it in the morning dont forget
I bet he never saw a better pair of thighs than that look
how white they are the smoothest place is right there
between this bit here how soft like a peach easy God I
wouldnt mind being a man and get up on a lovely woman
O Lord what a row youre making like the jersey lily easy
O how the waters come down at Lahore . . . (p. 770)

Stephen, at twenty-two, is unready for the eloquence—elemental, formulaic, and pulsating—that Molly represents: under her roof in "Ithaca," this post-bardic classicist passes up
an invitation to take singing lessons from the muse herself.
But there is plenty of time—Stephen has not promised to
deliver a classic for another ten years.

Ulysses opens on a world that has been mis-ordered in
pursuit of phantoms. The modern world has its heart in the
right place: its mis-order has developed in the name of Hebraism and Hellenism, but it is the *forms* of Christianity and
classicism that modern Europe has adopted, while violence
has been done to their *content* and *elemental sources*. The
response to this official mis-order, historically (as also in *Ulysses*), was an unofficial chaos. As Wallace Stevens puts the
matter:

> A. A violent order is disorder; and
> B. A great disorder is an order. These
> two things are one. (Pages of illustrations.)[10]

The forces of chaos—Berkeley, Hume, Freud, Einstein—had
no objection to being thought heresiarchs against the old order. But Joyce would show these rebels to be soldiers on behalf
of an order that looked entirely novel in form but was entirely
familiar in content. The future will not be Christian and classical; it will not even be Hebraic and Hellenic. It will, however,
be continuous with the whole past of man down to its most
elemental roots, and it will be, above all, affirmable. The

history of civilization plots the "greatest possible ellipse" and, in "Circe," Stephen calls its end-point "The ultimate return" (p. 505).

But the years of wandering—the years between Homer and Joyce—are not viewed as a "waste sad time" and negated, for these comprise the largest part of the human entelechy, of the self that man was "ineluctably preconditioned to become" (p. 504). The process, the history, discloses an elliptical pattern, but the pattern emerges from the process and is meaningful only in relation to it. Joyce in *Ulysses*, like Rousseau in *Julie*, would have us begin at the beginning and enjoy the exquisite nurture of confusion.

· · ·

STEPHEN DEDALUS begins his soliloquy in "Proteus" where he might argue the conscious Western mind began—with Aristotle's affirmation of objective, perceivable reality—and then he adds, "At least." He commences in the first paragraph by considering a world of comfortable certainties, where identity is stable and describable, where common-sense distinctions can be made between opposite states, where scholastic logic is an effective means of ascertaining truth, and where it is possible to use a word as though its precise meaning could be found in a dictionary. No sooner has he established this cozy Aristotelian reality than he determines to test its validity in the age of epistemology and solipsism, the age which considers objectivity a fiction and continuity a *trompe l'oeil*.[11] The first paragraphs of the episode, then, are an inside-out version of Hamlet's "to be or not" soliloquy: Hamlet wonders whether to assert himself against the enormous, ineluctable reality outside, while Stephen lives in an intellectual world that assumes the self to be the larger reality and he wonders whether to affirm any reality outside his own closed circle. Stephen's question is not, "To be or not to be," but "Is it or isn't it?" In order to answer his question, Stephen conducts an experiment—a test which, as Robert M. Adams has noted, bears some resemblance to Dr. Johnson's (Kick it; if it makes a thud, it's real). But Stephen's conclusion, "There all the time without you," affirms only a modified Aristotelianism, for the shut-eye observations he makes lead us back to his initial response: "At least that if no more."

When his eyes close, when he enters the dimension of the audible—that is, of time—space and time become less and less distinct to Stephen. He speaks of the shape of the audible, he cuts space into times and time into spaces, he listens to the audible sounds made by tapping on objects in space. He finds it possible to think the words, "Sounds solid"—a quasi-sentence in which the verb can refer only to the *nacheinander* and in which the adjective belongs to the realm of the *nebeneinander*. The same, in reverse, is true of "see now." Stephen is not thinking these words accidentally; he is well aware that time and space are so closely knit that they pun, even in nature. "Rhythm begins, you see," he muses, and then adds, "I hear." He wonders, "Am I walking into eternity . . . ?"—into the state of timelessness and spacelessness—but then he hears the sound of the "wild sea money" under his boots, an audio-visual phenomenon which suggests that the opposite is true, that he is strolling in a world where time and space are ine-luctable, but inextricably intertwined. For a while, Stephen's perceptions in the realm of time are purely abstract and au-ditory—he hears a "catalectic tetrameter of iambs"—but these soon begin to gallop and his mind's eye conjures up an image from the visible dimension, Madeline the mare. "*Deline the mare*," he sings, and that is precisely what he has done: de-lined the visible into the abstractly audible and then re-lined it into a horse. The visible signatures that the artist must read and the auditory rhythms that he must perceive are made almost indistinguishable, time and space are made very nearly interchangeable, and we are made witnesses to a most ex-traordinary scene: the nose-to-nose confrontation of an old, glabrate Aristotle and a young, setaceous Albert Einstein.

Here, on the first page of the "Proteus" episode, is a pattern for the chapter—in fact, for the book. First, Joyce posits a central tenet held by the Western conscious mind—in this case, the ineluctability of the sensible. Then he puts it to test, casting real doubt upon its validity; next modifies it to take account of modern philosophy, modern psychology, and modern science; and, finally, reaffirms it in a way that is simultaneously ironic and sincere.[12] This pattern is followed in at least three settings. On page one of this episode, Stephen posits, challenges, and then reasserts the objective reality of what men perceive through their senses, but with the caveat that Aristotelian time and space give way to the Einsteinian concept, and with the recognition that this question is, in any case, largely one of nomenclature. In the chapter as a whole, we begin with Stephen's qualified affirmation; which then is challenged by the protean realities of change, metamorphosis, and process; and which finally is reasserted at the chapter's close in the traveling, but solid, reality of the visible ship and in the concrete, but kinetic, sentences that create it. At the level of the book's structure, the sense of order established in the first half is shaken to its roots between "Wandering Rocks" and "Circe" and, at last, is reintroduced with the orgasmic "Yes" that concludes the book. Each time the pattern is repeated, the challenges to the traditional, Western idea of order become greater; the compromises necessitated become more basic; and the reaffirmation is all the more improbable and, therefore, all the more stunning.

It is in this sense that it is possible to view *Ulysses* as a theodicy, as an artistic affirmation of cosmology. Homer's *Odyssey* is no less and, if *Ulysses* is an odyssey of some sort, it might not be inaccurate to describe it as an odyssey of modern Western history: a species of epic proposed as early as the mid-eighteenth century by the founders of the "German historical school."[13] Homer was, for Joyce, not merely a scaffold but a device for interpreting modern cultural history as a Viconian process of *ricorso*. The crucial relation of *Odyssey* and *Ulysses*, of epic and novel, is a relation of pattern to history or, as Seidel formulates it, of "remembered and potential conditions."[14] The *Aeneid* imposes a Homeric structure on historical events of the years between the Homeric epics and itself—Vergil's poem is a theodicy, based on the Homeric patterning and affirmation, of Augustan Rome. In a precisely parallel way, *Ulysses* is the theodicy of an emerging post-

Christian cosmology, of an order that the book first sorely tests, reinterprets, and reconstructs in order to ensure that it is the artist's own Ithaca.

The challenge to order in this third chapter is the one that Proteus perpetually represents to the stability of common-sense categories. The most important of these to Stephen Dedalus the writer is language. Joyce told his readers through Stuart Gilbert that the art of this chapter is philology, and the episode opens with five resoundingly self-assured words. In the chapter's preludium, Stephen employs words and technical terms from several languages with the confidence that comes from knowing that their proper use has been precisely defined and petrified in dictionaries for centuries. Furthermore, the words correspond directly to static phenomena: Stephen is able to experiment with the nature of the *nacheinander* using numbered steps and he concludes his text with the word, "Exactly." However, by the end of the second paragraph, we can already sense the tension building. The words, true sons and daughters of Proteus, are already trying to shake loose. The protean resonances of the words Stephen uses render his scholastic logic all but ridiculous, and the gist of his soliloquy is lodged in the surface of its prose rather than in its logic. The clearest case of this is Stephen's thought, "Rhythm begins, you see. I hear." More important than its place in the logical progression of ideas are the connections this phrase establishes—through the resonance of the multiple meanings of the words "see" and "hear"—among hearing, sight, and cognition.

It should be noted immediately, however, that Stephen is aware of these resonances and that he frequently uses them deliberately to undermine his own (mock) scholastic logic. Nevertheless, the flow of Stephen's thought often follows the tug of his words rather than the direction indicated by strict logic. From the observation of the Pigeonhouse (p. 49), he proceeds to think of Mary and Joseph discussing her relations with the dove of the Holy Spirit, and then he moves on to reminisce about Kevin Egan, "son of the wild goose"—yet another bird. We have been exposed to this "stream of consciousness" logic from the first in *Ulysses*, but here we meet it in direct juxtaposition with medieval, Aristotelian logic. We can comprehend best what Joyce is saying with this juxtaposition by examining a turn-of-the-century linguistic study by Ernest Fenollosa—edited by Joyce's patron, Ezra Pound. Fenollosa writes of "the discredited, or rather the useless, logic of the Middle Ages," and he goes on to describe both it and what he believes should replace it in the age which discovered that mass is energy:

> According to this logic, thought deals with abstractions, concepts drawn out of things by a sifting process. . . . It was as if Botany should reason from the leaf-patterns woven into our table-cloths. Valid scientific thought consists in following as closely as may be the actual and entangled lines of forces as they pulse through things. Thought deals with no bloodless concepts but watches *things move* under its microscope.[15]

Fenollosa longs for, and Joyce provides, a concrete and kinetic language that reflects the Einsteinian view of object-as-process, to replace the abstract language that lost its usefulness when subject, object, and verb all came to be seen as parts of a space-time continuum. It is a language leading toward that of *Finnegans Wake*:

> No, they will pass on, passing chafing against the low rocks, swirling, passing. . . . Listen: a fourworded wave-speech: seesoo, hrss, rsseiss, ooos. Vehement breath of waters amid seasnakes, rearing horses, rocks. In cups of rocks it slops: flop, slop, slap: bounded in barrels. And, spent, its speech ceases. It flows purling widely flowing, floating foampool, flower unfurling. (p. 49)

The number and force of the gerunds indicate the author's desire to evoke things in process. According to medieval, Aristotelian logic—in which, Fenollosa writes, "It is impossible to represent change . . . or any kind of growth"—this scene in *Ulysses* would have to be presented in terms of something-under-the-classification-"Man" coinciding with something-under-the-classification—"Things Urinating." But in the sentences cited we see and hear the process *qua* process with the doer hardly distinguishable from the done and the doing. The point is made most clearly by comparing the opening and closing lines of the chapter, each of which serves to affirm the reality of the sensible world—at the opening, verbless and in abstract, scholastic fashion: "Ineluctable modality of the visible"; while, at the end, concretely and with time and space united in the process of movement: "Moving through the air high spars of a threemaster, her sails brailed up on the crosstrees, homing, upstream, silently moving, a silent ship" (p. 51).

What occurs between the "ineluctable modality" and this concluding paragraph has determined the nature of the "silent ship" and of the language that presents it. Its message is larger than that the sensible world exists ineluctably; it also affirms the possibility of identity in a world of continual energy-transference and constant flux. But before the solutions come the questions. How is it possible to claim individual identity when all things are in process? "We thought you were someone else," nuncle Richie's servant tells Stephen and scarely a page later Stephen is metamorphosed into the bald priest of Joachim's prophecy. Though Stephen desires his own identity ("I want his life still to be his, mine to be mine," he reflects on the drowned man), he finds it possible to think, in other circumstances, "*Lui, c'est moi.*" And it is not Stephen's identity alone that is challenged. Few things in this chapter remain for very long what they first seem to be. The living dog that examines the dead dog is compared in the space of one page (p. 46) with a horse, a hare, a bear, a faun, a wolf, a calf, a vulture, and the panther from Haines's dream. Alongside these and other metamorphoses, the wind blows and Proteus' tides wash the beach, each time accompanied by a change in the direction of Stephen's thought.

The protean process is sometimes creative, sometimes destructive, but in no case does it ever lead anywhere. We are not permitted even the small comfort of a *telos*. Joyce writes

that the falling leaves are "to no end gathered" and in two
sentences devastates Hegel:[16]

> He stopped, sniffed, stalked round it, brother, nosing
> closer, went round it, sniffing rapidly like a dog all over
> the dead dog's bedraggled fell. Dogskull, dogsniff, eyes
> on the ground, moves to one great goal. (p. 46)

The process is goal-less because endless, and it has no end
because it feeds upon itself, endlessly. "God becomes man
becomes fish becomes barnacle goose becomes featherbed
mountain" (p. 50), Stephen muses over the drowned man,
much as the live dog had nearly debated Hegelian teleology
over his dead brother's carcass—and we realize not only that
the process has no "one great goal" but, more disconcertingly,
that everything is consubstantial with everything else. We are
nothing but the re-formed, energized matter of what came
before us. In such a situation, distinctions fail. Life and death
unite to form an "all-Wombing tomb." "Mother Sea" becomes "Father Ocean." The time/space and verb/noun distinctions collapse in a crash of "shattered glass and toppling
masonry."

The point of ultimate disorientation is reached when the
Good Principle becomes topsoil, when the Evil Principle comes
crashing through the vacant interstellar spaces, and when Stephen admits that he, too, will die—is already, like his teeth,
in the process of decay. It is then—at the moment of gravest
epistemological doubt—that Stephen picks his nose, and his
ship comes in. Arriving where it does in this chapter, Stephen's
gesture makes much the same statement as that which one of
the ladies in Rousseau's *Confessions* makes when she remarks
on her sickbed, "A woman who can fart is not dead." We are
already back in the world of common-sense reality when Stephen spies the Rosevean sailing majestically into port. It is a
specific, concrete, named object, no longer the five-word "medieval abstruosity" that opens the chapter, and it is viewed
simultaneously in space and time. The ship is a large, solid
representative of the visible, yet it is in the process of moving
from one place to another. As John Eglinton says of Shake-

speare—on behalf of Joyce, about himself: "He . . . makes Ulysses quote Aristotle" (pp. 211–12).

• • •

CHALLENGES to common-sense reality exist in other episodes of the first half of *Ulysses*—the headlines in "Eolus" are a good example—but these are tame when compared with what is still to come. The two triads that follow "Scylla and Charybdis" sorely disrupt whatever comfortable assumptions are made in the first half of the book. The "Circe" episode, in particular, culminates and intensifies the challenges to the traditional sense of reality built up in the preceding chapters, yet it is also the locus of the Western mind's reintegration. "Circe" enunciates the terms in which Joyce's improbable theodicy will seek to make its impossible affirmation. Those disruptions are so hugely complex, their resolution accomplished at so high an altitude, that Joyce eventually felt the need to explain them in the language of catechism. As rationalism and Hellenism followed on fifth-century creativity, and neoclassicism on the Renaissance, so, after "Circe," we must back up and pin down. It will take some category-happy scholasticism to demonstrate how orderly chaos can be.

To begin with, "Circe" disrupts seven categories of common-sense reality: time, the identity of individuals and things, the laws governing the physical universe, language and human communication, literary convention, the privacy of personal thought and experience, and the bourgeois surface of everyday life. Of these, the first to implode is the category of time. Even more disconcerting than the question of *where* we are in this episode is the question of *when*. The chapter reviews—systematically, chaotically—what has come before it, in token of which the Daughters of Erin summarize for us the novel's chapters:

Kidney of Bloom, pray for us.
Flower of the Bath, pray for us.
Mentor of Menton, pray for us.
Canvasser of the Freeman, pray for us.

Charitable Mason, pray for us.
Wandering Soap, pray for us.
Sweets of Sin, pray for us.
Music without Words, pray for us.
Reprover of the Citizen, pray for us.
Friend of all Frillies, pray for us.
Midwife Most Merciful, pray for us.
Potato Preservative against Plague and Pestilence, pray for us.

(pp. 498–99)

It is often difficult to decide what chapter we are in and, consequently, what hour of the day.[17] Perhaps the most "flash-backed" episode is "Proteus" (especially around pp. 560–98). From Stephen's experience of the hour from 11:00 A.M. to noon, we find: references to Aristotle and Berkeley (p. 560), to the Boehme "signatures" (p. 562), to the Hegelian *telos* (p. 563), to tooth decay and dentistry (p. 563), to Parisian perversion (pp. 570–71), to the "fubsy widow" (p. 571), to "shattered glass and toppling masonry" (p. 583), to the gypsy poem (p. 598), and to the ubiquitous dog. "Circe" even doubles back on itself: Zoe's query "Who'll dance?" (p. 575) flashes back to the "Wha'll dance . . . ?" of the chapter's Scottish End of the World (p. 507). Also included under the subheading of flashbacks are several repetitions from an earlier Joyce novel.[18] There are also *flash-forwards* in "Circe"—a kind of foreshadowing let loose. Mr. Bloom, for example, offers chocolate to Zoe (p. 525) and this event is followed closely by a similar offer to Bloom by Zoe and, eventually, by an offer of cocoa by Bloom to Stephen.[19] There is at least one event, furthermore, that qualifies as both flash-forward and flashback: the sacrilegious introit (p. 431) foreshadows the "black mass" of the chapter's end and after-shadows Mulligan's introit at the epic's invocation.

Joyce harries our temporal sense, in addition, with seven categories of "time collapse." There is the collapse of "generational time," as when Bloom's ancestors are present simultaneously (pp. 437ff.) and also the collapse of "historical time," as when Wellington, Nelson, and Gladstone appear together (pp. 433–34). The time represented by grammatical tenses cannot survive such lines as "What now is will then tomorrow as now was be past yester," just as "Christian time" cannot coexist with "Jewish time" (p. 515). "Sequential time" topples when Stephen suddenly ages (p. 582) and Bloom feels pain before its infliction (p. 434). Time loses its absolute, Aristotelian impersonality when "The Hours" are taught to dance (pp. 576–77). Finally, the existence of time itself, in any form, is threatened by apocalypse. The mark of the beast (p. 459), the arrival of Antichrist (pp. 492, 505–6), and the complete destruction of time and space (p. 583)—all testify to time's impermanence, to its imminent demise.[20]

Even more disconcerting than time's nervous breakdown are the disruptions of identity and selfhood, for the ultimate axiom of Western logic is that "*a* = *a*." First, there are the famous metamorphoses. The omnipresent dog undergoes some thirty-two transformations in "Circe."[21] Mr. Bloom is metamorphosed, most impressively, into a policeman (p. 435), an Austro-Egyptian (pp. 455, 463), an upper-class maid-pincher (pp. 460ff.), the child Moses (p. 463), a Mongolian mongoloid (p. 463), an infant (p. 500ff.), Jesus Christ (p. 507), a pig (pp. 534ff.), a rooster who lays eggs (p. 563), and William Shakespeare (p. 567).[22] Then there are the melding and division of individual identities. Mr. Bloom unites with Mrs. Bloom and calls her "I"; he also becomes a Mr. Higgins and thus, we assume, a relative of Zoe Higgins (p. 485). Kitty and Kate become Kitty-Kate (p. 508), Zoe and Fanny become Zoe-Fanny (p. 509), Florry and Teresa become Florry-Teresa (p. 509), Bloom and Bella become Bloombella (p. 578).[23] The cases of identity division are no less startling. Bloom has a "quadruple existence" (p. 460), shows up as several different participants in the hunt for Stephen (pp. 586–87), and appears simultaneously with his *alter ego/nom de plume*, Henry Flower (p. 517). In similar fashion, Stephen splits into the Siamese twins, Philip Drunk and Philip Sober (pp. 518–21).

Small wonder that amnesia, early in this chapter, is of epidemic proportions (pp. 456–75). Bloom, for instance, cannot recall who he is or where he is from, and he carries an incorrect

I.D. It is hard to keep track of one's name and address when one cannot even keep control of one's sex. Bloom begins to act like a woman near the beginning of the episode (p. 449) and even gives birth (p. 494). "Extremes meet" (p. 504) is a general principle in "Circe," where opposites, coalescing, cease to oppose. This principle, and all others that govern the chapter, are in some sense ideal or devoutly-to-be-wished, but together they wreak havoc on the order of the physical universe. The impossible becomes the likely. Male mammals gestate and give birth to infant mammals; objects in space of a given mass pass through other objects in space of the same mass; a human being covers his left eye with his left ear while both are attached to his head, and he hangs from the top ledge of Nelson's Pillar by his eyelids; the sun is eclipsed, and with a minimum of human effort. The assertion that "circumstances alter cases" (p. 550) contradicts the common-sense law that cases control circumstances, though the shock to our system of this violation is not unbearable. Devout Aristotelians, like Thomas Aquinas, have long found a place for miracles in a well-run universe. Less bearable: the law that inanimate objects and concepts have no personal will is violated on more than a dozen occasions.[24] In all these instances, the order unbalanced is Aristotle's and the universe disrupted is Newton's.

The disruptions of Aristotelian-Newtonian physical reality in "Circe" are related causally to the upheaval of language and human communication. The coalescence of opposites brings about such linguistic concoctions as "pornosophical philotheology" (p. 432) and "mudflake" (p. 435). The principle that "circumstances alter cases" leads to phrases like "lugubru Booloohoom" (p. 434), which express not only lasting identity but also transitory mood. The collapse of simple time relations results in such lines as "Past was is today" (p. 515). Names like "Bloombella" are caused by the phenomenon of personality melding. Words like "piggledy" and "Viragitis" are produced by the suspension of common order and the establishment of an uncommon order based upon the development of special thematic elements (e.g., in these cases, "pig" and

"Virag"). Because of the independent, personal will in all things, Stephen comes to say "Circe" when he means to say "Ceres" (p. 504) and Zoe says "gimlet" when she should say "ghost" (p. 561), while Bloom and Stephen discuss "this" and "that" as though they were nouns rather than noun-referents (p. 558).

These linguistic disruptions are themselves the cause of an occasional collapse in communication, as when Bloom and his paternal grandfather converse (pp. 512–16) or as in the chapter's breakdown of literary formal conventions. The characters' minds sometimes spill over into objective, authorial preserves—as, for instance, when standard stage directions begin suddenly to appear in Bloomthink (p. 462) or when, also in a stage direction, Bloom's and Stephen's memories become confounded (p. 579). These disruptions of literary convention are related to the more general phenomenon in "Circe" of experience-sharing. Marion exclaims "Nebrakada! Feminimum" (p. 440) as if she had (mis-) heard Stephen's *nebrakada femininum* of an earlier chapter (p. 242). Zoe knows Bloom is looking for Stephen (p. 475), Bello knows Bloom's deepest secrets (p. 536), and Stephen and Bloom cooperate in the vision of Mananaan MacLir (p. 510).

All of which shakes our conceptions of reality to their roots, but Joyce is unsatisfied merely with deep transformations and insists, in addition, upon razing the surface. The bourgeois superficies of reality are more than disrupted—they are savaged: savaged by the satire of middle-class progressivism explicit in the new Bloomusalem (i.e., the Victorian Crystal Palace),[25] savaged by stripping off life's *politesse* leaving only the *grosserie* ("The Honourable Mrs. Mervyn Talboys . . . In amazon costume"),[26] savaged by the satire of middle-class parental desires (e.g., the birth of eight handsome male corporate executives),[27] savaged by making the clichés of rational liberalism ridiculous ("university of life," "simply satisfying a need"),[28] savaged by matter-of-fact discussions of the undiscussable,[29] savaged by random appearances of wandering pigs (pp. 452, 463, 469, 477, 499, 502, 508–9, 515, 516, 517, 531, 533, 551, 554).

But none of the seven categories of reality-disjunction cat-
alogued here is a disruption for the sake of disruption. Each
can be attributed to some tenet of modern science, either
physical or psychological. If we take Nighttown as the Freudian unconscious, which, waking or sleeping, operates according to the "logic" of dreams, much that is inexplicable according to Aristotelian-Newtonian and bourgeois surface
standards becomes practically straightforward in psychoanalytic terms. For example, the principles of unconscious "wish-
fulfillment," "anxiety-fulfillment," and "punishment-fulfill-
ment" obviously control the whole of Leopold Bloom's bizarre
career in "Circe." He regains potency (p. 482), becomes a
ladies' man (pp. 444ff.), and resumes paternity (pp. 486, 609);
he even takes his revenge on Mrs. Bloom. In the course of his
ultimate apotheosis (pp. 478–90), Bloom unites all humanity
under his bourgeois, liberal, nonreligious Judaism; ascends
the thrones of David, St. Edward, and Muscovy; and succeeds
Parnell as leader of the Irish Nationalists.[30] Anxiety-fulfill-
ments include his bisexuality and maternity (pp. 493–94), his
sexual torture by a masculine and superior-positioned female
(pp. 534–35), and his location at the keyhole during Molly's
adultery with Boylan (pp. 564–67). Examples of punishment-
fulfillment are everywhere, though often thinly disguised. The
unconscious always represents suppressed elements in symbolic form and frequently symbolizes self-accusation and guilt
feelings as trials, hunts, persecutions, or denouncements. Hence:
the Caffrey twins' hunt (p. 437), the fox hunt and the hunt
for Stephen (pp. 583ff.), and the several trials of Bloom for
breach of promise (pp. 456ff.), plagiarism (pp. 458ff.), sexual
perversion (pp. 465–85), and obscenity (pp. 538ff.).[31]

Other mysterious phenomena are explicable if Joyce, in
composing "Circe," was guided by the principles of the Freudian dream-work. In lecture 11 of the *Introductory Lectures
on Psychoanalysis* (delivered in 1916, some four years before
Joyce finished "Circe"), Freud conjectured that the dream-
work has a grammatical structure with subordinate clauses,
principal clauses, and interpolations. Subordinate clauses, Freud
said, often serve as preludes to more detailed main clauses or

provide the motives for them.[32] In this way, Bloom's incorrect Biblical quotation, "The voice is the voice of Esau," leads to the distorted liturgical quotation, "Jacobs Vobiscuits" (p. 473). The whispering of the Yews leads, according to dream logic, to the Irish Nationalist interjection about the "trees of Ireland" (p. 547). Moreover, as Florry says, "Dreams go by contraries" (p. 571). The reversals of order during the "black mass" scene (pp. 595ff.) may be attributable to Freud's lecture 11: "We find in dreams reversal of situation, of the relation between two people—a 'topsy-turvy' world. . . . Or again we find a reversal in the order of events, so that what precedes an event causally comes after it in the dream. . . . The order of sounds in a word can be reversed, while keeping the same meaning."[33]

Many of the disjunctions of time and identity in this chapter may have derived from Joyce's interest in psychoanalysis.[34] Freud's refusal, for example, to deny, finally and categorically, the prophetic nature of the dream state may have encouraged Joyce in his temporal machinations. The metamorphoses, already examined, may be accounted for with Freud's lecture 11 on "The Dream-Work":

> You will have no difficulty in recalling instances from your own dreams of different people being condensed into a single one. A composite figure of this kind may look like A perhaps, but may be dressed like B, may do something that we remember C doing, and at the same time we may know that he is D. . . . The dream-work, . . . tries to condense two different thoughts by seeking out (like a joke) an ambiguous word in which the two thoughts come together.[35]

In the same way, we can gloss the division of personalities in "Circe" with a line from Freud's lecture 14 on "Wish-Fulfillment": "a dreamer in his relation to his dream-wishes can only be compared to an amalgamation of two separate people who are linked by some strong element in common."[36] Freud likewise elucidates the chapter's coalescence of opposites:

Contraries are treated in the same way as conformities, and there is a special preference for expressing them by the same manifest element. Thus an element in the manifest dream which is capable of having a contrary may equally well be expressing either itself or its contrary or both together.[37]

More useful: many of the episode's individual characters and props have, for Freud, specific dream-symbol meanings. A bloom represents the female genitals, especially in the virgin state. A hat is a phallic symbol; so are a key, a hanging lamp, a weapon, or an ashplant. A small child can represent human genitals of either sex. Dancing symbolizes sexual intercourse. Piano-playing signifies masturbation (and tooth removal, the punishment for it). A pig is an emblem of fertility—and wild animals, in general, suggest "people in an excited sensual state, and further, evil instincts or passions." A king connotes fatherhood. A rescue symbolizes the delivery of an infant. A house represents a whole human figure. Implied in this list is a hazy summary of what Freud can do to help us make sense of "Circe." Bloom's virginal bisexuality, his feelings of paternity toward Stephen, and his potential recovery of masculinity through that paternity, are implied. Stephen's movement from autoeroticism and self-containment toward intercourse, both sexual and social, is implied. A general motion from sterility and evil passion toward fertility and love is implied. That the mind whose unconscious produces the activity of Nighttown may be that of a "person" who is not a character in the book is, perhaps, implied. The Freudian dream-interpretation of a house like Bella's (that it is a whole human body), the phenomenon of experience-sharing in this episode, and the existence of Joyce's chapter/organ charts, all would tend to support this last conclusion. On the Linati organ chart, the composite human being created in the background of *Ulysses*—Ulysses himself?—has had a brain since "Scylla and Charybdis." In "Circe," we may conjecture, this Ulysses is developing an unconscious mind.

Joyce's interest in Einstein accounts for some of this chapter's upheavals, but they are less complex than those that Freud inspired, and Einstein's influence has already been treated in relation to the "Proteus" episode. In "Circe," as in the earlier chapter, Einstein's transformation of the common time/space conception leads to disjunctions in identity, for the self cannot be portrayed as continuous when all things are in continual process. The breakdown of Aristotelian–Newtonian certainty, and the collapse of common-sense times and tenses, tend to follow the fomulation of "four-dimensional space" presented in Minkowski's lecture, "Space and Time" (1908), well-known in Joyce's day: "Henceforth space by itself and time by itself, are doomed to fade away into mere shadows, and only a kind of union of the two will preserve an independent reality."

To chart the impact of the physical and behavioral sciences on modernist literature is a familiar exercise, but "Circe" tests more than our ingenuity. Freud and Einstein have much in common, and Joyce extrapolates from the implications of the correspondence. Both scientists are twentieth-century, Jewish disruptors of the longstanding Western sense of order, and, in "Circe," it is the Jews—Bloom, Bella Cohen, Zoe (who speaks Hebrew), Elijah, Christ, Antichrist, the Wandering Jew—who disrupt the unconscious peace in the mind whose "thoughts" comprise Nighttown. On one level, it is possible and consistent to consider the mind of this episode—the mind of Ulysses—as a pre-Jungian "collective unconscious" for Western culture, and the events of the episode, as the nightmare of history of which Stephen speaks and in which the chapter's Jews are the subversives and the bad conscience. An embryonic version of this outlook appears first in "Nestor"—also the episode in which Stephen enunciates the line, "History . . . is a nightmare from which I am trying to awake" (p. 34), and in which the theme of anti-Semitism begins to take shape. Dedalus connects the nightmare and the anti-Jewish feeling explicitly (his famous line about history, it is seldom noted, comes in response to Mr. Deasy's anti-Semitic remarks) and in "Nestor," he introduces an image of the Jews that recurs again and again in *Ulysses*: of men who flash "mocking mirrors" on the "obscure soul of the world" (p. 28).

These Semites represent "a darkness shining in brightness which brightness could not comprehend" (p. 28),[38] and Deasy proves Stephen's point when he says of the Jews, "They sinned against the light. . . . And you can see the darkness in their eyes" (p. 34). They are underworld creatures—creatures of depth—and Stephen uses similar images to describe the mind's underworld:

> Fed and feeding brains about me: under glowlamps, impaled, with faintly beating feelers: and in my mind's darkness a sloth of the underworld, reluctant, shy of brightness, shifting her dragon scaly folds. (pp. 25–26)

The Jews' depth and darkness share much with the unfathomed profundities of the mind. On the other hand, "thought," or the mind's daylight side, is the "Tranquil brightness . . . candescent" (p. 26) in which darkness, we are told, shines. Consciousness would seem to be Gentile; the unconscious, Semitic.

The conscious mind of Europe appears both to want and to despise what its unconscious, its Jews, have always offered it (the new Bloomusalem); the Semitic unconscious appears both to fear and to enjoy the persecution it has always received. The relationship is perceived as sadomasochistic. The mind of "Circe" allows Mr. Bloom periodic apotheoses but brings him to an anti-Semitic trial (p. 459), accusing him (a Christ figure) of being Judas and Antichrist, and convicting him according to the laws of the *stone* Moses (pp. 470–71): "When in doubt persecute Bloom." It makes the Jew a comic stock-figure (Wandering Jew name of Reuben, magician, pilgrim, carries a wallet, first-born and only son, has notable nose) who has returned to end the world and to persecute the persecutors (p. 506). The Jew is jester and hobgoblin, ideal-offerer and heaven-intimator, savior, bad conscience, scapegoat, avenger, and—primarily—radical disruptor of the *pax conscientiae* and of physical, philosophical, psychological, and bourgeois reality.

This Jewish theme dominates the Nighttown episode and melds completely with the theme of Circe's island. The unconscious mind, both individual and collective, is the repository of both the kosher and the non-kosher, of both the superego and the id; it is the island of bestiality and the divine temple, where Mr. Bloom is destroyed and reborn. To make this "temple" analogy requires no poetic license. Cohen in Hebrew denotes descent from Aaron and refers to priests of the ancient Jewish Temple on Jerusalem's Mt. Moriah. As Mrs. Cohen says of her whorehouse, "This isn't a brothel" (p. 584). In "Ithaca," the chapters of *Ulysses* are reviewed in terms of activities associated with the Jerusalem Temple (pp. 728–29). Upon entering the house of Cohen, Stephen chants the paschal introit associated with Temple sacrifice (p. 431). Bloom's father Rudolph, "an elder in Zion," wears spectacles horned like the altar and a cap that smokes like an offering (p. 437). Mr. Bloom is referred to as a scapegoat (p. 457) at paschal time and, upon arrival at Cohen's house (p. 475), thinks he hears church music. On the porch, Oriental music is playing and the principal images of the Song of Songs are presented in a stage direction (p. 477)—following which, Zoe identifies herself in Solomon's Hebrew as a black but comely Israelite inside the gates of Solomon's Jerusalem. The gramophone accompanying the second coming of Elijah sings an amalgam of the Hebrew word for Jerusalem (*Yerushalayim*) and the English word "whore" (p. 508). The whores themselves are referred to as angels (p. 570). There is much talk of priesthood and Zoe says she has given penance even to priests (p. 520).

Bella Cohen, in particular, is cast distinctly in the role of High Priest(ess): Bloom calls her "nurse" (p. 533); she knows his sins before being told (p. 536); she presides over his cathartic ordeal as torturer, as restorative nymph, as chief of the "angels"—even of the one named Life (Zoe: Ζοη) in Greek— and she appears to have had dealings earlier in the day with death-symbol Corny Kelleher (p. 606). As a priestess of the bestial side of life, Bella is a Circean figure; as an ordeal-directress, concerned with redemption through recognition of bestial sins and sacrificial atonement for them, Mrs. Cohen is an anti-porcine Jewish priest(ess). Bella's roles are not contradictory: the superego is a creature of the id and, in the psyche, they are reconciled in a way that is familiar to us from the underworld descent/rite of initiatory passage/incorporation/catharsis myths. Nighttown is the underworld: Bloom walks with the (guardian?) dog "toward hellsgates" (p. 449) and Hades is invoked (p. 464). But it is the multilevel underworld of Freud's irrational unconscious mind, inside which Bella Cohen is ruler, both in her Circean aspect, as goddess of the desires repressed by civilized man, and in her aspect as Jewish priest(ess), presiding over the soul's painful rehabilitation and reincorporation into human society.

Bloom's descent commences at the top of Freud's underworld, the ego, in which "circle" he experiences a shamanic initiation and apotheosis (pp. 478–90)—an expression of the ego's most characteristic sin: pride. Even when the id seeps through (in the accusations and new Bloomusalem dissension), the ego is in control; Bloom's enemies are killed and he emerges from the trials as a "hero god." His hesitation upon entering Cohen's house is a traditional part of these myths, but Zoe (Life) insists he enter the second "circle"—the id— and she takes away his moly-esque resistance (pp. 501–2). From this point until his recovery of self and potato fifty-one pages later, the ego has no control over events and Bloom takes instructions from the angel/demons. From the last ego assertion (p. 527) where Bloom replies, "Yes. No," to Bella's fan from different circles of the unconscious, the ego is absent entirely. Bello makes him consider his "many . . . Hundreds of sins" (p. 537), makes him live out his undesirable id desires. The process of descent destroys Bloom (p. 544) and he is pronounced (symbolically) dead by the "circumcised."

Next commences the process of rebirth, catharsis, ascent, initiation, and incorporation—all through the agency of the "transformative feminine": an ancient mythic principle outlined by Jung and diagrammed by his disciple, Erich Neumann, in *The Great Mother* (see chart). The entrance of Bella (p. 527) marks Bloom's descent into the "feminine negative

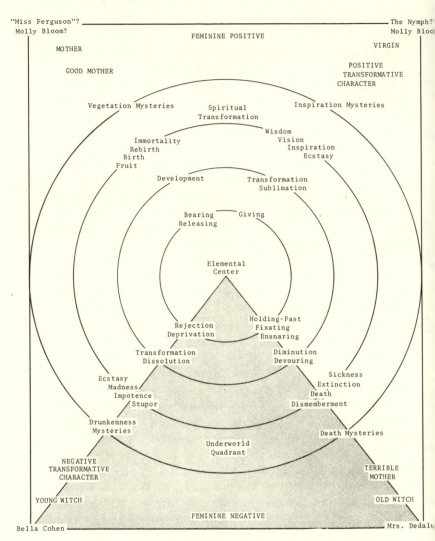

"Miss Ferguson"? ———————————————————————————— The Nymph?
Molly Bloom? Molly Bloo

FEMININE POSITIVE

MOTHER VIRGIN

GOOD MOTHER POSITIVE
TRANSFORMATIVE
CHARACTER

Vegetation Mysteries Spiritual Inspiration Mysteries
Transformation

Wisdom
Immortality Vision
Rebirth Inspiration
Birth Ecstasy
Fruit

Development Transformation
Sublimation

Bearing ——— Giving
Releasing

Elemental
Center

Rejection Holding-Fast
Deprivation Fixating
Ensnaring

Transformation Diminution
Dissolution Devouring

Ecstasy Sickness
Madness Extinction
Impotence Death
Stupor Dismemberment

Drunkenness
Mysteries Death Mysteries

Underworld
Quadrant

NEGATIVE TERRIBLE
TRANSFORMATIVE MOTHER
CHARACTER

YOUNG WITCH OLD WITCH

FEMININE NEGATIVE

Bella Cohen ———————————————————————————— Mrs. Dedalu

Chart based upon Erich Neumann, *The Great Mother*, Schema III,
Bollingen Series XLVII (Princeton University Press, 1955)

transformative character," into the "mysteries of drunkeness" (painful ecstasy, madness, stupor, impotence, rejection, deprivation, dissolution). Called upon by the Nymph (p. 545)—with the word "Mortal," reminding him that he is no longer the "hero god" of his ego wish-fulfillment—he crosses the elemental center-point of consciousness, emerging into the "feminine positive transformative character," into the "mysteries of inspiration" (unmitigated ecstasy, giving, sublimation, vision, wisdom). Dead and reborn, Bloom now can respond to the feminine as an adolescent (pp. 551–52) and he sexualizes the Nymph/Nun. Having purged his deepest psycho-sexual anxieties, he redescends briefly to purge his anxiety about his wife's adultery (pp. 564–68). Upon reascent, he is masculine and assertive with Bella/Bello/Nymph/Nun and ready to take his place again as an initiate in society. Hence the allusions to masonic initiation rites (e.g., on pp. 456, 526, 609): Mr. Bloom has completed his own rite of initiatory passage and is ready to assist Stephen through his. Stephen's ego-circle apotheosis (pp. 574ff.) comes immediately after Bloom's final transformation, and is followed closely (pp. 579ff.) by his descent into the id's "terrible mother death mysteries": dismembering, devouring, diminution, ensnaring, fixating, holding fast. (Note that Mrs. Dedalus is called only "The Mother" in this episode.) Stephen is symbolically killed and Bloom acts as "secret master" (p. 609) in his rebirth, even providing Stephen with an as-yet-non-existent Miss Ferguson to act as agent of his transformation. (He will also attempt an introduction of Stephen to his son-bereaved and love-hungry wife.) Stephen has as yet neither wife nor nymph, and the effect of his underworld descent is not as direct as Mr. Bloom's.

Predictably, Joyce satirizes this *Ewig-Weibliche* synthesis as he does all other abstractions: when Bloom charges Cissey Caffrey to speak as sacred life-giving Woman, as link of nations and generations, she responds, "Amn't I with you? Amn't I your girl? . . . Police!" (p. 598). And it is significant that the reintegration undertaken in "Circe" is accomplished at the psychological level—it is an accommodation, an incorporation or reincorporation into the social world. *Ulysses'* dramatic episode, as Hugh Kenner has observed, serves "cathartic needs."[39] "Circe," and the final triad that follows it, do not solve the dilemmas raised by Hume, Einstein, and Freud—the presences that haunt the middle reaches of the novel: at least, not in their own terms. Cartesian doubt informs the bulk of *Ulysses*, and Descartes' little fiction, the "evil deceiver," is a patron saint to Joyce's larger one:

> I will therefore suppose that . . . a certain evil spirit, not less clever and deceitful than powerful, has bent all his efforts to deceiving me. I will suppose that the sky, the air, the earth, colors, shapes, sounds, and all other objective things that we see are nothing but illusions and dreams that he has used to trick my credulity. I will consider myself as having no hands, no eyes, no flesh, no blood, nor any senses, yet falsely believing that I have all these things. . . . and [I] shall prepare my mind so well for all the ruses of this great deceiver that, however powerful and artful he may be, he will never be able to mislead me in anything.[40]

"Circe" is the epistemologist's nightmare—the world of persuasive deception—but it is, in addition, the psychoanalyst's dream. Joyce does not, like Descartes or Kant, bring us from epistemological doubt to a set of certainties; he brings us face to face, as Freud does, with the single, psychic root of our fictions and truths. Freud's accomplishment, from this perspective, was to incorporate Descartes' "evil deceiver" into a psychological model—to render doubt, fiction-making, and misperception a permanent and functional part of the psyche. As ontology gave way historically to epistemology, so epistemology gives way, in the twentieth century, to new approaches, some psychological and some still undefined in Joyce's day. *Ulysses* is a post-epistemological novel: it does not answer the epistemologist's questions but it "unpacks" many of them, and it moves us from doubts about our knowledge to knowledge about our doubts.

After the "Circe" episode, philosophy, science, and common sense itself can be readmitted only as ways of seeing—

from 9:00 to 5:00, on weekdays. Theirs is not true vision in the ultimate sense but a useful (even, perhaps, a necessary) illusion. The truer vision, the one to which the poet can give his unqualified assent, is one that precedes Newton and Aristotle, precedes Hebraism and Hellenism; it even precedes consciousness. That is a vision which only the *vates* can apprehend, and even he must perceive with merely human, 20/20 apparatus. Yet the theodicean poet is a social creature who holds, with Igor Stravinsky, that "Universality necessarily stipulates submission to an established order,"[41] and so his task is to transform the culturally accepted cosmology into something true and visionary and affirmable. After all that has occurred, however, both in Western history and in *Ulysses*, the "Penelope" episode is as much an act of defiance as one of affirmation. The traditional bases of the culture have been cleansed only by having been demolished, and our world can overrule its detractors only by re-emerging out of its original source.

• • •

When the trumpet blasts its opening "YES" on the first page of the "Penelope" episode, the old dispensation has breathed its last, and something new seems about to take place. Molly is agitated over Bloom's nearly unprecedented behavior and she thinks of earthquakes and thunder and the world's end. She returns to apocalyptic thoughts twice more (pp. 741, 769) and, later (pp. 772, 780), admits to being "sick of Cohens old bed"—restless, that is, in the constricting order lifted by her Catholic forebears from ancient Judaism. Yet her thoughts are not apocalyptic in the denotative sense: the old order may have ended with a whimper but a new one is about to commence with a bang and, in any case, life surges on. Each thought of doom or discontinuity is followed immediately by an appeal ("O Jesus wait") to keep things going and, after considering her own end, she immediately feels the menstrual flow of life's blood. Like Eliot's, this end appears to be an old beginning. Her soliloquy and the book itself conclude with Molly's recollection of the first moment in her serious relationship with Bloom and, as Diane Tolomeo has observed, her eight "sentences" mark the beginning of a new world cycle.[42]

In Molly's fifth sentence, human history seems to have returned to its first day:

> I had that white blouse on open at the front to encourage him as much as I could without too openly they were just beginning to be plump I said I was tired we lay over the firtree cove a wild place I suppose it must be the highest rock in existence ... those frightful rocks and Saint Michaels cave with the icicles or whatever they call them hanging down ... Im sure thats the way down the monkeys go under the sea to Africa when they die ... yes the sea and the sky you could do what you liked lie there for ever he caressed them ... in broad daylight too in the sight of the whole world you might say they could have put an article about it in the Chronicle ... Lord what a bang all the woodcocks and pigeons screaming coming back ... round by the old guardhouse and the jews burial place pretending to read out the Hebrew ... (pp. 760–61)

Read in this context—the familiar context of a Chronicle (unitalicized) concerned with a mischievous couple in a scorpion-infested "wild place"—Molly's adultery with Boylan marks June 16, 1904, as day one of a fresh human history. And, it seems, this fall, like its Biblical precursor, is a *felix culpa*, for from it result Bloom's underworld purgation (in "Circe") and the wandering from Eccles Street that leads him into symbiosis with Stephen.

At the same time that she heralds both an end and a new/old beginning to history, Molly in the last two episodes represents both the motive force for a new human being (the Ulysses of *Ulysses*) and, as Penelope, the aboriginal starting point to which man must return. So the radically new "union" of Stephen, Bloom, and Molly would appear, after all, to be a reunion. The Blooms knew Stephen as a child: Molly remembers him from eleven years before, at age eleven, during the year in which Rudy Bloom lived for eleven days—and, at the end of "Circe," Mr. Bloom sees his eleven-year-old son resurrected over Stephen's fetal-positioned body. That this reunion takes place only in the novel's most satiric chapter ("Ithaca") and in the mind of Molly Bloom, that Stephen declines the invitation to spend the night in Milly's bed, are important facts, but they are overwhelmed by Odyssean magnetism: by the urge to return. Joyce blurs the union of Bloom, Stephen, and Molly presumably to eschew the embarrassment of didactic transparency and, in a conceptual matter like this one, no action is necessary outside the mind—a lesson Stephen taught us in "Circe." Furthermore, by the time we reach "Penelope," the "new man" has been equipped with every bodily organ (of both sexes) and endowed with a mind whose unconscious machinations we have witnessed in the "Circe" episode.

After nearly seven hundred and fifty pages of parallel voyaging, we can guess pretty well what Blephen amounts to. Among other things, he would seem to be an artist of almost Shakespearian empathy and almost Abelardian critical intellect, a good Samaritan and a rebel, a Jew and Greek. But what does "Penelope" add to this creature in order to yield the final product, "Stoomolly?" Simply stated, Molly Bloom provides a soul, a "ground of being," or, in a more Joycean parlance, the sexual motive-power. As such, she presides over the reunion. It is in her womblike mind that the new being is fleshed out (Gilbert said that "flesh" was this chapter's organ) and, as Joyce gives Molly the oracular last word, it is she who gives the reader his lasting impression of the triunion by selecting the features of each man that will meld into the "new man." She approves of her husband's "spunk," his kindness and charitable spirit, his consideration and polite manners, his extraordinary understanding of the way others think (even his cat), his "way with words," his Mediterranean (i.e., Jewish) origins, his frugality and sense of family responsibility, and his comprehension of womanhood, while she dislikes his cold feet and sleeping habits, his mimicry, some of his "cracked ideas," his impotence, and his agnostic socialism.[43] Molly thrills to imagine Stephen's poetic creativity, his high intelligence, his personal distinction, his princely curls and handsome boyish face, his youth, his facility with languages, his Mediterranean name, and his status as a teacher, but she hopes he will be neither Bohemian nor stuck-up.[44]

To this still vague and inanimate amalgam Joyce adds the color and life-force of Molly Bloom. Blephen's self-consciousness and self-questioning are qualified by Molly's spontaneity (p. 766) and complete self-satisfaction (p. 763). Bloom's hyperconcern for the here and now, and Stephen's for the then and there, are balanced by Molly's timelessness and spacelessness. (She tells us her life's story with little reference to chronology and with locations confused, and—on pp. 751, 761, 779—we are told that she never ages, never changes.) Blephen's reliance on both common and uncommon sense is opposed by Molly's intuition and superstition (she reads cards and noses), just as Blephen's more or less detached observations about sexual love are countered by Molly's passionate cravings. In contradiction to Blephen's politico-economic radicalism, Molly affirms the extant (e.g., on pp. 738, 743, 748); with Bloom, impotent, and Stephen, loveless, she prepares to share her natural fertility; and she counters their contemplations about death with her prayers for eternal continuance (pp. 738, 769). Her earthiness reduces the pretensions of Stephen's philosophizing and Bloom's "scientizing"—after the learned philosophical speculations of Stephen's "Proteus" episode, the enormous psychological complexity of Bloom's "Circe" episode, and the technological calculations of Blephen's "Ithaca" episode, Molly's "Penelope" chapter is a considerable and invigorating relief.

Thus, these three Mediterranean Dubliners correct and complete one another. We have heard a good deal about keys from both Stephen and Bloom all through *Ulysses*, but only inside Molly's house do we hear anything of locks ("inserting the barrel of an arruginated male key in the hole of an unstable female lock"),[45] and the symbolism is more than obvious. Molly is poised to act as the "transformative feminine" (in Neumann's language but with Dante and Goethe—Joycean *maitres*—in mind as well) for both her husband and Stephen: for Bloom, as the "positive transformative character," and, for Molly's Rudy-replacement, as both "good mother" and muse, while she expresses a desire for the intellectual and artistic outlets that the men can provide her. Examined separately, Joyce's "heroes" are a middle-aged, masturbating cuckold; a menstruating adulteress; and a young, self-advertising *artiste*. Taken together, they are a self-completing and complementary trinity of humanity's best essences—an association of sensibility; they are Odysseus, Penelope, and Telemachus—the Holy Family of modernism.[46] Three final assertions remain to be made about this human trinity. First, both because of the "Penelope" episode's Eden imagery and because the triunion restores "Rudy" to the Blooms, this trinity represents nature as it once was and ought to become again—it is almost Adam with his rib put back. Second, Molly and the wanderers are held together (at least in her mind— the only place the union becomes vividly actual) by copulation. Molly imagines intercourse with both her husband and her surrogate son. Third, this trinity is a human (i.e., Joyce's, or the Blooms') creation—or re-creation—of something close to Creation's own heart.

Which neatly defines for us the terms of *Ulysses*' religious faith—the faith that this theodicean epic seeks to affirm. As Ellmann has said of the Joycean Genesis, God creates a world that forever requires re-creation: physical re-creation through sexual love and spiritual re-creation through imaginative art.[47] Molly hopes to receive a love letter (a definition for art that unites both sorts of human creativity) because it would make for a "new world" (p. 758). And the human act of re-creation participates in the natural processes of the divine creation, while being in addition the highest form of religious observance. As Molly tells us, atheists are those divorced from nature and, consequently, incapable of creation (p. 782). Her comments on religion are direct enough. She assaults the Roman Church for being divorced from (sexual) nature and she desires a religion in which the priest would make love with his flock (p. 741). She connects Jesus with basic sexual matters (p. 754), complains about the old bishop's sermon on women's higher functions (p. 761), and dismisses Mrs. Rubio's faith because she is a "mass of wrinkles with all her religion" (p. 759)— against which "mass of wrinkles" Molly proposes a new Mass of fertility and renewal, a Eucharist based on life rather than on crucifixion.

Ulysses proceeds from Mulligan's sado-narcissistic mock Mass to a conclusion comprised of the Eucharistic seedcake, the "crimson" red Mediterranean, and the Blooms' first sexual communion. Molly practically identifies the Passion with sexual flagellation (p. 752), an activity she finds repugnant (no doubt she prefers the "infant Jesus . . . in the Blessed Virgins arms" to the crucified Christ), and she nearly makes an erection out of the Host's elevation (p. 762). Through these ("seedcake," erection) and like associations, the "Penelope" episode makes of the Host a male sexual principle, while Molly's repeatedly invoked menstruation connects Eucharistic blood with the female sexual principle; thus even Christian communion becomes copulative.[48] Molly's religious impulses are sometimes Dionysian (she idolizes the semen of the young god), sometimes mythic-ritualistic (she wants a "new man every spring"), sometimes pantheist (her monologue moves from a rejection of "Cohens old bed" to a celebration of the fresh-vegetable market), sometimes simply reverent (she offers thanks for a cup of tea), and sometimes downright heathen (she recalls trying sex with a banana—a fertility rite mentioned in *The Golden Bough*), but always couched in Christian terms. Yet the Christianity of Molly Bloom is no cheat: the Frazerian deity whom Molly affirms is by no means the God by whose grace George V was King of Ireland. The Christ of *Ulysses* is curiously post-Christian.

The religion of "Penelope" is also curiously post-symbolist. Just as Joyce rehabilitates fecundity and sexuality as religious values, so he assigns to the imaginative artist a demi-godlike role not unlike the one that the symbolists and Flaubert ("high priest of art"), Wordsworth and Keats, had asserted was rightfully theirs. Stephen's ashplant in "Circe" is a "lifewand" that can control time and space, can even rule over the underworld

(p. 584). In "Oxen of the Sun" (p. 415), after several paragraphs of references to dead Hebrews and Hellenes, Stephen insists that only the artist can call "the past and its phantoms . . . into life across the waters of Lethe." If a *nostos* there will be, it is the artist who will bring it to pass. However, Joyce presents art in *Ulysses* as re-creation rather than *ex nihilo* creation—in the "Penelope" episode, in fact, nature has style and almost seems to turn into art spontaneously. Further, elitist symbolism to the contrary, almost everyone in *Ulysses* has a touch of the artist about him—an old Irish tradition but also a Joycean creed. Molly Bloom, whom many critics gloss as Nature herself, is spokeswoman for Joyce's ultimate "religious aesthetic" and her credentials are impeccable. She is an interpretive artist whose body produces music, and her artistry with words makes flora bloom out of the ditches. And as Molly observes (p. 774), if the creation of art on a higher plane is natural to the artist, then there is "no art in it." She virtually bathes art in its natural (almost sexual) source when she considers washing the piano keys with milk (p. 781), and she constructs her own aesthetic-axiological system, in which style is essential but pretense is unbearable: "sure you cant get on in this world without style . . . I hate that pretending of all things" (p. 751).

Art and nature are not easily distinguishable, and both are dependent on sexuality for their vigor. Nature is sexualized without a blush. Molly associates the mountains' natural heights with sexual love, female sexual organs with caves, and, when sexually aroused, she describes the flowers on the Rock of Gibraltar. Sex is made into an art form without a qualm. Molly's objection to Bloom's gluteal fetish is revealing; it is that "a womans bottom" hasn't "1 atom of any kind of expression" (p. 777). Reciprocally, the inspiration for art is in sexual nature and Molly fully endorses ancient muse theory (p. 775). Woman—or rather, the elements, the forces that she represents—is at the center of creation in all its forms: she is sexual procreator, inspirer of art, and (at least on p. 769, where Molly's menstrual blood seems to be the slime from which life emerged) the stuff out of which humanity was created.

Art, sex, and nature—with the female principle as the link among them—are intricately interrelated, and they unite to form Creation, the handiwork of the fun-loving God:

> if I am an adultress as the thing in the gallery said O much about it if thats all the harm ever we did in this vale of tears God knows its not much doesnt everybody only they hide it I suppose thats what a woman is supposed to be there for or He wouldnt have made us the way He did . . . then we can have music and cigarettes I can accompany him first I must clean the keys of the piano with milk whatll I wear shall I wear a white rose . . . I love flowers Id love to have the whole place swimming in roses God of heaven theres nothing like nature . . . primroses and violets nature it is as for them saying theres no God I wouldnt give a snap of my two fingers for all their learning why dont they go and create something . . . (pp. 780–82)

The trumpet blasts again, the dark dove is de-materialized, and the apostles of a new/old age go forth by land and sea, with the Chronicle in one hand, the pilgrim's ashplant in the other, and Gifford's *Notes* in a back pocket, to reawaken the world.

In our end is our beginning, and the ideal reader, with his ideal insomnia, puts down his copy of *Ulysses*, exhausted, refreshed, and even punchy—like Bloom and Stephen, after surviving the rigors of "Circe." *Ulysses* is a theodicy—a defense of the universal order—but it redefines theodicy just as it does the universal order: *Ulysses'* theodicy is a state of psyche. No mysteries have been solved, but many of our questions have been faced and defeated. When, for example, Stephen explains to Bloom the reason for his departure from home, for all departures that necessitate returns, he less solves than names the book's ultimate mystery:

> . . . why did you leave your father's house?
> —To seek misfortune, was Stephen's answer.
>
> (p. 619)

Stephen is telling Bloom the painful truth, but he tells it without rancor. Every inch of life has been inspected—its modern novelties, its eternal continuities—and, while much has been rejected *en route*, in the "*nostos* chapters" the whole seems a bruised but acceptable package. No longer is the ugliness that clots the flow of life an obstacle to assent. When Bloom, "returning to the range" in "Ithaca," vivisects the meaning of water—a substance that comprises two-thirds of planet Earth and almost the entirety of every organism—he admires *all* of its qualities: its "universality," "democratic equality," "constancy to nature," "profundity," and "utility," but also its "restlessness," "secrecy," "sterility," "violence," and "noxiousness."

The passage in praise of water—in praise of its hydraulic works and its plumbing no less than its glaciers and falls—contains some of the most winning poetry composed in our century:

> its hydrostatic quiescence in calm: its hydrokinetic turgidity in neap and spring tides: its subsidence after devastation: its sterility in the circumpolar icecaps, arctic and antarctic: its climatic and commercial significance . . . the multisecular stability of its primeval basin: its luteofulvous bed . . . its gradation of colours in the torrid and temperate and frigid zones: its vehicular ramifications in continental lakecontained streams and confluent oceanflowing rivers with their tributaries and transoceanic currents . . . its secrecy in springs, and latent humidity, revealed by rhabdomantic or hygrometric instruments and exemplified by the hole in the wall at Ashtown gate . . . its infallibility as paradigm and paragon: its metamorphoses as vapour, mist, cloud, rain, sleet, snow, hail: its strength in rigid hydrants . . . its docility in working hydraulic millwheels, turbines, dynamos, electric power stations, bleachworks, tanneries, scutchmills . . . its submarine fauna and flora (anacoustic, photophobe) numerically, if not literally, the inhabitants of the globe: its ubiquity as constituting 90% of the human body: the

noxiousness of its effluvia in lacustrine marshes, pestilential fens, faded flowerwater, stagnant pools in the waning moon. . . . (pp. 671–72)

As with every theodicean epic, *Ulysses* concludes with an affirmation, yet we well remember here, as in those earlier epics, what was lost in arriving at the concluding "Yes." As sleep envelopes a third of our lives, so "Circe" a third of *Ulysses*, and its disruptions, like our nightmares, are unforgettable, not meant to be forgotten.

The world of *Ulysses*—our world—is affirmed at the last, but it is a world which is, according to the narrating voice of the "Ithaca" episode, "ineluctably constructed upon the incertitude of the Void." Without the ineluctable construction, we have nihilism; without the Void, we have a too easy synthesis, fated to collapse into its empty basement. The former is a kind of idealism, or even romanticism; the latter a kind of academicism, or even neoclassicism. The ineluctable and affirmable incertitude—that is perhaps as close as we can come to *Ulysses*' implicit definition of classical authenticity: or of art, of beauty, of human existence.

Myth

The prologues are over. It is a question now
Of final belief. So, say that final belief
Must be in a fiction. It is time to choose.
    Wallace Stevens, "Asides on the Oboe"

THE "RETURN" implied by *Ulysses* operates most obtrusively
in the domains of genre and historical explanation, but it is
notorious that this novel also insinuates questions "of final
belief." The perennial, binary debate among Joyce critics, from
Lewis and Gilbert to Kenner and Ellmann, has been in part
reducible to extra-textual disagreements. *Ulysses* in the twentieth century, much as *Julie* in the eighteenth, indicates that
historical and aesthetic nostalgia cannot be isolated from similar reflexes that relate to issues in ontology and epistemology,
psychology, ethics, politics, and axiology. But the final belief
of *Ulysses* is entrusted to the ambiguities of narration: despite
the "Ithaca" eisode, the novel is less catechism than scripture.
Presumably this is what we mean when we describe the efforts
of Joyce and other modernists as "myth-making"—that their
narratives invite doxological readings—though this term, for
all its currency, has been an obstacle to critical commensur-
ability.

    Myth is among the ideologically charged words of almost
every European language, and its large significance for modern
intellectual history has been proportional to the confusion
surrounding its use since the late eighteenth century. "Myths
serve many purposes, almost any purpose," K.D.L. Burridge
wrote in an essay several years ago, and it certainly is true
that myth has been made to serve as a principal weapon of
the insurgents in a "great revolution" which, Friedrich Schlegel saw with uncanny prescience, would "seize all the sciences
and the arts."[1] *Myth*, *mythology*, and *myth-making* have been

key terms in the vocabulary of *nostos*: myth may be the ultimate genre of antiquity, and the literary critics, anthropologists, and psychologists who have fashioned myth-centered theories have been in no sense disinterested scholars. There have been two main sorts of approach to the study of myth in this period. The first, which we may call "mytheory" to distinguish it from the "theory of myth," is primarily interested in the implications of myth for psychology or "world view" rather than in myths as such, and this approach has given rise to what A. J. Greimas has called "a new ideological language."[2] The second, and more novel, approach—the scholarly investigation of myths—is dedicated to the study of myths *ante bellum*, without preconception and in empirical fashion.

The most successful attempt to make a scholarly approach possible has been that of G. S. Kirk, but even Kirk, in the end, is defeated by the ideological shrubbery. His studies, *Myth* (1970) and *The Nature of Greek Myths* (1974), are devoted in large part to debunking the universalist mytheories of the last hundred years, and the nature and extent of his failure to do so teach invaluable lessons about the central (and often unconscious) role that "myth" plays in the modern vocabulary. Kirk will not hear of Max Müller's meteorological theories, nor of Andrew Lang's notion of myth as primitive science. He assaults the Freudian dream analogies, the Cambridge School's "ritualism," Jung's "transpersonal unconscious," the Ernst Cassirer/Suzanne Langer "mythico-metaphorical dimension" of consciousness, Mircea Eliade's "creative era," and the "absurd . . . stringency" of Lévi-Straussian structuralism.[3] Kirk's "emphatic assertion" is that any monolithic theory of myth is doomed to fail the acid test of comparison with all the motley varieties of known myths. For Kirk, speculation on Myth in the abstract is a "learned waste of time" and he believes that "our sophisticated and literate intuitions on this topic are apt to be totally misleading."[4]

But even Kirk cannot help discussing Myth, as it has become, rather than myths, as they are; the special vocabulary of the mytheorists has been absorbed, to a surprisingly large extent, into the general vocabulary of modern intellectual discourse. Kirk holds his ground firmly when the discussion is theoretical but, when he must relate his anti-universalist theory to specific examples of Greek myths, he often loses control. He argues, for instance, that the Homeric epics are repositories of myth, rather than of historical legend, by pointing out "the special texture impressed upon legend by the presence of the gods" and by referring to the narrative's "archetypal mythical status."[5] This follows immediately upon his careful attempt to refute all monolithic theories that posit a necessary connection between myth (as opposed to legend or folktale) and ritual, or between myth and deity. Further, despite his denial of a mode of thought peculiar to myth, Kirk endorses what countless mytheorists have thought they saw behind these traditional stories—an associated sensibility:

> Myths in their primary forms may be held to involve something like poetical thinking, which proceeds by emotional as well as logical stages to achieve a quasi-intellectual end by impressionistic means.[6]

When writing enthusiastically about what seem to be his favorite myths (those to do with Heracles), Kirk permits himself to say that

> the central themes of contradiction—of madness and slavery, Nature and Culture, and the testing of the boundaries between life and death—single him out as a truly mythical being in the profounder sense, as one whose actions both express and determine men's attitudes to the central parts of their experience.[7]

We note with surprise the words "*truly* mythical . . . in the *profounder* sense"; the notion of a mythical being who can both "express *and determine* men's attitudes"; and the capital letters in the phrase, "Nature and Culture."

It appears that there are myths as linguistic constructs (the definition Kirk asks his readers to accept through most of his work) and there is Myth "in the profounder sense"—the product of a mysterious, archetypalizing dimension of consciousness. Kirk devotes much of his final chapter in *Greek Myths* to outlining the family tree of that "unnatural offspring of a psychological anachronism, an epistemological confusion, and a historical red herring"[8]—namely, "mythical thinking"—in order to make it forever anathema in myth scholarship. Yet here we find it, deaf to Kirk's bell, blind to his candle, and sitting in the pages of his own book. What moral we ought to draw from this discovery—from the presence of mytheorist notions in two, estimable works of counter-mytheorist scholarship—may be that the concerns which led to the modern obsession with myth still inform and compel our conversations about mythology and our fine art of myth-making. Ashley Montagu has written of Cassirer—and it may be said as well of almost any mytheorist in the romantic or modernist traditions—that his "approach to mythology is that of the neo-Kantian phenomenologist; he is not interested in mythology as such, but in the processes of consciousness that lead to the creation of myths."

The point is that mytheory and the psychology of the unconscious grew up together and that their necessary connection is a modern presupposition. The unconscious, as concept, has its roots in the idea of a "mythical imagination." William Blake, an important and early mytheorist interested in unconscious mental processes, provides (1793) a succinct list of those claims of the rationalist psychology that he and many other mytheorists have wanted most to refute:

> 1. That man has two real existing principles: Viz: a Body & a Soul. 2. That Energy, call'd Evil, is alone from the Body; & that Reason, call'd Good, is alone from the Soul.[9]

When a mytheorist expresses admiration for "mythical thinking" (the sort of thinking done when "Reason" and "Energy" are conjoined), he usually does not assert that such a thing exists in distinction to some other category of thinking. His claim is, rather, that the rationalist psychological model (in which thinking is an exclusive function of "Reason") has always been a false model: the last superstition of the Enlightened.

Of modernism's pet concepts, "mythical thinking" is the most treacherous to discuss in terms of the return ideologies. It is the aspect of modernism that has entered most directly into modern culture, has most influenced the daily life of modern society, and has given the most forceful impetus to the literary and artistic developments of the twentieth century. It seems that the modern motion toward a post-rationalist, post-Christian science of man has emerged out of a *nostos*-oriented poetic which, from the first, was devoted to myth, mytheory, and mythical thinking. But it is exceedingly difficult to say whether the transformation of modern mytheory into the behavioral sciences of psychology and anthropology has been a product, a cause, or an unwitting tool of modernism and its ideology of cultural *nostos*. What has resulted—in some cases coincidentally, in others hardly by accident—is a mass of observation and doctrine that looks strangely similar to the pre-rationalist, pre-Christian view of human nature. In *The Greeks and the Irrational*, E. R. Dodds describes the psychological model of pre-classical Greece and finds many points for comparison with the Freudian psychology. The emphasis on sexual energy, on the bond between *psyche* and *soma*, on the importance of dreams, on the extreme complexity of the simplest emotions—all these are shared by the *Iliad* and the *Introductory Lectures on Psychoanalysis*.

But the similarity of viewpoint may be, ultimately, a mirage. Dodds's vision—our vision—of the pre-Socratic psychology derives from that of Nietzsche, who himself was the founder of the post-Christian, post-rationalist science of humanity. In order to establish a pre-rationalist view of man that would be to his liking, Nietzsche had to assume a dissociation of sensibility taking place in the Greek mind at precisely the moment when, tradition had held for millennia, the Greek genius was reaching its acme. At this distance—both too far from Socrates and too close to Nietzsche and Dodds—we simply cannot know whether we have been deceived and burdened with unuseful concepts, unproven historical generalizations; or whether, after centuries, we have been enlightened, freed from the longest of all conspiracies of silence (Nietzsche's terminology), and restored to an understanding of our true nature through an encounter with the genuine antique.

• • •

WE cannot know the truth, but we can probe the facts. Nietzsche's whole theory of culture is built on a philosophy of history that projects a special relationship between the twentieth century-to-come and the Greek tragic age. Like almost all modernist historical formulae, Nietzsche's is based on an intuition of (or a passionate desire for) a *nostos*, back behind the Christian and rationalist and Hellenistic/Roman sensibilities, to the tragic Greek sensibility. But, with Malraux, Nietzsche shares the honor of being the most difficult of these philosophers of history, and to define him as a simple "return theorist" would do him (and the idea of a modernist *nostos*) a disservice.

Nietzsche proposes no simple substitution of Greek ideals for modern ones; what he does is propose a theory of tradition in which each age becomes itself by struggling for its life against the allure of the Greek accomplishment. In his *Philosophy in the Tragic Age of the Greeks* (written in the 1870's but posthumously published), Nietzsche argues that we must study the Greeks with a critical eye in order "to vie with antiquity"—for to accept antiquity whole, as the philologists of his age did, would leave antiquity "without any effect."[10] Nietzsche endorses—again, in the *Tragic Age*—the Heraclitean view of time, in which "every moment . . . exists only insofar as it has just consumed the preceding one, its father, and is then immediately consumed likewise."[11] A mere return to beginnings is unhealthy: "Everywhere, the way to the beginnings leads to barbarism. Whoever concerns himself with the Greeks should be ever mindful that an unrestrained thirst for knowledge for its own sake barbarizes men just as much as a hatred for knowledge."[12] Or, as he writes in maxim 24 of *The Twilight of the Idols*, "By searching out origins, one becomes a crab. The historian looks backward; eventually he also *believes* backward."[13] In *Beyond Good and Evil*, he asserts that the aim of Greek studies should be to "rise" rather than to "return," and that all present philosophical labors are directed at overcoming the philosophical labors of the past.[14] In regard to his own thought, Nietzsche admits that all of his work is an attempt to overcome the work of Socrates.[15]

These observations are not meant to belittle Nietzsche's devotion to the Greeks, nor to dilute the potency of his belief in their importance as a model antidote to both Christianity and rationalism. To Nietzsche, the Greeks represent the "highest authority for what we may term cultural health" and for the health of the individual psyche. "The Greeks," he writes, "remain the first cultural event in history: they knew, they *did* what was needed," and he continues—"and Christianity, which despised the body, has been the greatest misfortune of humanity so far."[16] This is the way in which Nietzsche generally uses the Greeks, as an antagonist worthy of the fight against Christianity: in *The Birth of Tragedy* he refers to Dionysus as the "Antichrist." All of this reinterpretation is done to clear the way for a specific kind of future. Nietzsche expects (hopes?) that the twentieth century will represent a new age, as contrasted with the Christian and bourgeois centuries—a new age which, according to the pattern history presents us, will parallel the Greek tragic one. The new age will be wrought by "philosophers of the dangerous 'maybe',"[17] but they will be only the culmination of a line that began with Descartes—with the beginnings of modernity—and whose work has been (usually without full consciousness)

> to assassinate the old soul concept, under the guise of a critique of the subject-and-predicate concept—which means an attempt on the life of the basic presupposition of the Christian doctrine. Modern philosophy, being an epistemological skepticism, is covertly or overtly, *anti-Christian*—although, to say this for the benefit of more refined ears, by no means anti-religious.[18]

Modern thought has been directed at undermining the philosophical underpinnings of Christianity, and Nietzsche expected that the philosophy of the twentieth century would base itself on a "religion" and a concept of the psyche diametrically opposed to those of Christianity—but close to those which underwrote Greek tragedy. In *The Birth of Tragedy*, one of Nietzsche's primary aims was to analyze the "powers to whose influence Greek tragedy succumbed," in order to make possible "the renascence of . . . the tragic world view."[19] Tragedy had succumbed to the optimism and scientific viewpoint of Parmenides and Socrates and Euripides, and this cheery world view Nietzsche associates, in *The Birth of Tragedy*, with the bourgeoisie socially and with proto-Christianity in religion. The decline of tragedy was followed not by a fall back into savagery but by a movement forward into decadence—in *The Twilight of the Idols* he says that decadence is almost a synonym for progress—a decadence that itself went through three states: Hellenistic, Roman, and Christian, or scientific, military, and religious. These were decadent phases because, instead of releasing the will to accomplish either creation or destruction, they chastised the will and turned its powers inside to do internal damage.

In the modern period, our civilization is undergoing this process in reverse—from Christian otherworldliness to Roman militarism to Hellenistic criticism, to a new tragic age (and then, one assumes, back to barbarism). This Nietzschean pattern is not cyclical in the same way that, for example, Vico's theory of history is. The going down cleanses for the way back up: we have learned from Christianity why we want no life-destroying illusions and there is decidedly an element of progress in that knowledge. Thus, once again, we have a three-period philosophy of history, founded on the *felix culpa* principle. In starkest outline, we have a primal ideal followed by an age of decadence and then a repetition of the ideal stage but at a much higher level. Nietzsche believed that the twentieth century would represent that second and higher ideal. *Beyond Good and Evil* bears the subtitle, "Prelude to a Philosophy of the Future," and he counts himself there with the "Europeans of the day after tomorrow . . . first-born of the twentieth century."[20]

"How soon," Nietzsche writes, "how very soon—all will be different!"[21] In *The Birth of Tragedy*, he is militant about the future:

> To what does this miraculous union between German philosophy and music point if not to a new mode of existence, whose precise nature we can divine only with the aid of Greek analogies? For us, who stand on the watershed between two different modes of existence, the Greek example is still of inestimable value, since it embodies the violent transition to a classical, rationalistic form of suasion; only we are living through the great phases of Hellenism in reverse order and seem at this very moment to be moving backward from the Alexandrian age into an age of tragedy.[22]

And in sum: "No one shall wither our faith in the imminent rebirth of Greek antiquity."[23] In other words, we are about to reassociate the sensibility that was divided in the Alexandrian age, more than two millennia ago. All modernist psychohistories posit a dissociation of sensibility, but this one (shared by Lawrence, Malraux, and others) has one of the earliest commencement dates—it begins even with the pre-Socratics. The later pre-Socratics (starting with Parmenides), and the Socratic line itself, "are the decadents of Greek culture, the countermovement to the ancient, noble taste (to the agonistic instinct, to the *polis*, to the value of race, to the authority of descent)."[24] In *The Birth of Tragedy*, Nietzsche assumes that the break came with Socrates and Euripides; in his *Philosophy in The Tragic Age of the Greeks* (of roughly the same period), he undertakes a more thorough analysis and places the break immediately after Heraclitus. What makes Parmenides "un-Greek" is his "absolutely bloodless abstraction," methodologically speaking, and, in theoretical terms, his positing of "that wholly erroneous distinction between 'spirit' and 'body' which, especially since Plato, lies upon philosophy like a curse."[25]

With Parmenides, then, begins the wholly un-Greek distaste for the phenomenal:

one even develops a hatred for phenomena including one-self, a hatred for being unable to get rid of the everlasting deceitfulness of sensation. Henceforth truth shall live only in the palest, most abstracted generalities, in the empty husks of the most indefinite terms, as though in a house of cobwebs. And beside such truth now sits our philos-opher, likewise as bloodless as his abstractions, in the spun-out fabric of his formulas. A spider at least wants blood from its victims. A Parmenidean philosopher hates most of all the blood of his victims, the blood of the empirical reality which was sacrificed and shed by him.[26]

Such is Nietzsche's vehemence on this subject. In *The Twilight of the Idols*, he even asks the question, "Was Socrates a Greek at all?"[27]—so sure is he of what the Greek must consist, and of the philosophic tradition's divergence from that essence. An absurd rationality developed, he postulates, because the psycho-cultural situation in Greece was "desperate."[28] The Greeks' strength was degenerating rapidly and, therefore, the psychology of reason was born: "one must imitate Socrates and counter the dark appetites with a permanent daylight—the daylight of reason. One must be clever, clear, bright at any price: any concession to the instincts, to the unconscious, leads *downward*."[29]

While this hyperrationality may have been necessary, his-torically, on account of the Socratic "idiosyncracy"[30]—the mysterious degeneration in the Greek soul, the loss of strength and will—it was certainly incorrect as a description of the human psyche. "Socrates was a misunderstanding; *the whole improvement-morality, including the Christian*, was a mis-understanding." And this was so because, "To *have* to fight the instincts—that is the formula of decadence: as long as life is *ascending*, happiness equals instinct."[31] This decadence Nietzsche calls "The first yawn of reason. The cock-crow of positivism."[32] With the abundant references in his work to positivism and Christianity, it becomes obvious what Nietzsche meant when he said that his examination of Greek phenomena was not undertaken out of historical interest or for the purpose of imitation, but in order to "rise."

Though much of Nietzsche's work is a discussion of ancient intellectual and cultural history, all is presented in modern terms. He identifies the source of both modern positivism and Christianity in one Greek thinker, and we are reminded of Joyce's effort in *Ulysses* to show how all modern antinomies (rationalism vs. Christianity, for instance) are the result of single, root misunderstandings. Nietzsche locates this particular misunderstanding in Plato: "Plato is boring. In the end, my mistrust for Plato goes deep: he represents such an aberration from all the basic instincts of the Hellene, is so moralistic, so pre-existently Christian—he already takes the concept 'good' for the highest concept—that for the whole phenomenon Plato I would sooner use the harsh phrase 'higher swindle,' or, if it sounds better, 'idealism,' than any other."[33] In *The Birth of Tragedy*, Nietzsche locates the Greek spirit in the Dionysianism of Aeschylus and provides a symbol for its death: the triumph of Euripidean Socratism.[34] From the hour of that triumph and onward, we have a new mode of existence—"theoretical man"[35]—by which, one assumes, Nietzsche means both the man who is interested only in pure theory (he calls Socrates a "mystagogue of science") and also Man as seen only through the lens of theory.

With the advent of Euripides and "theoretical man," we are already beyond the perimeter of the Greek world and are in the world of the Hellenistic empire, the Alexandrian world of fake classicism. (Nietzsche uses the opposition of tragedy and opera to describe what has occurred.) This new world insists upon calling itself Greek in order to keep under covers the dangerous phenomena of a truer and younger Greece. It is Alexandrianism that was passed to the Romans and thence to the Middle Ages and modernity—passed off as being Greek, as being the "founding attitude" of our culture: "So much depends on the development of Greek culture because our entire occidental world has received its initial stimuli from it. An adverse fate decreed that the late and decadent forms of Hellenism should exert the greatest historical force. On their account, earlier Hellenism has always been misjudged. . . . others have *discovered* the Greeks and later *covered them up* again."[36] The task which Nietzsche sets for twentieth-century philosophy—for the Antichrist to which Nietzsche thought himself an anti-St.-John-the-Baptist—is to uncover the younger Greeks (Homer, Heraclitus, Aeschylus, Sophocles), and to contrast their estimate of the human psychology with the rationalist and Christian ones, both of which had descended from the Platonic error.

In doing this, Nietzsche says that moderns will put themselves in the position of Oedipus: a curious anticipation of Freud, who would take Nietzsche one step further and proclaim that all men are Oedipuses. This king of Thebes became, in the span of a very few years in the late nineteenth century, one of modern Europe's culture heroes. That this should occur is astonishing, that we should make a hero of a man who killed his father and married his mother and became the progenitor of his siblings. But we are not, much, astonished and the reasons for our lack of surprise are of the first importance to an understanding of modern cultural history. In an excellent series of articles in *Arion* (1965–66), Thomas Gould outlines the most important of these reasons, namely, that the interpretation of *Oedipus Rex* in Aristotle's *Poetics* has for centuries kept most readers of the play from seeing it with appropriate horror.[37] Gould argues that, in setting forth his description of tragedy, Aristotle chose the *Oedipus* for his prime example, not because it was the most perfectly constructed of tragedies, nor because it was his favorite, but because it was the most horrible thematically. He did so, Gould continues, in order to defuse Plato's argument against the arts—to demonstrate that *even this play* was not damaging to the public's faith and morals. To assert that Oedipus possessed a tragic flaw and, therefore, deserved what the gods dispensed is, in Gould's opinion, absurd. All that Sophocles' chorus, indeed, can make of what has happened on stage is that unhappiness can fall on absolutely anyone, however virtuous, and at any time, however unpropitious.[38]

The opinion of Sophocles' chorus opposes the (Socratic)

view that justice is done in this world and that virtue and happiness are one. Oedipus is basically a good man—he flees his native land, or what he thought was his homeland, in order to meet no opportunity to fulfill the gods' decree against his family. The lesson of his subsequent experience, if we can call such devastation a lesson, can be only that there is no escape from fate. Other critics (Cedric Whitman and Maurice Bowra, for example), who want to find an upbeat lesson in the *Oedipus*, have tried other tacks, but to succeed in giving this play a moral different from that of Job is unlikely if not impossible. What we see in *Oedipus*, says Gould, is the destruction of a man for being human—and other humans seem to thrill at the sight. To admit this is to undermine, utterly, the rationalist psychology and poetics; it is to undermine the centerpiece of rationalist ethics, that virtue yields happiness.

The glee with which moderns have reinterpreted this play is evidence of their affirmation of the classical tradition in mythology and creative literature, just as it is evidence of their dislike of the classical tradition in philosophy. The proclamation of Oedipus as "a new divinity"—by Yeats, in *A Vision* (1937)—is symptomatic. Yeats contrasts Oedipus with Christ (as Nietzsche had contrasted Jesus with both Oedipus and Dionysus). Oedipus, Yeats writes, is the god who lies down on the earth, bound to the phenomenal world, while Jesus is the god who stands up in crucifixion pointing eternally upward. The opposition is, for Yeats, one of the concrete and earthly vs. the abstract and sky-bound. And he projects, in an open letter to Pound, that the espousal of Oedipus as a god to replace Jesus marks the beginning of an historical *ricorso* like the one in Pound's poem, "The Return."[39] To affirm the divinity of Oedipus is to affirm the supremacy of man over the gods: of humanity made divine rather than divinity humanized. (To the riddle of the Sphinx, after all, the answer was Man.) Gide's *Oedipe* and *Thésée* make a similarly radical revaluation of classical humanism.

The godfather of all such speculation is Nietzsche—though, for Nietzsche, it was Oedipus at Colonus rather than Oedipus the King who made the perfect emblem for modern man: the last, solitary philosopher. For Nietzsche, Oedipus is the man who looks back on the terrible past of humanity and, resigned—even happy—sees what it all has meant.[40] In *Beyond Good and Evil*, Nietzsche considers the meeting of Oedipus with the Sphinx, and he decides that humanity is not only the question-answerer and the answer to the question, but the questioner—the Sphinx—as well. In the twentieth century, Nietzsche asserts (in *The Birth of Tragedy*), wisdom will be the crime that we—like the unnatural, incestuous, murderous, regicidal, patricidal Oedipus—will commit against the natural order. That is, we will arrive at what we seek only if we are not squeamish about what we will find, and this lesson Freud too would attach to the myth of Oedipus: that life is a tale of biological, even genetic, terror. What the questioner—Nietzsche—found, or rather, what the questioner rediscovered, is that the human psyche is a biological, rather than a spiritual, substance. Nietzsche denies the Platonic-Christian concept of a spiritual self: the human being is not spiritual but sexual. As all organisms have a will to life—a will to power—so it is with the human organism, and all organic functions, Nietzsche claims, can be traced to that one, reproductive urge.[41] The basic urge is sexual (or, as he says in *Twilight*, Dionysian) because the will to live requires the reproduction of the self into other, reproducible selves.

These revolutionary postulations seemed, to Nietzche, entirely reactionary. The true Greek religion was based upon the pieties of sexuality, upon the holiness of reproduction and birth.[42] If the will to life and power is our basic urge, we might as well affirm it to be holy, as the Greeks did, and accept the consequences of such a recognition. This Nietzsche does in *Twilight of the Idols*, where he asserts that the passions are good—once they have passed through the phase when they are "merely disastrous"[43]—and that the sexual instinct must never be castrated as the Christians have done. "An attack on the roots of passion means an attack on the roots of life."[44] Moreover, the internal oppositions that the passions can cause are highly productive ("The price of fruitfulness is to be rich in internal opposition")[45] and—more heretical still, from the rationalist's viewpoint—thinking itself is nothing more than the clash of these passions: ". . . thinking is merely a relation of these drives to each other."[46] There is no independent faculty of reason in the psyche. Further, in a healthy psyche, the instincts are generally correct: "All that is good is instinct."[47] In *Beyond Good and Evil*, Nietzsche asserts that psychology must cease to concern itself with right and wrong but only, in view of the human organism's main concern, with what is or is not life-giving. Man must embrace all the things that he is, even if some of those things are contrary to a socially endorsed morality: ". . . everything in him that is kin to beasts of prey and serpents serves the enhancement of the species 'man' as much as its opposite does."[48]

In order to accomplish this revaluation of the psyche, we must be fervently anti-Christian. We must see things in a pre-Christian way: "Suppose we could contemplate the oddly painful and equally crude and subtle comedy of European Christianity with the mocking and aloof eyes of an Epicurean god, I think our amazement and laughter would never end: doesn't it seem that a single will dominated Europe for eighteen centuries—to turn man into a *sublime miscarriage*?"[49] When we have accomplished this revaluation, we will have made a kind of return: we will "take up again an ancient religious formula in a new and more profound sense."[50] Our destiny, Nietzsche proclaims, is to reinstate psychology as the most important of studies—and now as "queen of the sciences." "For psychology," he writes, "is now again the path to the fundamental problems."[51]

· · ·

WITHIN a generation, Nietzsche's prediction was reality: psychology had become central to our culture and was established as a behavioral science. Freud had fulfilled not only Nietzsche's prophecy but also Schlegel's: symbolist/romantic ideology had conquered even the natural sciences. Yet Freud was by no means as aware of his participation in the modernist ethos as Schlegel or Nietzsche or even Frazer. It is possible to argue that Freud is more the "tool" of the modernists than he is a colleague. Some of Freud's ideas are positively opposed to those of the modernists and to their ideology of history. His theory of parallel development between the individual and the culture is progressivist rather than nostalgic: a return, in Freudian psycho-history, is negative, a neurotic regression. In *Totem and Taboo* (1913), he outlines a kind of historical ideology but it represents nothing the mainstream modernists would approve:

> The animistic phase would correspond to narcissism both chronologically and in its content; the religious phase would correspond to the stage of object-choice of which the characteristic is the child's attachment to his parents; while the scientific phase would have an exact counterpart in the stage at which an individual has reached maturity, has renounced the pleasure principle, adjusted himself to reality and turned to the external world for the object of his desires.[52]

The scientific phase is, for Freud, the mature phase of civilization and any return to the religious or, worse yet, to the animistic/mythic phase is regression. Nietzsche, for one, would not have admired this formulation. For Freud, insofar as he is willing to express it, the goal of the individual and of mankind is the one he posits in the *New Introductory Lectures on Psychoanalysis* (1933): "reclamation work, . . . the draining of the Zuyder Zee."[53] In other words, he strives to make the scientific/positivist evaluation of Man ultimately a true one. As Freud knew, the positivist vision could never be fully realized and achieving it would involve strenuous efforts, but it is more correct to say that Freud possessed a rationalist's appreciation of consciousness than to assert the opposite: that he saw the unconscious past of humanity as its special glory. On the other hand, and despite all these qualifications, Freud's emphasis fell heavily on the importance and vastness of that unconscious past. When his disciples (Jung, in particular) endeavored to make the symbolic-mythic unconscious a benign and even blessed part of psychic life—and devalued consciousness and reason in the process—Freud should not have been nearly so surprised and indignant. For the importance or origins and sources and fundamentals is the heart of the Freudian psychology, as it is also of the more self-conscious, return-oriented modernisms.

As much as Freud was imbued with the historical credo of liberalism, positivism, and science—with the credo of progress—he became increasingly convinced that the return to origins was not only a psychological tendency but also a biological fact. In *Beyond the Pleasure Principle* (1920), he practically made the *nostos* myth a part of animal physiology: "It would be a contradiction to the conservative nature of the instincts if the goal of life were a state of things which had never yet been attained. On the contrary, it must be an *old* state of things, an initial state from which the living entity has at one time or other departed and to which it is striving to return by the circuitous paths along which its development leads."[54] As early as 1923, in *The Ego and the Id*, Freud had assumed the psyche's ability to "resurrect" the shapes of its former egos and, in anticipation of Jung, he wondered in print whether the id was capable of inheriting the "residues of . . . countless egos."[55] Freud never applied this group of observations to culture (though for him culture and the individual operate on roughly parallel bases), and perhaps he did not do so in this instance because of the havoc that application could have wreaked on his view of historical progress. However, the cultural significance of Freud's discovery—of his observations about the psyche's reactionary instincts—was not lost on the modernists, as the circular construction of *Finnegans Wake* perhaps indicates.

The reactionary quality of Freudian germ cells was not Freud's only relation to the ideologies of return. It is clear that Freud thought the psychological model he was developing had some important connection to psychology as understood by the Greeks, though it is equally clear that he thought the Greeks said better than they knew. In his analysis of *Oedipus Rex* in the *General Introduction to Psychoanalysis* (1916), Freud presumed that Sophocles did not comprehend the reasons for the impact of his play. Freud believed that Sophocles' interest in the myth was in what he ("the reverent Sophocles") could do to make it a moral tale about bowing to the will of the gods. The real cause for the magnetism that this tragedy has exerted is, in Freud's judgment, one that would have been as inexplicable to the playwright as it has been to the play's viewers. In fact, had Sophocles known that his play was "immoral" ("it sets aside the individual's responsibility to social law, and displays divine forces ordaining the crime and rendering powerless the moral instincts of the human being which would guard him against the crime"),[56] he would never have put it on the stage.

Still, at almost every major juncture in his thought, Freud would return to the Greeks for his terminology (Oedipus complex, Electra complex, narcissism, eros) and for illustrations of his views. To what extent he was aware of this phenomenon—or, rather, to what he would attribute it—is unclear, but it is certain that Nietzsche was correct when he predicted that the long-awaited, new vision of human nature would emerge from an agonistic encounter with the Greek heritage. That kind of encounter takes place throughout the pages of Freud's twenty-four volumes of writings, but especially in *Totem and Taboo*, where he analyzes primitive and classical conceptions of the sacred and proposes that such terms as *taboo, sacer,* ἄγος, and the Hebrew *kadesh* indicate both horror and veneration, both the impure and the holy. It is on the basis of this observation that he proposes that, except at the high level of ego consciousness, the human mind does not differentiate opposites—that the unconscious operates in an undifferentiating, "Greek" way. It is also in *Totem and Taboo* that Freud examines the hero-chorus relationship of the earliest Greek tragedies and proposes that the hero is a substitute for the primal father, and the chorus for his sons, so that the destruction of the hero is a scapegoat venture, undertaken to relieve the audience of unconscious guilt.

Freud's sense of superiority in approaching his Greek subjects is sometimes mildly amusing. For one thing, Sophocles might find some of the conclusions Freud drew from the Greek idea of a sexually determined self to be somewhat naïve: the fatalism of the Freudian Oedipus shares little with the robust independence of Sophocles' statesman, son, and father. And although Freud assumes that the substance he extracts from Greek texts has not been placed there with conscious intent, his Greek authors often beat him to his ultimate conclusions. In *The Ego and the Id*, written more than a decade after his earliest formulation of the "Opedipus complex," Freud was continuing to struggle with the notion of the superego as a product of the id. His conclusion, there, is that Oedipal desires are repressed in order for the individual to achieve maturity and that, in the process, the transformation of Oedipal desires becomes an ego ideal that forms the basis for the superego. Thus, guilty desires become the foundation of morality and social behavior.

But the supposedly ignorant poet of *Oedipus Rex* was also author of *Oedipus at Colonus*, a play that dramatizes almost precisely Freud's solution to the Oedipus-complex dilemma. The horrible Oedipus, grown old and surpassing wise, is taken the gods-know-where to die and be buried beneath Athenian soil. He is, thus, repressed—even his daughters do not know his place of burial—but he is, also, ultimately hallowed and hallowing. Athens, the great and good City of Man, is sanctified and protected by the presence of Oedipus' remains; he has become a creature of society (only the king and his descendants will know the location of the grave). Freud did not give Sophocles' last play the credit it deserves but either he knew the play well, or else he did not and his conception of superego origins, far from being original, was anticipated by some twenty-five hundred years. Concerning Freud's awareness of Greek influences and parallels, it is worth reiterating Lionel Trilling's observation about the Freudian view of man: that Freud's psychology is far closer to that expressed in Greek literature (as opposed to post-Socratic Greek philosophy) than to either the rationalist or Christian/moral psychologies of the modern age.[57]

That Freud, like Nietzsche, was reacting against these modern psychologies should be obvious, if only from the extreme anti-Freud reaction, which has even yet to cool. Freud was well aware of his status as a rebel and even seemed at times to relish it. As Freud once told his friend, Wilhelm Fliess, "I am actually not a man of science, not an experimenter, not a thinker . . . but a conquistador." Freud knew, for example, that his view of consciousness flew in the face of centuries of contrary doctrine, in both philosophy and in some brands of liberal Christian theology. He argued that consciousness represents only the tiniest fraction of the psyche and that, therefore, the mental process must be conceived as happening largely at the unconscious level. In the *Outline of Psychoanalysis*, he addressed his opponents directly: "The majority of philosophers . . . as well as many other people, dispute this and declare that the notion of something psychical being unconscious is self-contradictory."[58] Freud would not stop there. He went on to show that the ego is an *adjunct* to the id—its agent for sorting-out its conflicting urges, for perceiving external reality and determining how to achieve to the degree possible the id's desires in that external world.[59] Worse still from a rationalist's viewpoint, Freud asserted that the id, though chaotic and even (without its agent, the ego) self-destructive, "expresses the true purpose of the individual organism's life. This consists in the satisfaction of its innate needs."[60] In this opinion, Freud follows Nietzsche's insistence that the highest value of any organism is its will to life—though, for Freud, the id also has a will to death.

Aside from the instinct for sexual union (for binding together) and the instinct for death (for undoing connections), the human psyche has no other instincts. Freud the rebel is perhaps baiting Christians, or the religious in general, when he states: "It may be difficult . . . for many . . . to abandon the belief that there is an instinct towards perfection at work in human beings. . . . I have no faith, however, in the existence of any such internal instinct and I cannot see how this benevolent illusion is to be preserved."[61] Human "progress" is to be explained by the unceasing energy of erotic and violent instincts to strive for complete satisfaction even after their repression; Freud terms this process sublimation and insists that its product is what we call civilization. Conscience (the superego), social relations, philosophy, cultural institutions, the arts, religion, and morality—all derive from the primeval patricide described in *Totem and Taboo*. Even less appealing to the Enlightenment sensibility would be Freud's view that all love is sexual—even the love of parents—[62] and that there is no such thing as love uncolored by aggression, selfishness, incestuous desire, hostility, and bisexuality, because the psyche is whole, despite all the talk of its parts.[63] And, as for Nietzsche, the sexual instincts are for Freud entirely healthy: "They are the true life instincts."[64] Even the process of thinking is to a great extent sexual.[65] Man is an animal; there can be no mind/body distinction. The mind lives off the body's energies,[66] and "It thus seems natural to lay the stress in psychology upon those somatic processes, to see in *them* the true essence of what is mental."[67]

Each of these Freudian positions is problematic for Enlightenment psychology and many present severe problems to a Christian psychological model. Few of them, however, would have troubled Aeschylus; few would have much troubled even Plato or Aristotle. Or so many post-Nietzschean writers on the classics—E. R. Dodds is the most visible example—would ask us to believe. To muse about these possibilities for parallelism is, of necessity, pure speculation, like the view sometimes expressed that Hegel and Marx based their dialectic on the trilogic structure of Greek tragedies. And if we are to leave Freud on a speculative note, there are speculations more immediately relevant to cite—Northrop Frye's for example:

> It looks now as though Freud's view of the Oedipus complex were a psychological conception that throws some light on literary criticism. Perhaps we shall eventually decide that we have got it the wrong way round: that what happened was that the myth of Oedipus informed and gave structure to some psychological investigations at this point. Freud would in that case be exceptional only in having been well read enough to spot the source of the myth. It looks now as though the psychological discovery of an oracular mind "underneath" the con-

scious one forms an appropriate allegorical explanation of a poetic archetype that has run through literature from the cave of Trophonius to our own day. Perhaps it was the archetype that informed the discovery: it is after all considerably older, and to explain it in this way would involve us in less anachronism. The informing of metaphysical and theological constructs by poetic myths, or by associations and diagrams analogous to poetic myths, is even more obvious.[68]

The moving irony Frye describes has not escaped its victims' notice and they invariably explain its existence with some formulation of the modernist historical ideology. In observing how the modern science of human nature developed out of the study of primitive mythologies, Claude Lévi-Strauss has expressed the behavioral scientist's version of the myth of return:

We have had to wait until the middle of this century for the crossing of long separated paths: that which arrives at the physical world by the detour of communication, and that which, as we have recently come to know, arrives at the world of communication by the detour of the physical. The entire process of human knowledge thus assumes the character of a closed system. And we therefore remain faithful to the inspiration of the savage mind when we recognise that, by an encounter it alone could have foreseen, the most modern form of the scientific spirit will have contributed to legitimize the principles of savage thought and to re-establish it in its rightful place.[69]

It is in this context, also, that we should understand Jung's assertion, in *Modern Man in Search of a Soul*, that the twentieth century is living through "one of those swings of the pendulum which, as history has shown, set matters right again."[70] And in the provocatively titled *Essays on a Science of Mythology*, which he wrote in collaboration with Jung, Carl Kerényi, the classical scholar, demands that "science herself . . . throw open the road to mythology that she blocked

first with her interpretations and then with her explanations."[71]

What all these myth "scientists" have in common is their
conviction that the study of myth, like the process of Freudian
psychoanalysis, will in the end lead to a condition that Lévi-
Strauss calls "*Superrationalism*, which will integrate [the per-
ceptive] with [the rational], without sacrificing any of its properties."[72] The study of myth will lead to the reassociation of
sensibility—and that is because, according to Jung, the science
of "mythical thinking" has proven to us, once and for all,
that

> The deeper layers of the psyche lose their individual
> uniqueness as they retreat farther and farther into dark-
> ness. "Lower down," that is to say as they approach the
> autonomous functional systems, they . . . are universal-
> ized and extinguished in the body's materiality, i.e. in
> chemical substances. The body's carbon is simply car-
> bon.[73]

The unique properties of mythology teach us that spirit and
matter, mind and body, are one.

• • •

As JUNG was well aware, to make such a statement is, in the
broad sense, to make a religious commitment: a commitment
to a world view and to an estimate of the human potential.
The preoccupation with myth as world view has been due
largely to the enervation in the modern era of Christianity as
a myth-system. The belief in mytheory as science was simultaneous with a belief in the possibility of myth-making, and
both are, perhaps, cultural wish-fulfillment fantasies. Certainly both are substitutes for Christian theology. In his essay
on "D. H. Lawrence and the Apocalyptic Types," Frank Kermode poses the important question of why theologians "got
really deeply into de-mythologizing" just when literati "began
to go overboard for mythology."[74] There are numerous historical reasons why theology and art should have adopted
different tactics during the increasingly difficult "spiritual cri-

sis" of the modern period, but the fact is that both responded with a feeling of urgency to the same vision: the imminent implosion of Western Christian civilization.

The theologian's approach and that of the artist are simply two ways of re-enforcing or replacing the flooring and, sometimes, of furnishing the basement as well, to soften the fall and make life livable underground. For a moderate de-mythologizer, such as John Macquarrie:

> More important than the influence of any particular philosophy [i.e., logical positivism] in driving the apologists to consider the question of meaning has been the increasing remoteness of Christianity from the thinking of the ordinary man of today. The Christian religion is not so much rejected as merely disregarded. It does not seem to say anything which has meaning for contemporary life. De-mythologizing represents one of the ways in which the Christian apologist seeks to respond to this situation.[75]

The radical de-mythologizer, Fritz Buri, goes so far as to second Oswald Spengler's theory that every organic myth-system must serve its purpose, then decay and be replaced during some extraordinary period of cultural death and rebirth:

> In the sea of mythological ideas . . . there are only a few really great redeemer-myths of the kind which we have in the story of the eschatological Christ. As archetypes they emerge from the unconscious in great moments of humanity, they are formulated by prophets, then they grow old and die.[76]

For a Christian theologian to hold this view of the Christian *mythos* is tantamount to a disclaimer of faith in the eternal truth of his religion's most basic tenets. Buri's solution to the dilemma, of which his outlook is a symptom, is to render Christianity relevant to modern concerns by translating its *mythos* (and, in opposition to his movement's founder, Rudolf Bultmann, the *kerygma* as well) into the terms of contemporary philosophy.

Artists generally have taken another approach, which, for convenience, we may call "re-mythologizing." Their attitude toward the de-mythologizer, throughout the modern centuries (for this enterprise was nothing new, despite the considerable stir it caused), has been that of Pope to the fourth *Dunciad*'s

> ... gloomy Clerk,
> Sworn foe to Myst'ry, yet divinely dark;
> Whose pious hope aspires to see the day
> When Moral Evidence shall quite decay,
> And damns implicit faith, and holy lies,
> Prompt to impose, and fond to dogmatize.
>
> (459–64)

Re-mythologizing psychologists, too, have taken a dim view of Bultmann's and Buri's efforts. In his essay on "Psychological Aspects of the Mother Archetype," Jung observes that "Theologians would do better to take account for once ... of psychoanalytical facts than to go on 'de-mythologizing' them with rationalistic explanations that are a hundred years behind the times."[77]

Most European writers of this century have said something to the point. In the "Lotus-Eaters" episode of *Ulysses*, Joyce has the sometime Jewish, sometime Protestant, sometime Catholic Leopold Bloom watch Dublin ladies get prurient and masochistic thrills from the sacraments of the church—during which spectacle Bloom admires Rome's "clockwork" organization and a narrating voice observes that the holy water is at "low tide." At about the same time, T. S. Eliot recorded in quatrains his vision of a hippo ascending into heaven, leaving the church below in a putrefying fog; and, many years after his conversion, he still complained that bishops were a part of English society while horses and dogs were a component of English religion. In *Thor, With Angels*, Christopher Fry writes allegorically of pre-Christian British gods who "were too old" to be efficacious under radically changing conditions and, it is worth noting, two of Fry's three religious plays (*Thor* and *The First Born*) concern the collapse of a pre-Christian religious order in the face of a new religion, while the third

(*A Sleep of Prisoners*) deals more directly with the ordeal of Christianity in the era of fire-bombing and de-mythologizing.[78]

The noisiest and most sustained of these death knells for Christianity is that of D. H. Lawrence, the man whose gods Eliot thought the strangest:

> Down among the uneducated people you will still find Revelation rampant. . . . The huge denunciation of Kings and Rulers, and the whore that sitteth upon the waters is entirely sympathetic to a Tuesday evening congregation of colliers and colliers' wives, on a black winter night, in the great barn-like Pentecost Chapel. And the capital letters of the name: MYSTERY, BABYLON THE GREAT, THE MOTHER OF HARLOTS AND ABOMINATIONS OF THE EARTH thrill the old colliers. . . . today, Babylon means the rich and wicked people who live in luxury and harlotry somewhere in the vague distance, London, New York, or Paris worst of all, and who never once set foot in "chapel", all their lives. It is very nice, if you are poor and *not* humble—and the poor may be obsequious, but they are almost *never* humble in the Christian sense—to bring your grand enemies down. . . . If you listen to the Salvation Army you will hear that they are going to be very grand. Very grand indeed, since they get to heaven. . . . The Apocalypse has been running for nearly two thousand years: the hidden side of Christianity: and its work is nearly done. . . . This is the Christian community today, in its perpetual mean thou-shalt-not. This is how Christian doctrine has worked out in practice.[79]

And it is Lawrence's own exercise in myth-making that presents the modern reader with perhaps his greatest challenge.

It has been believed widely in this century that Christianity and the Christian era have concluded or are about to conclude, and that it is the duty of those who best understand Western man and his symbols to make way in the desert, by adjusting those symbols with care, the highway for a new religious mythology. As Lawrence writes, in *Apocalypse*:

> What was a creative god, Ouranos, Kronos, becomes at the end of the time-period a destroyer and a devourer. The god of the beginning of an era is the evil principle at the end of that era. For time moves in cycles. . . . The good potency at the beginning of the Christian era is now the evil potency at the end. . . . we are at the end of the Christian era.[80]

During most of his career, Lawrence's solution was to excoriate Christianity as a malevolent irrelevance and, in his fictions, to re-mythologize European life along lines that, after two millennia of Christianity, are no longer truly European. But at the end of his career, it appears, the most rabidly anti-Christian of modern myth-makers changed his mind—or at least his tack.

The Man Who Died (1928)—together with the very late essays, "The Risen Lord" (1929) and *Apocalypse* (1930)— represent Lawrence's last tactic in his lifelong battle with the near-corpse that refused to die. In these late pieces, Lawrence undertakes what G. S. Kirk calls a "literate reinterpretation of the myths," one that no longer pretends to be anything but "a literary creation, quite separate in form, method and intention either from spontaneous myths of the pre-literate past or from their transitional descendants." It would seem that, at the last, Lawrence recognized (in Kirk's words) that "the genuine mythopoeic urge lay in the hidden past,"[81] and that, as Victor White has written,

> It is idle . . . to suppose that our psyche can be rid of the Christ-symbol by an intellectual disavowal of Christianity. Christ is, whether we like it or not, the *Kulturheros* of our Western civilization.[82]

Or, perhaps, Lawrence came to ask himself seriously the question he had Ursula ask Birkin in *Women in Love*: " 'And if you don't believe in love, what *do* you believe in? . . . Simply in the end of the world and grass?' "[83] In any case, Lawrence evidently decided to concentrate his attention on the miracles of which the great artist actually is capable: resurrection and transfiguration.

It is clear, too, that Lawrence considered *The Man Who Died* his essential statement. He could have written a philosophical, demythologizing tract on the alterations he would have liked made in Christianity and, in fact, it is possible to read *Apocalypse* (published shortly after the *nouvelle*) as a partially de-mythologized gloss on his own New Improved Testament. But Lawrence had no use for the de-mythologizer:

> When the great figures of mythology are turned into rationalized or merely moral forces, then they lose interest. We are acutely bored by moral angels and moral devils. We are acutely bored by a "rationalized" Aphrodite.[84]

Lawrence was not giving up on myth when he turned from the homemade variety—he was simply more interested at this time in influencing his reader's psyche through the mysterious "power of suggestion" he attributed to the traditional, culturally accredited myth:

> the older a myth, the deeper it goes in the human consciousness, the more varied will be the forms it takes in the upper consciousness. We have to remember that some symbols ... can carry even our modern consciousness back for a thousand years. . . . The power of suggestion is most mysterious.[85]

If one suggests the proper symbol to a human subject, one can touch the springs of psychic life and, from those depths, a change in his "upper consciousness" (which contains the multiple "forms" of the symbol) may arise that could alter his course of action. "The old meanings control our actions," Lawrence wrote, "even when our minds have gone inert."[86] By remaking the conclusion to the Gospels, Lawrence was attempting to remake a pivotal construct in the Western "transpersonal unconscious" and, thereby, to effect a fundamental change in the way Europeans think and behave. Probably the most important of these thought/behavior complexes to Lawrence (and one of the most important for Freud and Jung) was Christendom's attitude toward love and the feminine. Lawrence believed that "the great woman of the pagan cosmos was driven into the wilderness at the end of the old epoch, and she has never been called back." On account of that error,

> All women today have a large streak of the policewoman in them. . . . poor modern Andromeda, she is forced to patrol the streets more or less in policewoman's uniform. . . . Andromeda at least had her nakedness, and it was beautiful. . . . But our modern policewomen have no nakedness, they have their uniforms.[87]

Lawrence's great pagan woman, expelled from the Christian cosmos, "must hide in the desert since she cannot die.—And there she hides, still during the weary three and a half mystic years"—which, apparently, Lawrence hoped to have some part in ending with his last testament of 1928.

In part two of *The Man Who Died*, a priestess of Isis dressed in hymen yellow and white, kept all her life in "immaculate loneliness . . . , and pure brightness" by the inadequacy of contemporary mankind, stands proudly in the "royal sunshine" of a sexualized Mediterranean landscape:

> the light stood erect and magnificent off the invisible sea, filling the hills of the coast. She went towards the sun, through the grove of Mediterranean pine-trees and evergreen oaks, in the midst of which the temple stood, on a little, tree-covered tongue of land between two bays. It was only a very little way, and then she stood among the dry trunks of the outer-most pines, on the rocks under which the sea smote and sucked, facing the open where the bright sun gloried in winter. . . . The hand of the wind brushed it strangely with shadow, as it brushed the olives of the slopes with silver.[88]

We know from the first that beneath those flowing robes and that linen tunic there beats no policewoman's heart. When the Lady of Egypt observes two of her young slaves making love in the manner Eliot derided as a "sexual operation . . . analogous to Kruschen Salts," she is repelled and turns to the shrine of the goddess whose "womb . . . waits for the touch of that other inward sun that streams its rays from the loins of the male Osiris."[89] She is the "rare" woman who waits "for the re-born man."

And who should arrive but the lately arisen Jesus—though not the Christ of the Gospels: a Lawrentian Jesus who has been convinced, it seems, by the Grand Inquisitor to renounce the "greed of giving," of universal loving—and the priestess assures him he is the reborn Osiris, son and lover of the goddess Isis. What transpires then is no surprise and the brotherly love of Christianity goes the way of all flesh, transforming its symbology on the way out. The priestess serves up a "First Supper" of warm eggs and diluted wine; Jesus forgets Peter and proclaims of the woman that "On this rock I built my life"; he complains to the Father in his New Passion, "why did you hide this from me?"; he experiences an erection and exclaims, "I am risen!"; and he is transformed from a human Son into a cosmic sun that "shall come again, sure as Spring." The heralding paraclete of the new age ushered in by this union is the escaped cock of part one—the bird for which Lawrence originally named his *nouvelle* and which is its emblem for "the greater life of the body."[90] Love cut off from its natural, carnal roots exists only by a dry exertion of will and produces only people who speak fluent catechism:

". . . how will he ascend?"
"As Elijah the Prophet, he shall go up in a glory."
"Even into the sky?"
"Into the sky."
"Then he is not risen in the flesh."
"He is risen in the flesh."
"And will he take flesh up into the sky?"
"The Father in Heaven will take him up."
The man who died said no more, for his say was over, and words beget more words, even as gnats.[91]

These are the people of the "little, narrow, personal life" to whom Christ bequeaths the earth in the Authorized Version and against whom Lawrence fulminates in *Apocalypse*; just as the priestess has libidinous slaves to ruin her view of the Mediterranean, so Lawrence's Jesus has his lower-class eunuchs. No democratic, brotherly ethos in this religion, since "The Christian, the democrat *cannot* love. Or, when he loves, when she loves, he *must* take it back, she *must* take it back."[92] Only aristocrats of the spirit may partake of the mysteries of life, which Lawrence extracts from the Christianity that he claims prevailed before John of Patmos wrote Revelation. To the mediocre masses, Lawrence leaves the mysteries of death, which the man who died found so much easier than his awakening to full-bodied life. Lawrence's alterations in the Christian *mythos*, then, would tend to engender a new religion centering upon a ritual of carnal, life-giving love; celebrating the great sensual mother/nymph and the sun-flooded magnificence of nature (not Wordsworthian: Mediterranean, pagan); excluding the proletarian and bourgeois from its mysteries; and banishing most of the "deathy" accoutrements and impulses of Christianity. Lawrence would integrate into the Western consciousness most of what Jung (and Joyce and Freud and Nietzsche) had suggested is "indispensable for human health and wholeness," the denial of which, by Protestantism especially, led Europe to become "the mother of dragons that devoured the greater part of the earth."[93]

This "paganization" of the Christian *mythos* was nothing new in Lawrence's day. As Theodore Ziolkowski writes in his *Fictional Transfigurations of Jesus*, it was "fashionable" after 1900 "to regard Jesus as the transformation of a pagan myth or cult figure." Moreover, *The Man Who Died* is, on the whole, unappealing as a work of art. The reader is too aware of the author's mockery and, while reading *The Man Who Died*, one cannot help recalling Lawrence's first description of Birkin in *Women in Love*: as a man "slightly ridiculous" when subordinating his imagination "to the common idea"— an idea that he characterizes in that novel as a "travesty."[94] However, the significance of this work does not derive either from its novelty or its artistic merit, but rather from its place in the history of the modernist myth of myth-making. In it, one of this century's foremost re-mythologizers moves from the practice of myth-making (the practice, for example, of *St. Mawr* or *The Plumed Serpent*) to that of myth-remaking and, furthermore, he attempts to delimit the scope of the modernist mania about mythology and mythologizing. When Jesus determines to leave his pregnant lover in Egypt and flee the Romans to unknown parts, we become aware of this other aspect of the *nouvelle*. The Cosmic Mother's priestess is pregnant with the future and we, like Yeats, cannot be sure "that twenty centuries of stony sleep" were not "vexed to nightmare by a rocking cradle." At the conclusion of the work that, surely, required greater *hubris* than any other fiction he wrote, Lawrence admits that even the most knowing exercise in mythologizing will bear uncertain fruit, for "the power of suggestion is most mysterious."

All along, this work has been a parable of the modern life of the Christian *mythos*, from its horrible death (during the Great War, perhaps?—in any case, at the hand of the same European imperialists who killed the fleshly Jesus), to its nauseated reawakening into the world as it is, to its aimless wandering in pursuit of the Father, to its future healing (the priestess salves the wounds of centuries when she applies her balm) by the feminine, pagan spirit. The correctness of this interpretation is suggested by Lawrence's essay, "The Risen Lord," in which he claims that only the resurrection can be an appropriate symbol for Christianity in the generation born after the First World War, for

> The young came into life, and found everything finished. Everywhere the empty crosses, everywhere the closed tombs, . . . those grey empty days between Good Friday and Easter.[95]

And he continues, in harmony with the *nouvelle*:

> In Sicily the women take into church the saucers of growing corn, the green blades rising tender and slim like green

light, in little pools, filing round the altar. It is Adonis.
It is the re-born year. It is Christ risen. . . . The Lord of
the rising wheat and plum blossoms is warm and kind
upon earth again, after having been done to death by the
evil and the jealous ones. . . . This is the image of our
inward state today.[96]

Yet the final outcome is left open—we know only that Jesus
(the quintessential spirit of the "lived myth") will come again
in spring. The most any "mythologian"—de-mythologizer or
re-mythologizer—can hope to do is represent or re-present the
myths whose actual creation and whose power to inspire right
action are beyond the scope of scholarship or of art.

· · ·

"MYTH-MAKING" is the most futile of enterprises: the features
of myth that distinguish it most sharply from other narrative
structures are its indeterminable authorship and its traditional, cultural accreditation. No modern writer can expect
that his self-conscious creations will acquire either characteristic, yet "myth-making" is a key term in the critical vocabulary and has been a principal aim of *nostos*-seeking writers
throughout the modern period. A return to cultural origins
and an escape from Christianity necessitate a return to myth—
though, in the age that invented agnosticism, mustard-gas,
and ping-pong, certain alterations in the quality of belief, and
in the myths themselves, become inevitable. The greatest of
modern myth "creators" have caught sight of the ironies
mocking them and have admitted the impossibility of their
enterprise. Yeats, for example, knew that the creation of a
"living myth" (in the sense of a traditional system of beliefs,
based upon a sacred narrative) was impossible without a new
manifestation of deity, without a Second Coming, but he went
on with his *Vision*, fully aware that it would represent an
ordering "more deliberate . . . , more systematized, more external, more self-conscious" than any myth could or should
be.[97]

Similarly, the man who wrote *The Golden Bowl* was also

author of "The Altar of the Dead," a story that can be read as a Child's Garden of Myth-making, for in it James illustrates each in turn the solemn and comic ironies of the myth-maker's undertaking, and he moralizes (with tongue bulging conspicuously in cheek) on their implications and consequences. James's George Stransom is a man whose "spiritual spaces" require filling in order to employ his native "piety" and satisfy his natural religious "inclination," but—"poor Stransom"—he is "very sure and not a little content" that he lacks the "domesticated gods" of "the religion some of the people he had known wanted him to have." Stransom is, in short, the modern man in search of a soul: a creator of myth. But instead of the "living myth," which all myth-makers dream of, Stransom creates a myth of the dead or, if you will, a dead myth, and he sets up his altar inside the temple of the fading faith to whose "old symbols" the myth-maker denies any possibility of "return."

This taut, grim comedy broadens when Stransom discovers that his personal myth has attracted a true believer, and the rest of James's fable traces the history of Stransom's faith from the first communion to nonconformity and schism. The myth-maker may yearn dearly for a flock but, as James knew, synthetic myths, however appealing aesthetically, are not made to sustain a community of souls. Finally, with impeccable taste, Stransom dies, for the sake of aesthetic symmetry, beside the shrine he has built—to "complete the subtle and complex relations," "to round it off"—and his lone disciple (the audience: the object of every myth-maker's designs) is left with her equivocal change of heart and an unlimited supply of candles, with a defunct myth-maker's head on her shoulder and a "great dread" of what is yet to come.

Thus, in 1895, on the threshold of the twentieth century, Henry James proffered his sympathies to the much put-upon modern reader, who must bear the burden of deriving order from the countless volumes of self-dramatic, and often comic, myth-making or mytheory. As his parting "touch," James determined to leave Stransom's disciple in the church where Stransom found her, for there is nowhere else to go. However much post-Christians may desire a new myth-system or the return to an older one, the Christian *mythos* is inescapable, pervades the whole culture. And the edifice in which we, James's readers, are left is described in the closing paragraph as a "dusky church," which, despite (or, perhaps, partly because of) the mythologian's services, becomes increasingly dusky all the time. In the absence of culturally accredited solutions (Lévi-Strauss to the contrary, the psychoanalyst has not quite replaced the priest), "fictive things" will "Wink as they will."[98] Personal fictions—private solutions—are by definition tentative, piecemeal, and partial.

The Politics of Return:
An Admonitory Postlogue

Pallas Athena was disturbed, and said:
"Ah, how bitterly you need Odysseus, then!
High time he came back to engage these upstarts.
I wish we saw him standing helmeted
there in the doorway, holding shield and spear,
looking the way he did when I first knew him. . . ."
Odyssey Book 1

The Classics! it is the Classics
. . . that Desolate Europe with Wars.
William Blake, "On Homer's Poetry"

TO UNDERTAKE a personal *nostos*, psychological and domestic, is cataclysmic enough, yet the urge to make that return communal appears to be either essential to the enterprise or else irresistible to its most devoted proponents. Serious people are not often satisfied with partial, piecemeal, or theoretical solutions to problems that seem, in origin, to be cultural. The varieties of personal, psychological *égarements* in Rousseau's *Julie* all derive from a societal *égarement* and, for each type, a return to personal health requires, simultaneously, a political solution. Even the personal *nostos* of the *Odyssey* requires a certain amount of social engineering: nostalgia, throughout the poem, is equivalent to slaughtering Penelope's suitors. Book 24 threatens to expand that engineering to the *polis* at large, and such a bloodbath impends that the gods are moved to impose a definitive public settlement between the claims of a cloying, parasitic present and an avenging, heroic past.

The "Book 24 aspect" of the modern *nostos* surfaces mainly in those theorists who identify the twentieth-century return with precedent epochs of Renaissance or renascence. Just before the onset of our daemonically driven century, Jacob Burckhardt introduced the conception of Western history as a single fabric in which there are places of special brightness and unexceptional darkness. Hegel, Ranke, Michelet, and other pioneers in the philosophy of history had viewed European civilization as a story in which the wise could observe the laws of its unfolding. But Buckhardt, as we have seen, found the story disappointing. Its plot was supposed to be circular—antiquity and modernity were meant to join at the Renaissance—but this elegant geometry had proved to be wishful thinking. Hence, Burckhardt could see no development in history but only a cultural ideal (the fifth-century Athenian) and the sustained failures or periodic successes in living up to it.

Burckhardt's supposedly objective definition of Athenian and Florentine brilliance was crafted to be the perfect antithesis of mid-nineteenth-century grayness. His volumes on the Italian Renaissance and his notes on Greek history are not mere descriptions of long-gone cultural configurations. For those who could make out their highest-frequency emissions—for those like Nietzsche, Burckhardt's friend and correspondent—these works were blueprints for a modern renascence. Taken in this way, Burckhardt's enormously influential studies (his *Renaissance*, in German alone, sold some half-million copies) do not seem especially benign. He strongly emphasizes, in the opening of his 1860 volume, that the humanists' revival of Greco-Roman culture would have led nowhere without the rebirth of the special kind of political order that cultural brilliance demands. The "state as a work of art" is how he describes that order, and he defines its principal elements, in various places, with perfect lucidity: the promotion of the artist to a position of public importance; the weakening of ecclesiastical authority and of absolute moral standards, in favor of a politically determined morality; the sudden birth of fiercely competitive nation-states, dominated by an "iron will," spurred "violently forward"; and, above all, the subordination of individual freedom to the good of the *polis* and its cultural aspirations.

These ideas were to have an awful future, one that would

culminate in the political career of Ezra Pound and other cultural fascists. The philosophy of history began to take on a combination of cultural and political significance with the rise of the *Action Française* group. For Charles Maurras, the Athenian dedication to Athena and to the intellectual life was the high point of world history.[1] In his *"Invocation à Minerve,"* Maurras defined the essence of Greek culture as wisdom and reason, clarity and precision, taste and harmony; but also as order and purity, power and violence. The Greek sensibility was unpitying, ruthless in its pursuit of simplicity and distinction. The Hellenic perfection required a severe axiological ranking of men and ideas in order to eliminate eccentricity—the mark of Semites, Orientals, and romantics.[2] That the romantics' vision of Hellas was utterly different— libertarian and democratic—from his own authoritarian one was only further proof of their eccentricity. Maurras claimed to be able to say what was or was not eccentric because, for him, objective nature and subjective tradition, when seen as the Greeks saw them, were one. Nothing essential had altered since Homeric times, certainly nothing had improved; modern times, in fact, must be less civilized than Homer's to the extent that modern men are the less Homeric.[3]

Like Burckhardt, then, Maurras viewed history as a general darkness with hours of brightness interspersed, and, he argued, the twentieth century could become a "privileged moment" if it would return to the authoritarian paganism of the Greco-Latin traditions (especially as embodied in the Roman Church).[4] And Maurras' solutions to the problems of post-Reformation modernity were neither theoretical in approach nor individual in thrust: the *Action Française* aligned its cultural classicism with the hypernationalism of the early twentieth century. Maurras' *nationalisme intégral* was based on a principle he learned from his mentor, Maurice Barrès (*Scènes et doctrines du nationalisme*), that nationalism is a kind of classicism, especially in the case of France. In the words of Maurras' *Romantisme et révolution*: "The old France had the classical spirit."

Much of this outlook passed directly into the mainstream

of fascist cultural thinking. The most notorious of the modernist "fascists" drew their politics, to a degree never fully explored, from their devotion to an ideology of return and to a Burckhardtian yearning for the cultural renascence which the "state as a work of art" could make feasible. Wyndham Lewis, for example, based his complex and protean politics on the *Action Française*/T. E. Hulme conception of the classicism/romanticism distinction. "If you asked a man of a certain set whether he preferred the classics to the romantics," Lewis notes in *Men Without Art*, "you could deduce from that what his politics were." In *The Art of Being Ruled* (note that governance and citizenship are arts), Lewis states that he was first attracted to the Italian fascist program because it claimed to revive the Roman imperial grandeur. (In 1925, for instance, Mussolini had arranged his squadrons into a facsimile of the Roman legions, instructing his troops to give the ancient salute. Nor was this attempt unique to Mussolini and the twentieth century; Cavour's political and military movement for the unification of Italy had been known as the *Risorgimento*.)

Lewis eventually gave up on Mussolini but, in both *Time and Western Man* and in his later journals, it becomes clear that, when Lewis rejected the fascists, it was because he had determined that Il Duce was not a genuine reviver of antiquity but a "Byronic *passéiste*." The authoritarian state in Germany seemed to Lewis, until the beginning of the war when he repudiated it in the *The Hitler Cult*, to be a political manifestation of the classic ideal of order and, also, a society in which a classicist art might flourish. In his *Hitler* book of 1930, Lewis refers, almost wistfully, to "the Hitlerist dream . . . of an eminent classical serenity," in opposition to those aspects of modern culture that Lewis himself loathed: romanticism, exoticism, and jazz. (Of course, the Nazis had worked their public-relations machine hard to acquire this image—particularly at the German-sponsored Olympics of 1936, where Aryan athletes were made to appear as "Greek" as possible.) When none of Lewis's political hunches proved correct, he withdrew somewhat from politics, became a "One

Worlder," and wrote in favor of a political system in which the artist could be left alone to do his critically important work. Even in political retreat, Lewis's assumption was Burckhardtian: that the interests of the arts—of the new renaissance—susperceded all others.

• • •

THE "BOOK 24 ASPECT" of the modernist *nostos* is nowhere more apparent than in the political writings of Ezra Pound, and nowhere is it a more instructive concept. After Pound read *Ulysses*, he determined that his *Cantos*, already in progress, would need reworking in order to fill in the part of Odysseus' story that Joyce chose to slight: the political settlement of Book 24. The *nostos* of Pound's epic is *polis*-centered: it emphasizes the building of the city of Dioce, "whose terraces are the colour of stars," in which man, nature, and the gods form an organic whole. We make our *nekuia* in "Canto 1"—we look back to our ultimate roots and repair the mistakes of the past—in order to reach, by an oceanic route (which, we note, is "flowing backward"), a city of "stone trees—out of water," a "forest of marble" like the Doric city of Athens. Following on the first canto (which ends "so that"), the remainder of the poem is a kind of *ut* clause. *The Cantos* look backwards to the culture's numinous source and to its periods of glowing renascence in order to help the twentieth century achieve its own renaissance. From beginning of Pound's career, this notion possessed him. In late 1912, Pound wrote his first, full-length social essay, *Patria Mia*, and its theme was that America could regain health if its national art could achieve a *"risorgimento."* For the young Pound, as for Shelley before him, it was not that art tends to flourish in a healthy society, but the reverse. Eventually, he would appreciate that a reciprocal relationship is involved ("Usura rusteth the chisel /It rusteth the craft and the craftsman"),[5] but at the start of his political involvement, it was the artist's role that impressed him.

In his 1915 "Chronicles" for Lewis's journal, *Blast*, Pound was still impressed—the public might struggle, but the London-Paris Vortex of *Blast* would lead them aright nonetheless:

> BLAST does not attempt to reconcile the homo canis with himself. Of course the homo canis will follow us. It is the nature of the homo canis to follow. They growl but they follow.[6]

And he was not merely reiterating the avant-garde/Philistine notions of an earlier generation of modernist writers. Pound was applying them to politics—applying them, in fact, to the First World War:

> BLAST alone dared to present the actual discords of modern "civilization," DISCORDS now only too apparent in the open conflict between teutonic atavism and unsatisfactory Democracy.[7]

The same idea, presented in much the same way, showed up again a dozen years later and, if anything, he expressed his belief then even more emphatically than he had under the immediate pressures of the Great War:

> The artist . . . is always too far ahead of any revolution, or reaction, or counter-revolution, or counter-reaction for his vote to have any immediate result; and no party programme ever contains enough of his programme to give him the least satisfaction. The party that follows him wins; and the speed with which they set about it, is the measure of their practical capacity and intelligence.[8]

It is evident that Pound's more sympathetic critics (Hugh Kenner and Noel Stock, for example) are correct to assert that Pound accepted much of what the fascists did in early years on the assumption that Mussolini would end up by following his régime's leading poet into a new renaissance. Until his last years (the years of recantation and silence), Pound saw art as "the real history," artists as civilization's "registering instruments," and—especially after his arrest in Genoa—he assumed that he himself was the mind of Europe. Stock is perceptive to conclude that it was not the economic or political order as such which obsessed Pound from the mid-teens forward, but rather that

> In so far as there was a single factor which governed his thought for the next forty years and the direction he took in both poetry and politics, it was this ideal of the artist's place in a smoothly functioning society.[9]

Pound was at all times the artist first: the *homme politique* was always a subordinate persona—useful, in the main, when writing *The Cantos*, his "poem including history." When, in their much-touted meeting, Mussolini asked Pound why he wanted to set his "ideas in order," Pound's response was: "For my poem."[10] Pound made his priorities clear in print as well as in private. His "Introduction to the Economic Nature of the United States" commences with this highly significant statement:

> This is not a SHORT History of the Economy of the United States. For forty years I have schooled myself, not to write an economic history of the U.S. or any other country, but to write an epic poem which begins "In the Dark Forest", crosses the Purgatory of human error, and ends in the light, and "fra i maestri di color che sanno." For this reason I have had to understand the NATURE of error.[11]

And the first of the Pisan Cantos, which opens with a lament on the execution of Mussolini ("The enormous tragedy . . . / by the heels at Milano"), is essentially a poem of triumph, for—whatever has happened in the unstable realm of political events—"certain images be formed in the mind / to remain there" and will remain forever as part of *The Cantos* "in the stillness outlasting all wars."

It is safe to say of Pound what it probably is not even thinkable to say of any other modern writer involved in politics: that his social interests and convictions all were directed by his concern for art—for his own artistic work, for art in general, and, above all, for the twentieth-century renaissance.[12] In his 1933 article, "Murder by Capital," the greatest of literary instigators wrote that the unemployment question which had plagued him during the preceding quarter-century had been "the unemployment of Gaudier-Brzeska, T. S. Eliot, Wyndham Lewis the painter, E. P. the present writer, and of twenty or thirty musicians, and fifty or more other makers in stone, in paint, in verbal composition."[13] It was, he writes, only many years later that he decided the artist's unemployment problem had more general implications:

> If there was (and I admit that there was) a time when I thought this problem could be solved without regard to the common man, humanity in general, the man in the street, the average citizen, etc., I retract, I sing palinode, I apologise.[14]

He goes on to praise the solutions of Major Douglas and Mussolini in terms of their benign influence on art:

> C. H. Douglas is the first economist to include creative art and writing in an economic scheme, and the first to give the painter or sculptor or poet a definite reason for being interested in economics; namely that a better economic system would release more energy for invention and design.[15]

Mussolini receives applause, in "Murder by Capital," for emphasizing the "dimension of quality"; in *Guide to Kulchur*, for telling "his people that poetry is a necessity *to the state*"; [16] and, in the tract whose title Mussolini shares with the third American president, Pound commends Italian fascists for their architectural restoration projects.[17] In the same way, Pound's hatred of bourgeois values, liberal democracy, capitalism, usury, and Protestant Christianity derived from what he understood as their hostility toward the "better tradition"—the classical tradition—in aesthetics. A bourgeois with political power is a disaster for civilization: the *Guide to Kulchur* informs tourists that "we have been governed by boors, we have been governed by pot-bellied vulgarians" and that, therefore, no English or American government since the First World War would do anything "in any way however slight or remote" that might "conduce to support . . . of art or letters."[18] And democracy—a system in which sovereignty rests with a "bourgeois mass" insufficiently civilized to resent its governors' bungling—is likewise inimical to the arts. Worse yet, the capitalist (economic democrat) will invest only in a fast-selling melodrama or a sentimental novel, while his familiar companion, the usurer, will underwrite only works that tend to blur discrimination.[19]

These examples of the way in which artistic considerations could lead Pound to adopt certain social and economic positions seem fairly reasonable from the modernist's point of view. But Pound also was capable of making connections between aesthetic and social concerns that were dubious, to say the least. In the second number of *Blast*, Pound reported the story, mildly amusing, of an inconsiderate, bell-ringing Anglican clergyman: "Lest the future age be misled." Twenty-three years later, he included this "note in very small print" in *Guide to Kulchur*, as explanation of his anti-Protestant bias:

I was brought up in American school and sunday school. Took the stuff for granted, and at one time with great seriousness. Questionings aroused by the truly filthy racket imposed on denizens of Kensington, W. 8, by a particular parson. It appeared to me impossible that any clean form of teaching cd. lead a man, or group, to cause that damnable and hideous noise. . . . Vigorous anti-clerical phase ensued. NOT based on noise itself but on the states of mind necessary to induce that gross and piglike tolerance of infamous sound. . . . But for the noise I shd. not have been started investigating.[20]

And the next paragraph (in regular-size print) begins, "I am talking about civilization."

In like manner, Pound could dismiss whole epochs of human history and whole national cultures on account of the noise, stench, or eyesores produced in them. "Anyone," Pound wrote, "who has seen the furniture at Schönbrun ought to understand the flop of the Austrian Empire, and anyone who saw it before the flop ought to have known that the flop was coming. . . . a people who could tolerate such an emperor and an emperor who could put up with such furniture were well ready for the ash-can."[21] By the mid-to-late 1930s, when he produced *Jefferson and/or Mussolini* and *Guide to Kulchur* (probably his most important social essays), Pound was convinced that— while the highest "volitional" genius could overcome any cultural situation—good artists with less forceful personalities could be harmed seriously by a perverse social ambience. This is so, at least in part, because the artist requires that his culture accept mythical concepts and ethical values of a sort which can be included in his aesthetic "mechanism."[22] Pound, furthermore, argued that a new cultural construct, based on the ancient and Renaissance constructs, was needed urgently, both to furnish the missing external cogs for the artist's mechanism and to alter current patterns of taste in order to encourage a higher standard of artistic production.

On second thought, "argued" is perhaps not the word for what Pound does in his *Guide*. Pound makes his "points" there about cultural urgencies in much the same way as he does in his poetry, and the poetic procedure of his ideological prose tells us much about the direction of his politics. After several long paragraphs presenting exempla taken from medieval and Islamic history—each intended to illustrate an historical moment when usury was firmly under some wise thumb—he lurches suddenly into the modern world and commences to ridicule its most vulnerable monument:

> The black darkness of Europe occurred not in the "dark ages", hitherto so called, but in the ages of usury. By that I mean when usury was subterranean, unnoticed, undenounced, camouflaged under thrift propaganda, mercantilist tosh, down to the filth of Manchester and the slop of Victoria's time.
>
> This is not rabid prejudice against Mrs. Albert Memorial. I hold (naturally) that the pseudo-gothic was the result of causes.[23]

Pound's meaning is lodged in the opposition of the healthy, medieval/aristocratic leadership and the diseased, modern/bourgeois "filth"; it is manifest in the contrast of "dark ages" and the genuine Gothic with "black darkness" and the "pseudogothic." Many long passages—sometimes whole essays—out of Pound's socio-economic corpus must be read in this way: must be read, in fact, as we read *The Cantos*.[24] Pound made no bones about the fact that he constructed these social pieces out of the "good bits" that did not make it into his epic, much as Eliot composed his first quartet out of leftovers from his dramatic writing:

> In fact the records of rascality (as conserved in fragments of law records) are so good one grudges them to the prose page, and wants to reserve them for poetry.[25]

Moreover, Pound's social essays, like Eliot's, have a markedly musty, Man of Letters-ish scent. Both writers assumed that the poet's political responsibility is of a different order from that of ordinary commentators and, in the *Guide*'s "Digest of the Analects," Pound defined that responsibility as making certain "that the terminology" of public discourse "was exact." Pound believed that the poet could do no greater service to the social order than to make a "precise use of words," for that enterprise "is bound in the long run to be useful to the state and the world at large."[26] It is instructive to recall that Olga Rudge, in Pound's post-war defense, published a selection of the poet's Rome Radio broadcast transcripts under the title, *If This Be Treason*, and that—to the shock of many ill-informed anti-Poundeans—they addressed almost exclusively questions about the arts. Of course, Miss Rudge was careful to exclude certain speeches, but it is nonetheless crucial to realize the extent to which Pound risked prosecution for a capital crime in order to broadcast literary propaganda. Almost a generation before, Pound already had decided that the "necessary elements" for a new renaissance were "an indiscriminate enthusiasm" and "a propaganda."[27]

To come to terms with details of this kind out of Pound's own life requires a sympathetic exertion more strenuous than any demanded by his poetry, and yet the life and the poem are, in some sense, identical. The most elusive allusions in *The Cantos* derive not from Pound's erudition but from his personal experiences. The idea behind *The Cantos* was that the poet's life, in process of *nostos*, and the life of the West, in process of *nostos*, should coincide, and that together they should become one with a schematic, Odyssean poem which would celebrate that coincidence and enact that union. Pound was unwilling even to appropriate the expedient that his masters, Homer and Dante, had adopted—to prophesy events of the near past from an imaginary vantage point in more distant history—so confident was he that the twentieth century was the epoch of ultimate return. Probably no other artist had ever attempted so energetically and on so large a scale to reorganize both his own life and that of his entire civilization according to the principles of art. Nor is it mere psychological speculation to attribute this motive to Pound's behavior. In the first number of *Blast*, Pound wrote that "the DESIGN of the future" was already "in the grip of the human Vortex."[28] His alliance with *some* revolutionary political movement was in the cards from the beginning, for he could not implement his design alone. It was only a question of which movement was the most aesthetically appealing or historically inevitable and, as William Chace has shown, Pound's attraction to the radical Left was genuine and continued for some time.[29]

It sometimes seems that Pound decided in favor of the fascists because, artistically speaking, "The fascist revolution is infinitely more INTERESTING than the Russian revolution because it is not a revolution according to preconceived type."[30] Stock's biography also reports that certain statements by the fascist and Nazi finance ministers encouraged Pound to believe that those régimes eventually would adopt the Douglasite/Gesellite economic structure: never mind that such a structure would be based upon specious objections to the free market, what mattered was that the system would be as self-consistent as a symbolist poem and would lay emphasis where it belonged—on the state's "cultural heritage."[31] Moreover, the fascists had "style," and Pound was inclined to associate style with truth.[32] In *Guide to Kulchur* he further associated "form sense" with his "discovery" of Mussolini and with Lewis's discovery of Hitler,[33] while, in *Jefferson and/or Mussolini*, he insisted upon analogies between Il Duce and Remy De Gourmont,[34] and between former journalist Mussolini and an ideal little-magazine editor.[35] But Pound was most explicit when contending that no "estimate" of Mussolini would be valid

> unless it *starts* from his passion for construction. . . . Treat him as anything save the artist and you will get muddled with contradictions.[36]

What Pound could have hoped to accomplish by the use of such tortured similes is made clearer in an autumn 1934 letter to the editor of *The Criterion*, in which he attempted to manipulate Eliot's Burkean sensibility ("One element of the Duce's gamut is the continual gentle diatribe against all that is . . . against historic process") and his post-symbolist taste (Pound compared Mussolini's recent "Milan speech" to a Brancusi sculpture), while minimizing fascism's totalitarian claims and the threat it posed to international security. Then, aiming directly at *The Criterion*'s readership, Pound issued a challenge to "Lily-liver'd literati" to "exercise their perception of style" in matters of politics and, by strong implication, to join him in an all-Europe, fascist-sponsored renaissance. This letter is far from being Pound's only published volley in the campaign to shame the modernist avant-garde into organizing itself as a political vanguard. Pound obviously was thinking of the art work (and drawing upon personal experience as a literary impresario) when he wrote of the state, in *Jefferson and/or Mussolini*, that

> when a single mind is sufficiently ahead of the mass a one-party system is bound to occur *as actuality* whatever the details of form in administration. . . . One might speculate as to how far any great constructive activity CAN occur save under a *de facto* one-party system.[37]

Elsewhere in the same book, he practically identifies government and verse: "The real life in regular verse is an irregular movement underlying. Jefferson thought the formal features of the American system would work. ...."[38] Like the state, "poetry is totalitarian."[39] And like verse, the state should put order first, above all other priorities. In 1911, Pound exerted himself in the interest of a classicist verse "as much like granite as it can be ... austere, direct, free from emotional slither"; in 1933, he campaigned with equal fury on behalf of the "lovers of ORDER" in politics, and in 1940, for statesmen whose concern was "not less" for "order than liberty."[40]

But Pound did not dream up his art/state analogy merely to provide "outside support" for an ideology he wanted to foist on his fellow writers. He believed in an objective universe organized along the lines of a modern poem, where each element relates in a specifiable way to each other constituent element and to the poem as a whole. Thus the analogy of poetics and politics, like the analogy he perceived between metaphor and nature, "is more than an analogy, it is identity of structure."[41] Twenty years before the publication of the *Anthropologie structurale*, Pound wrote of "immoral geometries" and of what he viewed as the highly civilized desire "to regulate terrestrial law on [the] heavenly model."[42] He thought that, through complete mastery of the laws governing verse (a mastery Pound probably could claim without *hubris*), he was in contact with an objective and universally applicable paradigm. What Pound did not apprehend (or, more likely, refused to account for) was cosmic incorrigibility: the certainty that our universe will defeat any explanation and every theory. Pound's tragedy was that he realized many years too late that human life is impervious to schematization and that he was for many years unaware of the possibility that it was just that realization (of imperfectible imperfection) that drove the world's first artist to invent fiction.

It is only after the fall of fascist Italy that *The Cantos* betoken any understanding, however dim, that in the real world the poet *qua* poet can only lament, pray, fantasize, record, refresh, or—the muses permitting—create out of ugliness and chaos a beautiful (though fictional) order:

That maggots shd/ eat the dead bullock
DIGENES, διγενές but the twice crucified
               where in history will you find it?
yet say this to the Possum: a bang, not a whimper,
    with a bang not with a whimper,
To build the city of Dioce whose terraces are the colour
                    of stars.
The suave eyes, quiet, not scornful,
               rain also is of the process.
What you depart from is not the way
and olive tree blown white in the wind
washed in the Kiang and Han
what whiteness will you add to this whiteness,
                       what candor?

. . . .

"I believe in the resurrection of Italy" quia impossible est
    4 times to the song of Gassir
          now in the mind indestructible[43]

But Pound still believed ("Canto 84") that "out of all this beauty something must come," and it was not until the 1960s, when he had settled down once more in the (now democratic) Republic of Italy, that his resignation became complete and the oracle fell silent. "Words no good" were the only words which the author of *The Cantos* spoke to the interviewer from the *New York Times*, but in their eloquent concision they bestowed the contrite blessing of modernism's last survivor upon the post-modernist experiment.

• • •

POUND's fundamental notions about the poet's social role were entirely commonplace in post-Shelleyan Europe, and yet he was to spend a quarter of his working life behind bars for the commission of political crimes. More curious still, that mainstream modernist would find himself opposed with the greatest virulence by a majority of the intellectual-artistic community. Even Jean Genet enjoyed the support of his fellow writers, but Pound's offenses proved to be less forgivable. The reasons for this are complex. It is entirely possible that, just as literati had flocked to Freud and Jung in an act of mass narcissism, so they may have retreated from Pound's side in an act of horrified self-recognition. Pound represented (albeit, in a most radical way) the historical viewpoint of modernism and, in defense of that ideology, was more than willing to join a political movement which, he believed, would restructure Europe in ways that would make it once more a place where the arts could flourish. The postwar reaction to Pound, and to modernist aesthetics in general, began as a kind of self-accusation—an act of penance—by modernists who saw in the ideology they shared with Pound a totalitarian *telos*.

For within the world of a modernist art work, there is no right to free assembly or free speech, little social mobility, and no guarantee of a fair trial: yet all is done for a good cause. Seen from this angle, Western aesthetics, from Aristotle and Horace to Mallarmé and Pound, have been gnostic and totalitarian. As W. H. Auden has expressed this viewpoint:

> A society which really was like a poem and embodied all the esthetic values of beauty, order, economy, subordination of detail to the whole effort, would be a nightmare of horror, based on selective breeding, extermination of the physically or mentally unfit, absolute obedience to its Director, and a large slave class kept out of sight in cellars.[44]

—a statement that has the air of a retraction coming from the poet who a decade earlier had written of "necessary murder" for the just cause.[45] Auden continues, in his questioning of the classical tradition:

> The frightful falsehood which obsessed the Greeks and Romans and for which mankind has suffered ever since, was that government was a similar activity to art, that human beings are a medium like language out of which the gifted politician creates a good society as the gifted poet creates a good poem.[46]

What came between "Spain" (1937) and "Squares and Oblongs" (1948) was the Second World War. After reading "Spain," George Orwell suggested that the poet see firsthand "the struggle" about which he had written, then think again; and, when Auden did just that, his viewpoint altered dramatically.

In the aftermath of that war, an important segment of the avant-garde moved quickly to repudiate Pound and the other great modernists whose political attitudes had been equivocal or worse during the crisis. John R. Harrison summarizes this group's outlook:

> What Yeats, Pound, Lewis, and Eliot wanted in literature was barrenness, a hard intellectual approach ruled by the authority of strict literary principles. They rejected the humanist tradition in literature, and in society, the democratic humanitarian tradition. The same principles governed their social criticism as their literary criticism and led them to support the fascist cause, either directly as Pound and Lewis did, or indirectly.[47]

For some, the war experience required a complete repudiation of the artist-as-legislator and kindred concepts. "Poetry," Auden said in his postwar formulation, "is a game of knowledge"—and the operative element in that sentence is the absent, though understood, word: *only*. Art has no special claims on our attention, can work no symbolist magic, cannot even produce effects that the most ancient authorities asserted it could: "If I understand," writes Auden, "what Aristotle means when he speaks of catharsis, I can only say he is wrong."[48] And the Western poetic tradition—which, according to the modernists, attained its apotheosis in the first half of the twentieth century—has been wrong, because catharsis (for example) "is an effect produced, not by works of art but by . . . monster rallies at which ten thousand girl guides form themselves into the national flag. . . . Orpheus who moved stones is the archetype, not of the poet, but of Goebbels."[49]

The revulsion felt in contemplating the war and its literary sideshows helped to engender a new aesthetic outlook, which—

in part to denote its antagonism toward Pound, his modernist colleagues, and their classicist forebears—has come to be known as "post-modernism." Geoffrey Barraclough contends that "harmonious balance was no longer acceptable" in the "post-Hitler, post-Hiroshima world," that "the preoccupations of the inter-war years, remote from those of the nineteenth century, were almost equally remote from those of the post-war world."[50] The contemporary German composer Karlheinz Stockhausen, for instance, has said he will not use regular rhythms in his music because they remind him of Nazi radio broadcasts, and his "anti-teleological," anti-harmonic compositions (e.g., *Stimmung*)—whose fragments musicians may play in any order they choose—are based in large part on postwar ideological considerations. The highly organized productions of the modernists are associated with political barbarism in many minds and their perfectionist, classicist aesthetic has been strongly repudiated.

Iris Murdoch and others reject purity and consistency in favor of messy, random particularity, and Murdoch joins Jean-Paul Sartre in chastising the earlier writers of the century for their loss of interest in freedom and humanity. For Sartre, the novel is written by a free man, presupposes a free man as its reader, and is about freedom; for Murdoch, the novel is a "house of fiction for free characters to live in." In a 1959 essay revealingly titled "The Sublime and the Beautiful Revisited," Murdoch claims that

> A great novelist is essentially tolerant, that is, displays a real apprehension of persons other than the author as having a right to exist and to have a separate mode of being which is important and interesting to themselves.[51]

Or, in Alain Robbe-Grillet's version of the same idea, the anti-novelist presents The Thing (*any* thing—not just the human person) as itself, without forcing it at quill-point to serve as a symbol for some other thing. In America for some years now, "painters" and "sculptors" have propped planks against gallery walls or signed pre-existing objects and have asserted that they are works of art according to the post-modern definition, whereby the artist has no poetic license to coerce his materials.

Members of the Black Mountain school, who sponsored a literary equivalent of this artistic "objectism," made it plain that a primary source of the new aesthetic could be found in their reaction to the Second World War. In a discussion with Donald Allen, Robert Creeley stated that

> in 1945 . . . a war had ended, and men of my particular generation felt almost an immediate impatience with what was then to be regarded as a solution. Many of us had been involved in this huge global nightmare, and we came back to our specific personal lives, situations, feeling a great confusion and at times a great resentment. . . . So we had that reason to move upon . . . a clarity that could confront these dilemmas more adequately. . . .[52]

Stephen Spender likewise has turned post-modernist under postwar pressures and has pointed a self-accusing finger at the role that the modernist art of myth-making played in Europe's greatest catastrophe:

> Modern life has imitated apocalyptic modern art . . . successfully. . . . When nature comes full circle and copies unnatural art, then art has to move on to something else. It may even have to move back to nature.[53]

Others will not go even this far, will not even make the effort to construct a new, untainted aesthetic: composer John Cage has offered us "Four Minutes and Thirty-three Seconds of Silence," while (more to the point) T. W. Adorno has demanded: "No poetry after Auschwitz." It is entirely possible, Claude Lévi-Strauss said in 1959, that art may vanish from Western civilization altogether and, like a good post-modernist, he questioned (as George Steiner continues to question) whether that necessarily would be an alarming development, for the greatest artistic achievements have occurred in the most despotic societies: a lesson Burckhardt taught us, though with another moral in mind.

The invention of writing itself, says Lévi-Strauss, tends to occur in societies

> consisting of masters and slaves. . . . When we consider the first uses to which writing was put, it would seem quite clear that it was connected first and foremost with power. . . . Therefore, the problem . . . becomes more complicated and appears two-dimensional. . . . the essential problem is to know whether, for the past few centuries, the evolution of . . . art has been a constructive advance, or whether it has been progressively destructive, so that, at this moment, we may be experiencing the last phase of the destruction.[54]

Lévi-Strauss does not question the modernists' claim to have been a "last phase"—does not question the modernists' historical ideology. What he and other post-modernists challenge is the value of what was "epiphanized" by the modernist achievement. They challenge the value of the Western classical tradition. The connection made between modernism and totalitarianism on the one hand, and between modernism and the classical tradition on the other, has led to a crisis in aesthetics that is, at base, axiological. Who is to prescribe what privileges to which sets of objects, and on the basis of what claims to superiority? Once the concept of a hierarchy of value is rejected in the name of democracy, it is reasonable to suppose that, in the end, there will be no art: no privileged class of objects. Already the *objet trouvé* is being considered too much a "singling-out" for a democratic world.

Recently, some traditionalist critics have endeavored to salvage the remains of what Donald Davie has called "literary cultre" by minimizing the charges against prewar modernism and its proponents. We may read Davie's latest book on Pound not so much as a general introduction to the poet's work as an attempt to undermine the post-modern outlook by reaching, through a popular series, a larger audience than he could have hoped for with a specialist study. His conclusion is that Pound's political viewpoint had in any case . . . nothing to do with his being "liter-ary"; and so Pound's case by itself gives no warrant for concluding, as some have done, that fascism is a political false solution that twentieth century literary men are par-ticularly prone to.[55]

It very well may be essential for the healthy development of our culture that we embrace Pound and his fellow modernists, but we must not do so on false grounds (Pound's politics, in Pound's view, had everything "to do with his being 'liter-ary' "): the issues at stake are crucial, and we are liable to end by devaluing the important lessons of the Second World War. Already this has begun to happen, and the flippant tone of these sentences, written by a lesser Pound scholar than Donald Davie, is deeply disturbing:

> We are often reminded nowadays that modernist litera-ture is the creation of men whose political views were anti-democratic or even patently fascist. . . . This puts admirers of modernist literature in something of a quan-dary, for we are not supposed to approve of fascism; after all, it was the fascists who started World War II and murdered millions of Jews. . . . I am inclined to regard the . . . fascism of literary intellectuals as something of a non-subject, by no means so scandalous as it is sometimes made out to be. . . . our mid-century critiques of mod-ernist Fascism . . . [are] simply a revisionist tactic by a younger generation in which to continue the difficult task of creating a post-modernist literature.[56]

Before we dismiss the World War, the Holocaust, and the resulting post-modern outlook, we must first resolve several urgent and profoundly troubling questions—and none more disturbing than the symbolism of Pound's silence during the 1960s. Davie formulates the matter with eloquence:

> noting in Pound's lifetime the false alternative of several "metapoetries" which have ended in silence, having de-stroyed the poetry that they thought to go "beyond" . . . Pound's significance . . . may be thought to turn . . . on

what we understand by "a literary civilization"; whether
we want any more of it; and supposing we do, what
chance we stand of getting it in any future that we can
foresee.[57]

Davie narrows our choices considerably. Either we embrace
Pound's achievement, the modernist apotheosis of tradition,
and continue to develop its subtleties for our own time, or
we pass over—partly from spite, largely from genuine fear
that return-oriented poetics are inseparable from reactionary
politics—into an entirely new order of civilization. And Davie
is, on the whole, correct. Every aesthetic movement that has
tried to make of poetry a nonprivileged utterance, which anyone can produce, has failed by succeeding too well. Most
recently, the "concrete poetry" movement has evaporated, as
its denial of a values-hierarchy predestined that it should, and
its leading spokesman, Ernst Gomringen, no longer publishes
poems or writes manifestoes but organizes advertisements for
a large German firm.

Sympathetic as we might be with the post-modernist viewpoint—especially when glimpsing, over our collective shoulder, the stark monument at Auschwitz—we must also ponder
Lévi-Strauss' unconcerned warning that imaginative literature
may someday disappear. We should, with Hannah Arendt,
try to survey to landscape through the modernists' eyes, for
the view from that elevation can be equally impressive:

> It would be rash indeed to discount because of artistic
> vagaries or scholarly naiveté, the terrifying roster of dis-
> tinguished men whom totalitarianism can count among
> its sympathizers, fellow-travelers, and inscribed party
> members. . . . Simply to brand as outbursts of nihilism
> this violent dissatisfaction with the prewar age and sub-
> sequent attempts at restoring it . . . is to overlook how
> justified disgust can be in a society wholly permeated with
> the ideological outlook and moral standards of the
> bourgeoisie . . . This whole world of fake security, fake
> culture, and fake life.[58]

The question is so impossibly complicated that every case presented on every side contains at least a partial truth—and yet, there is a sense in which the whole issue (at least, as regards Pound) is unnervingly simple. As Joseph Frank has written, the modernism/fascism association was not international and at no time involved a necessary correlation.[59] Pound's union of aesthetic and social concerns has no genuine logic other than that which existed in the poet's brain. "The record shows," writes post-modernist theoretician Harold Rosenberg, "that a living connection exists between questions of form in poetry, in conventions of the bedroom, in assaults on police stations. The logic of his admiration for Renaissance art patronage led Ezra Pound to a decade behind bars."[60]

But Pound and his critics both may have fallen victim to the Hegelian presumption that (in E. H. Gombrich's concise summary) "all aspects of a culture can be traced back to one key cause of which they are the manifestations."[61] It was entirely possible to affirm a return-oriented aesthetic, support the idea of a democratic society, move to Zürich, and write *Finnegans Wake*: after all, Greece was home not merely to Pisistratus but also to Cleisthenes of Athens. Though it was nearly irresistible to demand a *rappel à l'ordre* in an age that would see two, globe-consuming wars, we must recall the argument of Auden's "Squares and Oblongs" and observe that the poetics/politics identification need not have been made in Pound's day and, with his example in mind, need never be made again. The problem is that those who, like Iris Murdoch, assault return and reaction commit the same error as Pound when they attempt to build a post-modernist aesthetic on liberal-humanitarian foundations. Realists, symbolists, modernists, post-modernists—all have erred in presuming that the paradigmatic unity which Hegel finds in each era of cultural history could or should be the function of conspiratorial effort on the part of an era's politicians, theologians, scientists, and aestheticians. This error has been so pervasive that, if we sought an Hegelian unity in the facets of twentieth-century culture, it might be found in the practical adaptation of the philosophy of history to our culture and our cultural politics.

Moreover, there never was for Pound a poetics/politics connection of the type that "neo-liberals" and anti-novelists have
claimed to ameliorate with their greater respect for persons
and objects: "a leaf is a *LEAF*," Pound wrote in a postwar
letter from St. Elizabeth's Hospital, just as he had insisted in
1912 that, before it is a symbol for anything, "a hawk is a
hawk."[62] There is no reason, then, why contemporary writers
should not undertake a thoroughgoing rehabilitation of modernism's perfectionist aesthetic, being careful to dissociate
themselves from Poundean politics and to avoid remaking his
mistakes. Instead, we continue to fight the Second World War
on the battlefield of literature. Modernism roughly coincides
with the Crisis of Europe (1914–45: World War I, the Depres-
sion, World War II) and consists unmistakably of crisis art.
But the trauma is past and we must deal now with its after-
effects. To use the Odyssean metaphor: *nostos*-seeking Europeans have slaughtered the suitors only to discover that they
now must live on an island full of the dead men's relations.
As Odysseus discovers in the last book of Homer's poem, the
time must come to arrange a prudent truce.

Frank Kermode has suggested that one thing needed is for
writers to develop a healthy "clerical scepticism" about their
mythic fictions, for

> If we treat them as something other than they are we are
> yielding to irrationalism; we are committing an error
> against which the intellectual history of our century should
> certainly have warned us. Its ideological expression is
> fascism; its practical consequence the Final Solution.[63]

Yet, as Kermode says, skepticism is not enough: Pound was
himself a kind of clerkly skeptic. Nothing will do but a complete reconstruction of the modernist viewpoint in order to
bring it into harmony with postwar realities. But we have
been insufficiently self-conscious to manage the strenuous tasks
of renewal that have been laid upon us. Our "post-culture,"
seen in its historical context, may be little more than a futil-
itarian's projection of the modernist ideology of return.

Of "post-modern," "post-culture" artists, none is as self-conscious about his relation to modernist ideology as Samuel Beckett. His dramatic production, from *Waiting for Godot* to *Footfalls*, has for its major theme the nature of life in a world that exists after the literal fulfillment of the modernist apocalypse. In *Waiting for Godot*, written soon after the war, the return already has been effected, the climax attained, and the historical crisis passed. The temporal setting of the play is "post-": always after, always too late. Every important detail is given in the past tense: Estragon, for instance, *was* a poet. The End has passed, it seems, and, hence, teleological characterization is impossible: Pozzo, we note, is a liberal "this evening." Still, there is a sense of precise historical placement in the play. The "nineties" are said to have been "a million years ago" and, more crucially, the stage set has an eerily familiar look. A country road, a tree, a boy—Beckett takes up precisely where Yeats left off in *Purgatory*, the most apocalyptic of modernist dramas.[64] Modernism was a self-conscious Last Days phenomenon. When modernism passed from man's world, man's world was (somehow) expected to pass from God's universe. And that very nearly occurred, though not quite. Our culture survives: stubbornly, endlessly. And this is the sense one derives from all Beckettian drama—the sense, not of an ending, but of an inconclusible repetition of the moment before the end.

Even after modernism's passing, its view of history presides over the arts. Since this is (astonishingly) the case, perhaps we should consider the possibility that the modernist ideology of history has been a correct interpretation of events. More likely, however, that ideology has assumed the quality of a self-fulfilling prophecy, left by the modernists to be fulfilled through other selves. Beckett, after all, had once been Joyce's "literary secretary." In any event, that ideology's works remain with us—and our awareness of its operation, both conscious and unconscious, may be essential for our welfare. In his essay titled, "The Modern," Kermode reviews Eliot's last formulation of the historical ideology ("We have enlarged our conception of the past. . . . in the light of what is new we see the past in a new pattern"), and remarks: "In the end what

Simone Weil called 'decreation' (easy to confuse with destruction) is the true modernist process in respect of form and the past. Or if it is not we really shall destroy ourselves at some farcical apocalypse."[65] Our best defense is to understand thoroughly our conceptions of "the modern"—to apprehend their operation in the past and their continuing operation in the present. For, if we do not, we are likely, in our own earnest rejection of the modernists' historical viewpoint, to invent merely a new version of it, to inflict merely one more break in the creative traditions of our culture.

Like the history of our civilization, from which they sometimes appear to be indistinguishable, the ideologies of return make a compelling story: so compelling, in fact, that the twentieth century may have adjusted its own life to conform with the contours of the narrative. And whether fictitious or factual, spontaneous or artistically arranged, this is an old-fashioned story, one with a moral. We often think of our civilization as countless eons into hoary old age, yet if we were to gather one representative of each generation since the days of Homer—or of Moses—we would not even begin to fill the seats in a modern lecture hall. Samuel Beckett would sit, perhaps, a dozen rows behind Aeschylus, perhaps two rows behind Shakespeare. Human life—we are inclined to repress the fact—antedates the history of our civilization by something like one million years. Diversified as it may seem to us, who are inside that closed system, Western civilization forms a discrete unit and may possess its own entelechy. When we do gesture toward a first or final cause, we tend to think in terms of progress, but "progress" and "return" may not be opposed phenomena nor even opposite expectations. They may be concomitant, the components of a single cultural process. This, at any rate, would seem to be the implication of our paradoxical self-image—the appellation we have chosen for the years that inaugurate our age of progress is *renaissance*, a word that means, roughly, *return*. And behind this paradox of nomenclature lurks the insight which informs it: that our culture was relatively younger in antiquity than at present, that "modern" can mean old and "ancient," young.

The dynamic between progress and return—between social or technological change and the simultaneous devotion to authenticity and original sources—has conditioned much of modern history, and the dynamic requires a kind of attention we have not shown it. "Progress" has received considerable independent attention, as has the *nostos* aspect of the Renaissance, but the continuity of return-oriented phenomena has been perilously underrated. Panofsky has written, and the direction of post-modernism appears to confirm his speculation, that the "permanent" backward reach, set in motion by the Renaissance, would be "changeable only with a change in our civilization."[66] Most often, critics take the phenomena of Renaissance, renascence, classicism, tradition, and reaction to denote historical periods, literary or artistic movements; seldom as evidence of a culture's patterns of development. The modernist classicism of Eliot or Valéry, for example, is taken either as willful resistance to novel conditions or, worse, as proof of cosmetological talent. From the scholar's perspective, these approaches are of necessity the correct ones. But to do fullest justice to such phenomena may require that the scholar also become something of an anthropologist—that the scholar approach high civilization as, in the anthropologist's sense, culture. Tradition, the backward glance, may very well be involuntary; to proceed as if it were not may very well mandate an equal and opposite reaction—an overwhelming expectation of Return. This much, at least, we should have learned from the spectacle of the twentieth century: that there can be no escape from the prestige of beginnings.

· NOTES ·

Prologue

1. F. R. Leavis, *The Living Principle: 'English' as a Discipline of Thought* (New York: Oxford University Press, 1975), p. 9.
2. M. H. Abrams, "A Note on Wittgenstein and Literary Criticism," *English Literary History* 16, 4 (Winter 1974), pp. 541–54. Wayne Booth, *Critical Understanding* (Chicago: University of Chicago Press, 1979), pp. 139–74.
3. Ludwig Wittgenstein, *Philosophical Investigations*, trans. G.E.M. Anscombe (New York: Macmillan, 1958), p. 230.
4. Friedrich Schlegel, *Athenaeum* fragment 149 in *Friedrich Schlegel's Lucinde and the Fragments*, trans. Peter Firchow (Minneapolis: University of Minnesota Press, 1971), p. 181.
5. Erwin Panofsky, *Renaissance and Renascences in Western Art* (New York: Harper & Row, 1972), p. 113.
6. "Crites" [T. S. Eliot], "A Commentary," *The Criterion* 2, no. 7, p. 231.
7. Jean Seznec, *The Survival of the Pagan Gods*, trans. Barbara S. Sessions (Princeton: Princeton University Press, 1972), p. 322.

I

1. Homer, *The Odyssey*, trans. Robert Fitzgerald (New York: Anchor, 1963), pp. 235–36.
2. Giorgio Vasari, preface to *The Lives of the Painters*, ed. William Gaunt (London: Everyman, 1963), p. 18.
3. See, for example, G. S. Gordon, *Medium Aevum and the Middle Ages* (Oxford: Society for Pure English, 1925), tract no. 19; and P. Lehmann, "Mittelalter and Küchenlatein," *Historische Zeitschrift* 137 (1928), pp. 197ff. See also Erwin Panofsky's excellent synopsis of this literature and the succinct bibliography in his essay, " 'Renaissance'—Self-Definition or Self-Deception?" *Renaissance and Renascences in Western Art* (New York: Harper & Row, 1972), pp. 1ff. and esp. n. 4 of p. 5 and n. 1 of pp. 9–10.
4. Herbert Butterfield, *Man on His Past* (Cambridge: Cambridge University Press, 1955), p. 45.

5. Jacob Burckhardt, *The Civilization of the Renaissance in Italy*, trans. S.G.C. Middlemore (New York: Harper & Row, 1958), pp. 105, 106.
6. Ibid., p. 107.
7. Jacob Burckhardt, *History of Greek Culture*, trans. Palmer Hilty (New York: Macmillan, 1963), p. 227.
8. Hayden White, *Metahistory* (Baltimore: Johns Hopkins University Press, 1973), esp. pp. 93ff. on the historical "plot" of Hegel.
9. Joachite and other heretical or Gnostic sects often divided history into Trinity-related portions—the third age, the Age of the Holy Spirit, being the apocalyptic epoch. Cf. Norman Cohn, *The Pursuit of the Millennium* (New York: Oxford University Press, 1970); Eric Voegelin, "Gnosticism—the Nature of Modernity" in *The New Science of Politics* (Chicago: University of Chicago Press, 1952); and Frank Kermode, *The Sense of an Ending* (New York: Oxford University Press, 1967).
10. Burckhardt, *Renaissance*, pp. 102, 178, 235ff.
11. Burckhardt, here, is possibly paraphrasing Michelet.
12. Burckhardt, *Renaissance*, p. 184.
13. Friedrich Nietzsche, "Homer's Contest" (posthumously published), in *The Viking Portable Nietzsche*, ed. and trans. Walter Kaufmann (Harmondsworth: Penguin, 1954), p. 32.
14. Ibid., p. 34.
15. Ibid., p. 32.
16. Friedrich Nietzsche, *Philosophy in the Tragic Age of the Greeks*, trans. Marianne Cowan (Chicago: Henry Regnery Co., 1962), p. 79.
17. First published in *Westminster Review* (Jan. 1857).
18. Burckhardt, *Renaissance*, p. 199.
19. Walter Pater, *The Renaissance: Studies in Art and Poetry* (London: Macmillan, 1922), p. 199. And cf. Ezra Pound: "European civilization or, to use an abominated word, 'culture' can be perhaps best understood as a mediaeval trunk with wash after wash of classicism going over it. That is not the whole story, but to understand it, you must think of that series of perceptions, as well as of anything that has existed or subsisted unbroken from antiquity" (*The ABC of Reading* [New York: New Directions, 1934], p. 56).
20. Pater, *Renaissance*, pp. 206, 207.
21. Ibid., pp. 206, 222.
22. Ibid., p. 226.

23. Heinrich Heine, *Romantische Schule* (1836) in *The Works of Heinrich Heine*, trans. Charles Godfrey Leland (New York: Croscup, 1900), pp. 241, 243.
24. Pater, *Renaissance*, p. 226.
25. Ibid., pp. 226, 232.
26. Ibid., pp. 226–27, 223.
27. Ibid., p. 227.
28. Paul Valéry, "Letter from France: The Spiritual Crisis," *The Athenaeum*, 11 Apr. 1919, pp. 182–83 (published first in English).
29. Homer, *Odyssey*, pp. 8–9.

II

1. Geoffrey Hartman, "Romanticism and Anti-Self-Consciousness," *Beyond Formalism* (New Haven: Yale University Press, 1970), p. 307.
2. Jean-Jacques Rousseau, *Les Confessions*, ed. Jacques Voisine (Paris: Garnier, 1964), esp. pp. 515–16. (Author's translation.)
3. Ibid., p. 483.
4. Rousseau, letter to Philibert Cramer, 13 Oct. 1764, *Correspondance Générale de J.-J. Rousseau*, ed. T. Dufour and P. P. Plan (Paris: Armand Colin, 1924–34), p. 339. (Author's translation.)
5. Paul de Man, *Allegories of Reading: Figural Language in Rousseau, Nietzsche, Rilke, and Proust* (New Haven: Yale University Press, 1979), pp. 188–200, esp. n. 36 on p. 219.
6. My translations from *Julie* have been based on *Eloisa*, trans. William Kennick (London: Griffiths, Becket, and De Hondt, 1761), and on *Eloisa* (London: Allen and West, 1795), in order to maintain a semblance of eighteenth-century diction and tone. All parenthetical references in this chapter are to the French text: *Julie, ou La Nouvelle Héloïse*, ed. Michel Launay (Paris: Garnier-Flammarion, 1967).
7. *Hegel's Logic*, trans. William Wallace (Oxford: Clarendon, 1975), pp. 43–44.
8. Hartman, "Romanticism," p. 301.
9. *Eloisa* (1795), vol. 2, p. 230; see n. 6 above.
10. *The Works of Aurelius Augustinus*, ed. Marcus Dods (Edinburgh: T. & T. Clark Co., 1871–76), p. 105.

11. Julie calls her life with Saint-Preux a dreadful slavery (*"une servitude . . . redoutable"*): p. 269.
12. Rousseau, *Confessions*, p. 643.
13. Cf. ibid., p. 460 (the French text). Translation quoted from Jean-Jacques Rousseau, *The Confessions*, trans. J. M. Cohen (Harmondsworth: Penguin, 1954), p. 362.
14. *Hegel's Logic*, p. 43.
15. See chap. 1.
16. T. S. Eliot, *The Family Reunion* (New York: Harcourt, Brace & Co., 1939), p. 101.
17. Julie writes of her sons in her deathbed letter to Saint-Preux: "Do not make them scholars, make them charitable and righteous men": p. 566.
18. Anita Brookner, "Rousseau and the Social Contract," *Times Literary Supplement* (London), 8 Feb. 1980, p. 150; Lionel Gossman, "Time and History in Rousseau," *Studies in Voltaire and the Eighteenth Century* (Geneva) 30 (1964), p. 313.
19. See n. 3 above.
20. Roger D. Masters, *The Political Philosophy of Rousseau* (Princeton: Princeton University Press, 1968), p. 11.
21. Jean-Jacques Rousseau, *Émile ou de l'Éducation*, ed. François and Pierre Richard (Paris: Garnier, 1961), p. 356.
22. For some of these ideas about the genre of *Julie*, I am indebted to Joseph Frank.
23. Masters, *Political Philosophy*, pp. 5–6.
24. Gossman, "Time and History," pp. 326ff.

III

1. *Athenaeum* fragment 276 in *Friedrich Schlegel's Lucinde and the Fragments*, trans. Peter Firchow (Minneapolis: University of Minnesota Press, 1971), p. 201; Friedrich Schlegel, *Dialogue on Poetry and Literary Aphorisms*, trans. Ernst Behler and Roman Struc (University Park: Pennsylvania State University Press, 1968), p. 101.
2. Friedrich Schlegel, *Lectures on the History of Literature, Ancient and Modern*, trans. H. G. Bohn et al. (London: Bohn, 1859), vol. 2, p. 276.
3. T. S. Eliot, *For Lancelot Andrewes* (London: Faber, 1970), p. 7. C.-A. Sainte-Beuve: *"Autour de deux ou trois idées fonda-*

mentales, s'organisa chez eux un système de poésie formé du platonisme en amour, du christianisme en mythologie, et du royalisme en politique" ("Victor Hugo: Odes et Ballades," *Premiers Lundis* [Paris: Michel Lévy, 1874–75], vol. 1, p. 165).

4. Donald Davie, "T. S. Eliot: The End of an Era," *Twentieth Century* 159 (1956), no. 950, p. 362.

5. Northrop Frye, *Romanticism Reconsidered* (New York: Columbia University Press, 1963), p. 24.

6. Edmund Wilson, *Axel's Castle* (New York: Scribner's, 1969), p. 93.

7. T. S. Eliot, "A French Romantic," letter in the *Times Literary Supplement* (London), 28 Oct. 1920, p. 703.

8. T. S. Eliot, "Ulysses, Order, and Myth," *The Dial* 75, in *The Modern Tradition*, ed. Richard Ellmann and Charles Feidelson, Jr. (New York: Oxford University Press, 1965), p. 680.

9. T. S. Eliot, *The Use of Poetry and the Use of Criticism* (London: Faber, 1933), p. 74, and "Preface to the Edition of 1964," p. 10.

10. Ronald Schuschard, "T. S. Eliot as an Extension Lecturer, 1916–19," *R.E.S.*, n.s., vol. 25, no. 98 (1974), p. 165.

11. T. S. Eliot, "The Idea of a Literary Review," *The New Criterion* 4, no. 1, p. 5.

12. Jean Seznec, *The Survival of the Pagan Gods* (Princeton: Princeton University Press, 1953), p. 320.

13. G. E. Lessing, *Laocoön*, trans. Edward Allen McCormick (Indianapolis: Bobbs-Merrill, 1962), p. 27. Or see *Laokoön* (Stuttgart: Phillip Reclam, 1971), pp. 33–34.

14. Longinus, *On the Sublime*, chap. 3, in *Classical Literary Criticism*, trans. T. S. Dorsch (Harmondsworth: Penguin, 1965), p. 102.

15. Erwin Panofsky, *Renaissance and Renascences in Western Art* (New York: Harper & Row, 1972), pp. 110–11.

16. Seznec, *Pagan Gods*, pp. 320–21.

17. Panofsky, *Renaissance and Renascences*, p. 87.

18. Yvor Winters, "Explanation," *The Gyroscope* 1 (May 1929). (I want to extend my thanks to the Special Collections Department of the Stanford University Libraries for permission to read this journal's four mimeographed—and, therefore, extremely rare and fragile—issues.) The most interesting and perceptive article that *The Criterion* published during the classicism debate is Paul Jacobsthal, "Views and Valuations of Ancient Art Since Wickel-

mann, Chiefly in Germany" (3, no. 2), pp. 543ff. Other *Criterion* pieces on the subject include: Eliot, "The Idea of a Literary Review" (4, no. 1), p. 5; Eliot, "The Function of Criticism" (2, no. 5), pp. 31ff.; Eliot, "Notes" on teaching the classics (2, no. 5), pp. 104–5; "Crites" [Eliot], "A Commentary" on Hulme (2, no. 7), pp. 231ff.; J. Middleton Murry, "Romanticism and the Tradition" (2, no. 7), pp. 272ff.; H. P. Collins, "The Classical Principle in Poetry" (3, no. 2), pp. 389ff.; Eliot, "A Commentary" (6, no. 3), pp. 193–94; Bertram Higgins, letter (6, no. 3), p. 259; Max Rychner, "German Chronicle" on Stefan George as classicist (6, no. 6), pp. 540ff.; Charles Maurras, "An Essay on Criticism" (6, no. 6), pp. 204ff.; and the 1927–28 Murry articles and responsa.

19. Eliot, *The Use of Poetry*, p. 84.
20. Ibid., p. 85.
21. *Paul Valéry: An Anthology*, ed. James R. Lawler (Princeton: Princeton University Press, 1977), pp. 167–68. Or see Paul Valéry, *Vues* (Paris: Table ronde, 1948), p. 185.
22. He discusses Stendhal and Flaubert in "Beyle and Balzac," *The Athenaeum*, 30 May 1919, p. 392; James, in "In Memory of Henry James," *The Egoist*, Jan. 1918, pp. 1–2; the metaphysicals and *symbolistes* in "The Metaphysical Poets," *Selected Essays* (hereafter *SE*) (New York: Harcourt, Brace & World, 1964), pp. 241ff.; Jonson, in "The Comedy of Humours," *The Athenaeum*, 14 Nov. 1919, pp. 1180–81, and in "Ben Jonson," *SE*, pp. 127ff.; Marvell, in "Andrew Marvell," *SE*, pp. 251ff.; and the *Noh* drama, in "The Noh and the Image," *The Egoist*, Aug. 1917, pp. 102–3.
23. He discusses the unpleasant aspects of the Georgian poets in "Reflections on Contemporary Poetry, I," *The Egoist*, Sept. 1917, pp. 118–19; in "Verse Pleasant and Unpleasant," *The Egoist*, Mar. 1918, pp. 43–44; and in "The Post-Georgians," *The Athenaeum*, 11 Apr. 1919, pp. 134–36. He criticizes the Victorian novelists in "Beyle and Balzac"; Swinburne and Kipling, in "Kipling Redivivus," *The Athenaeum*, 9 May 1919, pp. 297–98, in "Imperfect Critics," *The Sacred Wood* (hereafter *SW*) (London: Methuen, 1969), pp. 17ff., and in "Swinburne as Poet," *SE*, pp. 281ff.; the early romantics, in "The Romantic Generation," *The Athenaeum*, 18 July 1919, pp. 616–17; the eighteenth century, in "Metaphysical Poets," *SE*; Milton, in "Notes on the Blank Verse of Christopher Marlowe," *SW*, pp. 86ff.; Yeats, in "The

Method of Mr. Pound," *The Athenaeum*, 14 Oct. 1919, p. 1065, and in "A Foreign Mind," *The Athenaeum*, 4 July 1919, pp. 552–53; Dryden, in "Metaphysical Poets," *SE*; and Shakespeare, in "Hamlet and His Problems," *SW*, pp. 95ff.

24. Eliot's letter to the editor of *The Athenaeum* in the 25 June 1920 number, concerning a response to his article on Massinger, should make us forever italicize the word "transformation" in this context.

25. The most complete statements of his technical criteria may be found in essays on writers whose technique he finds flawless but whose brains he finds "anemic": "Philip Massinger," *SW*, and "Swinburne as Poet," *SE*, especially. The quotation is from "John Dryden," *SE*, p. 274.

26. Eliot, "Philip Massinger," *SW*, p. 140.

27. Ibid., pp. 139, 143.

28. Eliot, "Metaphysical Poets," *SE*, p. 250.

29. The quotations are taken from Eliot, *SW*: "Ben Jonson," p. 104; "Philip Massinger," p. 136; and "Imperfect Critics," p. 131.

30. Eliot, "Beyle and Balzac," p. 392, and "Ben Jonson" in *SE*, p. 104.

31. "Simple . . . unknown": Eliot, "Beyle and Balzac," p. 393. Relationship of emotions in the *Commedia*: "Dante," *SW*, p. 168.

32. Eliot, "Metaphysical Poets," *SE*, p. 247.

33. Eliot, "Philip Massinger," *SW*, p. 131.

34. Surface unity: Eliot, "The Perfect Critic," *SW*, p. 14, and "Philip Massinger," *SW*, pp. 131–32. "Beautiful," "successful": "Dante," *SW*, pp. 162–63.

35. See esp. Eliot, "Philip Massinger," *SW*, pp. 134–35; also "Kipling Redivivus," p. 298; and "Prose and Verse," *The Chapbook*, Apr. 1921, p. 6.

36. Eliot, "A Sceptical Patrician," *The Athenaeum*, 23 May 1919, pp. 361–62; "Blake," *SW*, pp. 155–58 (for Blake) and 157 (for Milton); "A Foreign Mind," pp. 552–53.

37. Eliot, "Andrew Marvell," *SE*, p. 252.

38. Eliot, "Philip Massinger," *SW*, p. 140.

39. Eliot, "Blake," *SW*, p. 158.

40. Eliot, "Philip Massinger," *SW*, pp. 133–34.

41. Eliot, "Blake," *SW*, p. 158; "Philip Massinger," *SW*, p. 139 (for Yeats); and "Metaphysical Poets," *SE*, p. 248 (for Keats and Shelley).

42. Eliot, "Philip Massinger," *SW*, pp. 133–34.

43. Eliot, "Metaphysical Poets," *SE*, p. 247.
44. Ibid., pp. 248–49.
45. Eliot, "Andrew Marvell," *SE*, p. 252 (the remark on Latin culture was made about Marvell, but the Eliot of 1921 probably would not have minded its application to English literature in general), and "The Function of Criticism," *SE*, pp. 16–17.
46. Eliot, "Kipling Redivivus," p. 298. Other comments on the evils of provinciality appear in "Reflections on Contemporary Poetry, I"; "Verse Pleasant and Unpleasant"; "Disjecta Membra," *The Egoist*, Apr. 1918, p. 55. Note that his most general statement, "Provinciality of material may be a virtue. . . . provinciality of point of view is a vice," is found in his review of an *American* poet's book: "Contemporanea," *The Egoist*, June–July 1918, p. 84.
47. Eliot, "Blake," *SW*, p. 157.
48. Pound recalled that in his philosophical disagreement with Eliot, "each of us was accusing the other of Protestantism": Ezra Pound, "For T. S. E.," in *T. S. Eliot: The Man and His Work*, ed. Allen Tate (New York: Delacorte, 1966), p. 89. The word "Protestant" seems to have summarized for them everything wrong with the modern Western world.
49. Eliot, "Philip Massinger," *SW*, p. 136.
50. Wordsworth: cf. his note on the "Ode to Lycoris" of 1817 and his late work, *Laodamia*, which he based on *Aeneid* 6.
51. Walter Pater, as quoted in Harry Levin, *The Broken Column* (Cambridge: Harvard University Press, 1931), p. 22.
52. Arnold's neoclassical aspect is most apparent in his essay "On Translating Homer." There, he regrets England's lack of an academy "to introduce a little order into this chaos," though he is sufficiently modern to quote approvingly the aphorism of Menander that rejects too great a purism. Arnold's academicism is, perhaps, an inheritance from his father, the Head Master of Rugby.
53. S. T. Coleridge: ". . . the principle of Aristotle, that poetry is essentially *ideal*, that it avoids and excludes all *accident*" (*Biographia Literaria*, ed. J. Shawcross [Oxford: Oxford University Press, 1973], chap. 17, vol. 2, p. 33). Eliot compared Aristotle and Coleridge as critics in "A Brief Treatise on the Criticism of Poetry," *The Chapbook*, Mar. 1920, pp. 1–10.
54. Eliot, "Wordsworth and Coleridge," *The Use of Poetry*, p. 74.
55. Carlos Baker, "Shelley's Translation from Aristotle," *Modern*

Language Notes 61, 6 (June 1946), pp. 405ff. See also James A. Notopoulos, "Shelley's 'Distinterested Love' and Aristotle," *Philological Quarterly* 32, 2 (Apr. 1953), pp. 214ff.

56. Hugh Lloyd-Jones, "Nietzsche and the Study of the Ancient World," in *Studies in Nietzsche and the Classical Tradition*, ed. J. C. O'Flaherty et al. (Chapel Hill: University of North Carolina Press, 1979), p. 5.

57. Eliot, "Francis Herbert Bradley" (1927), *SE*, p. 404.

58. *Poetics* in *The Basic Works of Aristotle*, ed. Richard McKeon (New York: Random House, 1941), p. 1461.

59. Ibid.

60. Ibid., pp. 1463–64.

61. Ibid., p. 1472.

62. Eliot used the G. Biehl–O. Apelt edition of *De anima* during 1914–15 and, in a dedicatory note to John Hayward, explains the origin of his marginalia. He read Pacinus at the insistence of Harold Joachim. The volume is in King's College Library, Cambridge, and may be consulted with Mrs. Eliot's permission.

63. *De anima* in *Aristotle*, p. 587.

64. Ibid., pp. 587, 595.

65. Ibid., pp. 587–88.

66. Eliot, *The Use of Poetry*, pp. 78–79.

67. The hypothesis that the essence of romanticism is its anti-Newtonian internalization of reality is outlined most cogently in Northrop Frye, "The Drunken Boat," *Romanticism Reconsidered*, pp. 1–25. Gilbert Highet suggests that the romantics' lack of faith in systematic thought and their reliance on imagination and intuition may have been due to Oriental influence. But romanticism is a thoroughly Western phenomenon: Aristotle attributes the notion that imagination and judgment are identical with bodily sense perceptions—and, thus, necessarily correct in their observations—to Homer and Empedocles. Aristotle disputes the "ancients." (See *De anima*, pp. 585–87.)

68. Eliot, "Hamlet and His Problems," *SW*, pp. 121-26, esp. pp. 123–24.

69. S. T. Coleridge, "Hamlet," *Shakespeare and the Elizabethan Dramatists* (Edinburgh: John Grant, 1905), p. 204.

70. Eliot, "Hamlet and His Problems," *SW*, pp. 124–25.

71. Coleridge, *Biographia*, chap. 5, vol. 1, p. 73.

72. "Dazzling disregard": "Metaphysical Poets," *SE*, p. 249. "Crankiness": "Blake," *SW*, p. 157. "Short cut": "Imperfect Critics,"

SW, p. 31. Simplicity and terribleness: "Beyle and Balzac," p. 392.

73. Eliot, *The Use of Poetry*, p. 84. The most suggestive instance of this modernist tradition-blending is Eliot's own classical canon. Like the romantics, Eliot affirms the Greek supremacy, the supremacy of Aeschylus, but he also asserts that the most "classical" of poets is the Roman Vergil. See "What is a Classic?" *On Poetry and Poets* (New York: Noonday, 1957), p. 53.

74. Frank Elgar and Robert Maillard, *Picasso* (New York: Praeger, 1956), p. 74.

75. Grover Smith, for instance, notes that Eliot sometimes signed his name, "T. Stearns Eliot," and he concludes that "Prufrock" is a case of "mere self-masking." See Grover Smith, *T. S. Eliot's Poetry and Plays* (Chicago: University of Chicago Press, 1950), pp. 15–20.

76. Quotations are from Eliot, *SW*: "Imperfect Critics," p. 31, and "Tradition and the Individual Talent," p. 58.

77. Eliot's Lady alludes to Arnold's poem in II:12: " 'these April sunsets, that somehow recall / My buried life'." Arnold's affectations (of which, Eliot's most amusing imitation is his placement of quotation marks around the phrase "false note") include: inversion of conversational word order, overworking the exclamation point and question mark, deployment of uncalled-for word repetition, and use of a record 1⅓ expletives per page. Eliot plays with Arnold's life-flow ("The Buried Life," lines 1, 40, 88) in "Portrait," II:7.

78. Helen Gardner, *The Art of T. S. Eliot* (London: Faber, 1949), p. 83.

79. F. H. Bradley, as quoted in Eliot's note to line 411 of *The Waste Land*.

80. George Saintsbury, *A Short History of English Literature* (London: Macmillan, 1962), p. 413.

81. Remembering that Eliot may have been the most ingenious critic-baiter who ever wrote, it might not be farfetched to suggest that Prufrock's line, "It is impossible to say just what I mean!" is also a warning to those readers who would squeeze the persona into a formulated phrase—such as, for instance, "intellectual, internal, radical, modern romanticism."

82. Cf. Eliot's 1920 essay, "Swinburne as Poet," *SE*, pp. 281–85.

83. Eliot calls romantics "palpitating Narcissi" in "The Function of Criticism," *SE*, p. 16.

84. Compare these phrases from the "Portrait" ("Among the smoke and fog," "With the music coming down above the housetops," "This music is successful with a 'dying fall' ") with these from "Prufrock" ("The yellow fog" and "yellow smoke," "the smoke that rises from the pipes," "I know the voices dying with a dying fall"). Note that Eliot has placed quotation marks around "dying fall" in the "Portrait" but not in the earlier poem—it is, of course, also a quotation from *Twelfth Night*.

85. Perhaps Eliot's conversion to Anglo-Catholicism had been delayed by the connection in his mind between literary romanticism and sloppy humanitarianism. Just when he began to cling to the image of the Christian God ("The notion of some infinitely gentle / Infinitely suffering thing" in "Preludes"), his ironic intellect required laughter.

86. Eliot, "Dante," *SE*, p. 223. Cf. Eliot's introduction to his 1930 translation of *Anabase*.

87. The last words of Eliot's poem, "A Note on War Poetry" (1942).

88. Helen Gardner, *The Composition of Four Quartets* (London: Faber, 1978). For example, Eliot wrote to John Hayward that he would not drop a certain line that Hayward had queried because it alluded to *The Family Reunion* and the poem required a reference to that play at that point.

89. Eliot, *The Use of Poetry*, p. 81.

90. Gardner, *Composition*, p. 109.

91. Eliot, "Prose and Verse," pp. 3–10.

92. "Other creation" is taken from "Tintern Abbey," and that poem's phrase, "worshippers of Nature," may have supplied Eliot's "worshippers of the machine." For "many gods and many voices," see Wordsworth's *Prelude*, V, lines 106–7.

93. For "I have said before," cf. Coleridge, *Biographia*, chap. 3, vol. 1, p. 38, and others places. The tone of the passage is possibly meant to be that of Coleridge the critic.

94. The lines about the destroyer and preserver allude, perhaps, to similar lines in "Ode to the West Wind." In each poem, the lines refer to Vishnu.

95. Cf., for example, "equal mind," with *In Memoriam*, elegy 62, line 8.

96. For Kipling, see Gardner, *Composition*, p. 50.

97. Eliot's remarks about Spencer were made in the context of a 1948 sermon in the chapel of Magdalene College, Cambridge.

The text is available in the Bodleian and Cambridge University Libraries.

98. Huck's river leads upward out of slavery: see Eliot's preface to *The Adventures of Huckleberry Finn* (London: Cresset Press, 1950), and note the allusions to Twain's novel in the poem ("dead negroes," for example).

99. Eliot, "The Dry Salvages," II:104, 107, 114, 123; and III:126–28.

100. Eliot, "Blake," *SW*, p. 151.

101. Ibid., p. 158.

102. Cf. Eliot's argument about D. H. Lawrence in *After Strange Gods* (New York: Harcourt, Brace & World, 1934).

103. Cf., for example, the lines in part I about "The fog . . . in the fir trees" with "Marina," and the whole of part IV with the second section of "Ash-Wednesday."

104. See Gardner, *Composition*, pp. 54–55 and esp. n. 51 on p. 55. It was during the thirties that Eliot wrote *After Strange Gods*, a volume he refused to reprint. Eliot also came to repudiate the spirit lust of Harry Monchensey (created 1939) and called it, simply, priggishness: see T. S. Eliot, "Poetry and Drama," *On Poetry and Poets*, p. 91.

105. J. Middleton Murry, *Europe in Travail* (London: Christian Newsletter Books, 1940), p. v.

106. T. S. Eliot, *Knowledge and Experience in the Philosophy of F. H. Bradley* (New York: Farrar, Straus, 1964), pp. 147–48.

107. Eliot, "Little Gidding," III:156–57, 159, 163–65.

108. T. S. Eliot, "London Letter," *The Dial* 71, 3 (Sept. 1921), p. 455.

109. Longinus, *On the Sublime*, chap. 29, p. 138.

110. Aristotle, *Poetics*, p. 1478.

111. Longinus, *On the Sublime*, chap. 32, p. 141.

112. Eliot, "Baudelaire," *SE*, p. 376.

IV

1. August Wilhelm Schlegel, *Dramatic Art and Literature*, trans. John Black (London: H. G. Bohn, 1849), p. 52.

2. Ibid., p. 59.

3. Ibid., p. 71.

4. Ibid., p. 528.

5. *Mary Shelley's Journal*, ed. Frederick L. Jones (Norman: University of Oklahoma Press, 1947), p. 20.
6. Friedrich Melchior von Grimm, letter of 15 May 1768 in *Correspondance littéraire*, ed. Maurice Tourneux (Paris: Garnier, 1879), vol. 8, p. 74. (Author's translation.)
7. F. O. Nolte, *The Early Middle Class Drama* (Lancaster, Pa.: Lancaster Press, 1935), pp. 130–31.
8. Ibid., p. 25.
9. *Shelley's Poetry and Prose*, ed. Donald H. Reiman and Sharon Powers (New York: Norton, 1977), p. 490.
10. Ibid., pp. 491–92.
11. M. H. Abrams, *Natural Supernaturalism* (New York: Norton, 1971), pp. 299–307.
12. For both "Follow, follow!" and for points of comparison with "Circe," see *Prometheus Unbound* in *Shelley's Poetry and Prose*, p. 164.
13. Byron, letter to publisher John Murray in *English Romantic Writers*, ed. David Perkins (New York: Harcourt, Brace, Jovanovich, 1967), p. 810.
14. Byron, *Manfred*, act 2, sc. 1, lines 59–61.
15. Ibid., act 3, sc. 4, lines 31–41.
16. G.F.W. Hegel, *Werke*, vol. 12, pp. 257ff., as trans. by Walter Kaufmann in *Tragedy and Philosophy* (New York: Anchor, 1969), p. 245.
17. Friedrich Nietzsche, *The Birth of Tragedy*, trans. Francis Golffing (Garden City: Anchor, 1956), pp. 13, 120, 111.
18. Ibid., p. 71.
19. Ibid., p. 88.
20. Ibid., p. 35.
21. Ibid., p. 79.
22. Ibid., p. 49.
23. Ibid., esp. pp. 49, 53, 78, 106. "Artificial": p. 49. Chorus: pp. 49–50. Like Schiller, Nietzsche believed that the reintroduction of the chorus would be the "main weapon" against commonplace naturalism and the "illusionistic demand" upon dramatic poetry.
24. Ibid., p. 137.
25. Ibid., and for "tragic world view": p. 104.
26. Ibid., "constitutional democracy": p. 47; "at last . . . validity": p. 104.
27. Ibid., p. 29.

28. S. S. Prawer, *Karl Marx and World Literature* (Oxford: Clarendon, 1976), p. 65.
29. Ibid., p. 23.
30. Ibid., pp. 287–88.
31. Karl Marx, *The Grundrisse*, trans. David McLellan (New York: Harper & Row, 1971), pp. 43ff.
32. W. B. Yeats, *Plays and Controversies* (London: Macmillan, 1923), pp. 433–34.
33. Christopher Fry, "Why Verse?" *World Theatre* (Autumn 1955), p. 52.
34. E. E. Cummings, *i: six nonlectures* (Cambridge: Harvard University Press, 1953), p. 43.
35. "Plunge . . . social life": W. B. Yeats, *Pages from a Diary Written in Nineteen Hundred and Thirty* (Dublin: Cuala Press, 1944). "Powerful politically": reference to *The Dreaming of the Bones* in a letter to Lady Gregory of 11 June 1917, in *The Letters of W. B. Yeats*, ed. Allan Wade (New York: Macmillan, 1962), p. 626. Also see Yeats's letter to Stephen Gwynn (1918) on the same subject, *Letters*, pp. 653–54. *The Dreaming of the Bones* contains references to the Rising of 1916.
36. W. B. Yeats, *Samhain* of 1904 (theater notebooks), in *Explorations*, ed. Mrs. W. B. Yeats (London: Macmillan, 1962), p. 129.
37. Ibid. (1905), p. 187.
38. Ibid. (1906), p. 205.
39. W. B. Yeats, *Wheels and Butterflies* (London: Macmillan, 1934). See also the 1931 introduction to *Words Upon the Window Pane*, in *Essays and Introductions* (London: Macmillan, 1961), p. 10. Orient: in the preface to *The Cat and the Moon*, in *Essays and Introductions*, p. 136, he asserts that before the Battle of the Boyne, Ireland lived "in Asia."
40. *The Countess Cathleen*, in *Collected Plays of W. B. Yeats* (London: Macmillan, 1972), p. 30.
41. Yeats, *Samhain* (1905), p. 183.
42. Yeats, *A Full Moon in March*, in *Collected Plays*, p. 629.
43. "Traditional knowledge": Yeats, letter to Lady Gregory, in *Explorations*, p. 251. "Simple people": "The Theatre" (1900), in *Essays and Introductions*, p. 166.
44. Yeats, *The Great Herne*, in *Collected Plays*, pp. 649–50.
45. Yeats (1906), as quoted in Raymond Williams, *Drama from Ibsen to Eliot* (London: Chatto, 1952), p. 207.
46. Yeats, letter to Lady Gregory, in *Explorations*, p. 247.

47. Yeats, *Samhain* (1905), p. 189.
48. Nolte, *Middle Class Drama*, p. 212.
49. Yeats, letter to Lady Gregory, in *Explorations*, p. 251.
50. D. R. Pearce, "Yeats's Last Plays," *Journal of English Literary History*, Mar. 1951, p. 76.
51. Yeats, *The King's Threshold*, in *Collected Plays*, p. 125. The first two versions of this play (1904 and 1906) conclude with the restoration of the poet's rights but, as Peter Ure asserts in *Yeats the Playwright* (London: Routledge, 1963), pp. 31ff., the tragic ending of the 1922 version better suits the tone and structure of the whole play.
52. Yeats, *Countess Cathleen*, p. 21.
53. Yeats, *Samhain* (1902), pp. 96–97.
54. Ibid., pp. 86–88.
55. Ibid. (1906), p. 213.
56. "The theatre . . . scenery": Yeats, *Samhain* (1903), p. 107. "Anti-self": letter to Lady Gregory, in *Explorations*, p. 257. "Motto": 1920 preface to the *Four Plays for Dancers*, in *Plays and Controversies*, p. 333.
57. W. B. Yeats, *Ideas of Good and Evil* (London: Macmillan, 1903), p. 247. Yeats makes similar remarks about the uses of poetic rhythm in "The Symbolism of Poetry," *The Dome*, Apr. 1900.
58. The best exposition of Yeats's (and Auden's) use of alternating verse and prose is Denis Donoghue's, in *The Third Voice* (Princeton: Princeton University Press, 1959), pp. 26ff., and I am indebted to it.
59. Yeats, *Words Upon the Window Pane*, in *Collected Plays*, p. 603.
60. Conor Cruise O'Brien, "Passion and Cunning: An Essay on the Politics of W. B. Yeats," in *In Excited Reverie*, ed. A. N. Jeffares and K.G.W. Cross (New York: Macmillan, 1965), p. 247.
61. Yeats, *The Land of Heart's Desire*, in *Collected Plays*, p. 53.
62. Yeats's review of Apr. 1894, in *Uncollected Prose by W. B. Yeats*, ed. John P. Frayne (New York: Columbia University Press, 1970), vol. 1, p. 235.
63. Yeats, *Heart's Desire*, pp. 69–70.
64. Ibid., p. 62.
65. Ibid., p. 65.
66. The words "hearth" and "marriage" always indicate the safer of the opposed alternatives in Yeats's plays. Cf. *At the Hawk's*

Well (1917), in *Collected Plays*, p. 220: " 'The man that I praise', / Cries out the leafless tree, / 'Has married and stays / By an old hearth, and he / On naught has set store / But children and dogs on the floor . . .' "

67. Cf. *Cathleen ni Houlihan* and *At the Hawk's Well.*
68. Yeats, *Essays and Introductions*, p. 338.
69. "Common idiom": Yeats, as quoted in S. B. Bushrui, *Yeats's Verse Plays: The Revisions, 1900–1910* (New York: Oxford University Press, 1965), p. 214.
70. Yeats, *On Baile's Strand*, in *Collected Plays*, p. 276.
71. Yeats, *Purgatory*, in *Collected Plays*, p. 688.
72. Yeats, letter to Ethel Mannin of 20 Oct. 1938, in *Letters*, p. 918.
73. Yeats, *Purgatory*, p. 684.
74. Ibid., p. 683.
75. Ibid., p. 683.
76. Ibid., pp. 686–87.
77. Ibid., p. 689.
78. For Eliot's discipleship, see "Little Gidding," II, and the section on that poem in Helen Gardner, *The Composition of Four Quartets* (London: Faber, 1978). For the antagonism between Eliot and Yeats, see the chap. on Eliot in Richard Ellmann, *Eminent Domain* (New York: Oxford University Press, 1967).
79. T. S. Eliot, "London Letter," *The Dial*, Apr. 1921, p. 451.
80. T. S. Eliot, "Eeldrop and Appleplex," *The Little Review*, May 1917, p. 9.
81. T. S. Eliot, "Dialogue on Dramatic Poetry" (1928), *Selected Essays* (New York: Harcourt, Brace & World, 1964), p. 34.
82. T. S. Eliot, "The Poetic Drama," *The Athenaeum*, 14 May 1920, p. 635.
83. Eliot, "Dialogue on Dramatic Poetry," p. 35.
84. Nietzsche, *Birth of Tragedy*, p. 64.
85. Stage directions to part 1 of *The Family Reunion.*
86. T. S. Eliot, "The Noh and the Image," *The Egoist*, Aug. 1917, p. 10.
87. Nietzsche, *Birth of Tragedy*, p. 20.
88. Yeats, *Arrow*, in *Explorations*, p. 233.
89. Yeats, letter to Lady Gregory, in *Explorations*, p. 257.
90. Renato Poggioli, *The Theory of the Avant-Garde*, trans. Gerald Fitzgerald (Cambridge: Harvard University Press, 1968), esp. chap. 6.
91. T. S. Eliot, "Poetry and Drama" (1951), *On Poetry and Poets* (New York: Noonday, 1957), p. 90.

92. T. S. Eliot, "John Marston," *Times Literary Supplement* (London), 26 July 1934, p. 518.
93. T. S. Eliot, "Ulysses, Order, and Myth," *The Dial 75*, in *The Modern Tradition*, ed. Richard Ellmann and Charles Feidelson, Jr. (New York: Oxford University Press, 1965), p. 681.
94. Wallace Stevens, *The Necessary Angel* (New York: Vintage, 1951), p. 28.

V

1. Ian Watt, *The Rise of the Novel* (Berkeley: University of California Press, 1974), p. 239.
2. Ibid.
3. See esp. "An Essay on the Knowledge of the Characters of Men" (1743), in *The Works of Henry Fielding* (New York: Scribner's, 1899), vol. 11, p. 196; but also vol. 1, p. 299; vol. 11, p. 93; and vol. 12, pp. 258–59.
4. Hugh Kenner, *A Colder Eye: The Modern Irish Writers* (New York: Knopf, 1983), pp. 196–97.
5. See Jeffrey M. Perl, "Anagogic Surfaces: How to Read *Joseph Andrews*," *The Eighteenth Century: Theory and Interpretation* (Fall 1981), pp. 249–70. See also "Scylla and Charybdis" (*Ulysses* [New York: Vintage, 1961], p. 192), where there is a comico-serious reference to a possible Irish "national epic," centering on "A Knight of the rueful countenance here in Dublin."
6. Richard Ellmann, *Ulysses on the Liffey* (New York: Oxford University Press, 1972), pp. 117ff.
7. Gustave Flaubert, *Salammbô* (Paris: Gallimard, 1974), pp. 106–7. (Author's translation.)
8. Gustave Flaubert, *Lettres inédites à Tourgueneff*, ed. Gerard Gailly (Monaco: Éditions du Rocher, 1946), p. 45.
9. *Aeneid*: see Victor Brombert, *The Novels of Flaubert* (Princeton: Princeton University Press, 1966), p. 110. "*Prurits*": Gustave Flaubert, *Correspondance* (Paris: Conard, 1926–33), vol. 3, p. 321.
10. Stendhal, "Histoire de la peinture en Italie," *Du romantisme dans les arts*, ed. Juliusz Starzyński (Paris: Hermann, 1966), p. 12.
11. Tennyson, *Maud*. "Vast speculation": I.iii.9. "My life has crept. . . .": III.i.1–3, 11; iv.50–53; v.54–55.

12. Boris Eikhenbaum, *The Young Tolstoi*, trans. Gary Kern (Ann Arbor: University of Michigan Press, 1972), p. 120.
13. Parenthetical references to Tolstoy are to *Sebastopol*, trans. F. D. Millet (Ann Arbor: University of Michigan Press, 1972).
14. Homer, *Iliad*, trans. Robert Fitzgerald (Garden City: Anchor, 1975), p. 542.
15. Cf. ibid., p. 36, where the officers' gloves are "of doubtful whiteness," to the "irreproachable" pair on p. 8.
16. Homer, *Odyssey*, trans. Robert Fitzgerald (Garden City: Anchor, 1963), p. 201.
17. I am relying here on Eikhenbaum, *Young Tolstoi*, esp. pp. 75–79.
18. Rachel Bespaloff, "Troy and Moscow," *On The Iliad* (Princeton: Princeton University Press, 1970), p. 85.
19. Tolstoy, *Sebastopol*: see, e.g., the arrival of Volodia on pp. 133–34.
20. Henry James, "The New Novel" (1914), *Notes on Novelists* (New York: Scribner's, 1916), p. 328.
21. For references to James, see Joyce, letters to his brother Stanislaus of 19 Nov. and 3 Dec. 1904, and of 13 Jan. and 18 Sept. 1905. Joyce was reading a good deal of the elder novelist's work at this period and called him "that nice old Henry James," approving James's work being "damn funny."
22. James's "Preface" to *The Ambassadors*, ed. S. P. Rosenbaum (New York: Norton, 1964), p. 9. Parenthetical references to James are to this edition.
23. Stendhal, *Romantisme*, p. 12.
24. See, e.g., John Paterson's essay, "The Language of 'Adventure' in Henry James," *American Literature*, Nov. 1960, pp. 291–301.
25. Possibly the greatest of all these lines is ensconced, without so much as a second exclamation point, in the pages of *The Aspern Papers*: " 'Well,' she said mirthfully, 'my aunt is a hundred and fifty!' "
26. James, "Preface" to *Ambassadors*, p. 7.
27. Ibid., p. 8.
28. Amphibolous: credits to Mrs. Dorothy Bednarowska of Oxford. "Exciting and depressing": Henry James, "Alphonse Daudet" (1882), *Literary Reviews and Essays*, ed. Albert Mordell (New York: Twayne, 1957), p. 189.
29. As quoted in Alan Holder, *Three Voyagers in Search of Europe* (Philadelphia: University of Pennsylvania Press, 1966), p. 276.

30. Henry James, "Flaubert's Temptation of St. Anthony" (1874), *Literary Reviews*, p. 150.

31. Henry James, "Minor French Novelists: The Goncourts, Etc." (1876), *Literary Reviews*, p. 158.

32. "Lightness of soil": Henry James, *French Poets and Novelists*, ed. Leon Edel (New York: Grosset & Dunlap, 1964), p. 175. The reference is to Balzac.

33. Matthew Arnold, preface to *Culture and Anarchy*, ed. J. D. Wilson (Cambridge: Cambridge University Press, 1950), p. xxvii.

34. Cf. Alwyn Bergland, "Henry James and the Aesthetic Tradition," *Journal of the History of Ideas* 23 (July–Sept. 1962), pp. 407–19.

35. See also James, *Ambassadors*, p. 102, where "pagan" and "gentleman" are brought together (in Chad).

36. James, "Flaubert's Temptation," *Literary Reviews*, p. 150.

37. In *Ambassadors*, Book 2, James associates Mrs. Newsome with Elizabeth I and Miss Gostrey with Mary Stuart. Later, he will associate Mme. de Vionnet with Notre Dame. And Waymarsh, New England itself, believes that the Catholic Church was "the enemy, the monster of bulging eyes and far-reaching quivering groping tentacles—was exactly society, exactly the multiplication of shibboleths, exactly the discrimination of types and tones, exactly the wicked old rows of Chester, rank with feudalism; exactly, in short, Europe" (p. 38).

38. Little Bilham in conversation with Strether:
    ". . . It puts us back—into the last century."
    "I'm afraid," Strether said, amused, "that it puts me rather forward: oh ever so far!"
    "Into the next? But isn't that only," little Bilham asked, "because you're really of the century before?"
    "The century before that? Thank you!" Strether laughed. "If I ask you about some of the ladies it can't be that I may hope, as such a specimen of the rococo, to please them" (p. 123).

39. Waymarsh and his "sacred rage" are back to back with Mme. de Vionnet and her face like "some silver coin of the Renaissance" on pp. 159–60. As the reader remarks (using Strether's voice): "It's an opposition."

40. Note how Mme. de Vionnet's doorbell is "as little electric as possible."

41. See esp. *Ambassadors*, p. 64, where Europe is associated with memory.

42. *Ulysses* ("Eolus") also uses the Michelangelo analogy to point

up the difference between modern Christianity's "stone Moses" and the "supple" (Joyce's word), living Moses of the Hebrew Scriptures.

43. See: Lionel Trilling, "A Joy Whose Grounds Are True," *Matthew Arnold* (New York: Columbia University Press, 1949), p. 352.
44. James's "Preface" to *Ambassadors*, p. 7.
45. T. S. Eliot, "Ulysses, Order, and Myth," *The Dial 75*, in *The Modern Tradition*, ed. Richard Ellmann and Charles Feidelson, Jr. (New York: Oxford University Press, 1965), pp. 679-81. For Joyce's approval, see his letter to Harriet Weaver of 19 Nov. 1923.
46. Donald Fanger, *Dostoevsky and Romantic Realism* (Chicago: University of Chicago Press, 1965), p. 268.
47. Again, I must acknowledge a debt to Joseph Frank.
48. A. Walton Litz, "The Genre of 'Ulysses'," in *Theory of the Novel*, ed. John Halperin (New York: Oxford University Press, 1976), pp. 111ff.
49. T. S. Eliot, "Tradition and the Individual Talent," *The Sacred Wood* (London: Methuen, 1969), pp. 49–50.

VI

1. John Milton, *Paradise Lost* (Boston: Houghton-Mifflin Co., 1959), pp. 214, 70.
2. Victor Bérard, *Les Phéneciens et l'Odysée* (Paris: Colin, 1927).
3. Richard Ellmann, *The Consciousness of Joyce* (New York: Oxford University Press, 1977), p. 112.
4. *The Zionist Idea*, trans. and ed. Arthur Hertzberg (New York: Atheneum, 1977), pp. 122, 125, 133.
5. Richard Ellmann, *Ulysses on the Liffey* (New York: Oxford University Press, 1972), esp. pp. 1–23.
6. Parenthetical page references for Joyce are to *Ulysses* (New York: Vintage, 1961).
7. Michael Seidel, *Epic Geography* (Princeton: Princeton University Press, 1976), p. xi.
8. For the "wandering Jew" (whom Mulligan mentions on p. 217 and who shows up in "Circe" on p. 506) as an Odyssean figure, see "Nestor," p. 34.
9. Initially Joyce was enthusiastic about Nietzschean Hellenism but, as Ellmann points out, he later modified his judgment of Nietzsche

somewhat. See: Richard Ellmann, *James Joyce* (New York: Oxford University Press, 1959) pp. 178, 352ff.

10. Wallace Stevens, "Connoisseur of Chaos," *The Palm at the End of the Mind* (New York: Vintage, 1972), p. 166.
11. Cf. Ellmann, *Liffey*, pp. 93–96. I am indebted to Ellmann's study for its suggestive pairing of Hume and Aristotle.
12. Again, I am in substantial agreement with Ellmann.
13. Cf., e.g., J. G. Schlözer, *Vorstellung* and *Weltgeschichte*, as cited in the chap. on "The Rise of the German Historical School" in Herbert Butterfield, *Man On His Past* (Cambridge: Cambridge University Press, 1955), pp. 44–50.
14. Seidel, *Epic Geography*, p. xi.
15. Ernest Fenollosa, *The Chinese Written Character as a Medium for Poetry*, ed. Ezra Pound (San Francisco: City Lights, 1969), p. 12.
16. Note that Stephen has just been lectured on Hegel's theory of history in "Nestor" (p. 34).
17. Prominent examples of flashback from pre-Circean hours of Bloomsday include: the Yeats poem (p. 609) from "Telemachus," the arrival of the Nymph (pp. 545–53) from off the painting over the Blooms' bed in "Calypso," the Savior's face (p. 517) from "Eolus," the "creamy-dreamy" terminology (p. 510) from "Scylla and Charybdis," and the "Cuckoo" (p. 469) from the conclusion of "Nausicaa."
18. The earlier novel is *A Portrait of the Artist as a Young Man*. The repetitions include: the aesthetic discussion between the Cap and Stephen (pp. 504ff.), the Cap playing Lynch; the exclamation of "Hoopla!" (p. 557); and the appearance of Fr. Dolan (p. 561).
19. Other flash-forwards: Stephen smashes the brothel lamp (p. 432) and re-smashes it one hundred and fifty-one pages later. London burns (p. 434) and then Dublin burns (p. 598). Mrs. Bloom's friend, Mrs. Breen, says "yes" seven times in a row (p. 449) in anticipation of Molly's "yes" soliloquy (pp. 738ff.). Zoe predicts, "You'll know me the next time" (p. 476) and then Bella prognosticates the same, using the same words (p. 554).
20. Other indications of apocalypse: the opening of the angel's book (p. 465), the destructive construction of the new Bloomusalem (pp. 484–85), the second coming of Elijah (pp. 507–8), the End of the World approaching on its invisible tightrope (p. 507), the affirmation by Bella's fan that "all things end" (p. 528), the reference in "Ithaca" to "Circe" as "Armageddon" (p. 729),

newspaper reports (pp. 504–5), and the testimony of reliable witnesses (p. 506).

21. The dog's metamorphoses: spaniel (p. 432), retriever (p. 437), terrier (pp. 441, 448), whining dog (p. 449), retriever (p. 452), polecat/wolfdog/mastiff (p. 453), spaniel/bulldog/boarhound/educated greyhound/lion/thinking hyena (p. 454), hangdog/Bloom (p. 459), pig/dog (p. 469), beagle/Dignam/dachshund (p. 472), Dignam/RCA dog (p. 474), Christian mysteryman-dog (p. 485), Bloom/dog/pig (p. 497), spaniel/fox (p. 502), word-ending dog (p. 509), "dog sage" (p. 523), "cursed dog" (p. 560), beagle (p. 572), bloodhound (p. 586), dog-in-blasphemous-apotheosis (p. 599), retriever (p. 601), and barking dog (p. 609).

22. Other metamorphoses: Paddy Dignam becomes, in the space of two pages (473–74), King Hamlet's ghost, a rat, and a dog. Bella Cohen is privileged to see life from every angle: as Nymph (p. 545), as Nun (p. 552), and as man (pp. 530ff.). Virag leads a checkered career—as a king, a moth, a kitten, a lawnmower, a scorpion, and a baboon (pp. 517–21). Dedalus family transformations come as close as any to a logical rationale: Stephen appears as a cardinal and as a miniature cardinal (pp. 523–24), as Prince Hamlet, and as Shakespeare (p. 567), while his father is metamorphosed into the Fabulous Artificer (p. 572).

23. Other incidences of melding: J. J. O'Molloy acquires the cheekbones of John F. Taylor and the head, moustache, and eloquence of Seymour Bushe (pp. 464–65), while Stephen slowly becomes like his mother (p. 582) and then "unites" with Rudy Bloom (p. 609).

24. The occasions: when the bells speak (p. 435), when the wreaths speak (p. 452),when the kisses coo and fly (pp. 474–75), when a series of inanimates make cryptic remarks (p. 496), when the gramophone sings a song appropriate to the immediately preceding events (p. 508), when the gas jet becomes a character in the dramatic action (p. 510), when Bella's fan initiates a conversation with Bloom (p. 527), when the trick doorhandle turns of its own accord (p. 525), when the Sins of the Past enunciate themselves (p. 537), when the Blooms' painting comes alive (p. 544), when the yew trees whisper (p. 545), when the Echo speaks before being spoken to (p. 548), when the waterfall imitates Bloom in an Italian accent (p. 552), when the Halcyon Days cheer (p. 548), and when the boots mock and heckle (p. 564).

25. Joyce, *Ulysses*, pp. 484–85.

26. Ibid., p. 467.
27. Ibid., p. 494.
28. Ibid., pp. 459, 550.
29. Ibid., p. 594.
30. Bloom also assumes a "literary occupation" (pp. 458–59), acquires agility in conversation (p. 488), is acclaimed the funniest man on earth (p. 491), and seems to have invented kosher pork (p. 464). He, moreover, acquires an impressive war record, addresses the universe, modulates the weather, and eliminates his enemies.
31. There are also the anti-Bloom dissension in the new Bloomusalem (pp. 490ff.), the Carrollian pronouncement of "The King versus Bloom" (p. 460), and Bloom's denouncement before the civil authority (p. 498).
32. Sigmund Freud, *Introductory Lectures on Psychoanalysis*, trans. James Strachey (New York: Norton, 1966), p. 177.
33. Ibid., p. 180.
34. Joyce had two volumes of Freud's essays in his library and a number of other works of psychological theory. See: Ellmann, *Consciousness of Joyce*, p. 109.
35. Freud, *Introductory Lectures*, pp. 171–73.
36. Ibid., p. 216.
37. Ibid., p. 178.
38. Stephen refers to Maimonides and Averroes, both Semitic Aristotelians, though only the former is Jewish.
39. Hugh Kenner, *Ulysses* (London: Allen & Unwin, 1982), p. 118.
40. René Descartes, *Meditations on First Philosophy*, trans. Lawrence J. Lafleur (Indianapolis: Bobbs-Merrill, 1960), p. 22 (first meditation).
41. Igor Stravinsky, *Poetics of Music*, trans. Arthur Knodel and Ingolf Dahl (New York: Vintage, 1977), p. 77.
42. Diane Tolomeo, "The Finale Octagon of *Ulysses*," *James Joyce Quarterly* 10, 4 (Summer 1973), esp. pp. 440ff.
43. Spunk: p. 742. Kindness: pp. 738–39 and 768. Consideration: pp. 744 and 764. Understanding: p. 764. Mediterranean origins: p. 771. Frugality and responsibility: pp. 773–74. Comprehension of womanhood: p. 782. Feet and sleeping: p. 763. Mimicry: p. 771. "Cracked ideas": p. 777. Impotence: p. 780. Socialism: p. 782.
44. Creativity: p. 774. Intelligence: p. 775. Distinction: p. 775. Med-

iterranean name: p. 779. Teacher: p. 774. Bohemian and stuck-up: p. 775.

45. Joyce, *Ulysses*: "Ithaca," p. 703. But see also "Penelope," p. 757.

46. It is perhaps (foot-)noteworthy that this human trinity is based closely on its divine precursor. The similarity of Molly's function in the novel to that of the Holy Spirit in the New Testament is evident, and the Father/Son relationship of Bloom and Stephen is even more obvious. That Stephen and Bloom are at one moment King Hamlet (i.e., Shakespeare) and, at the next, his son of the same name—that they are Blephen and Stoom, yet not quite one person—is the best example of the Trinitarian, three-and-one mechanics of Joyce's characterology. Also, the Bloom's only-begotten son, Rudy, has died, and they rejoice some time later in his resurrection (as Stephen) by the "father." Stephen's departure from Eccles Street, then, may signify the Son's return to his responsibilities in the world on earth (namely, forging a conscience for the human race), without indicating a permanent separation of the novel's protagonists. Note also that Molly thinks Stephen attended Trinity College (p. 775).

47. Cf. Ellmann, "Why Molly Bloom Menstruates," *Liffey*, pp. 159–76.

48. This sentence represents a tentative idea with the serious reservations that Molly also thinks of occasions on which Bloom has bled (p. 738) and that menstrual blood (pp. 769, 783) and semen (p. 765) are united by a single symbol: the sea.

VII

1. K.D.L. Burridge in *The Structural Study of Myth and Totemism*, ed. Edmund Leach (London: Tavistock, 1967), p. 113. Friedrich Schlegel, *Dialogue on Poetry*, trans. E. Behler and R. Struc (University Park: Pennsylvania State University Press, 1968), p. 83.

2. A. J. Greimas, "Description de la signification et la mythologie comparée," *L'Homme* 3 (1963), as collected in *Du sens: essais sémiotiques* (Paris: Éditions du seuil, 1970).

3. G. S. Kirk, *The Nature of Greek Myths* (Harmondsworth: Pelican, 1974), part 1. Lang: pp. 17, 43. Freud: p. 72. Cambridge School: pp. 66ff. Jung: p. 74. Cassirer/Langer: p. 80. Eliade: p. 64. Lévi-Strauss: p. 84.

4. Kirk, *Greek Myths*, p. 50.
5. G. S. Kirk, *Myth* (London: Cambridge University Press, 1970), p. 34.
6. Kirk, *Greek Myths*, p. 292.
7. Ibid., p. 212.
8. Ibid., p. 286.
9. *The Writings of William Blake*, ed. Geoffrey Keynes (London: Nonesuch, 1925), p. 145.
10. Friedrich Nietzsche, *Philosophy in the Tragic Age of the Greeks*, trans. Marianne Cowan (Chicago: Henry Regnery, 1962), p. 6.
11. Ibid., p. 53.
12. Ibid., pp. 30-31.
13. Friedrich Nietzsche, *Twilight of the Idols* in *The Portable Nietzsche*, ed. and trans. Walter Kaufmann (Harmondsworth: Penguin, 1954), p. 470.
14. Friedrich Nietzsche, *Beyond Good and Evil*, trans. Walter Kaufmann (New York: Vintage, 1966), pp. 17, 136.
15. Nietzsche, *Tragic Age*, p. 13.
16. Nietzsche, *Twilight*, p. 552.
17. Nietzsche, *Good and Evil*, p. 11.
18. Ibid., p. 66.
19. Friedrich Nietzsche, *The Birth of Tragedy*, trans. Francis Golffing (Garden City: Anchor, 1956), p. 104.
20. Nietzsche, *Good and Evil*, p. 145.
21. Ibid.
22. Nietzsche, *Birth of Tragedy*, p. 121.
23. Ibid., p. 123.
24. Nietzsche, *Twilight*, p. 559.
25. Nietzsche, *Tragic Age*, p. 79.
26. Ibid., p. 80.
27. Nietzsche, *Twilight*, p. 474.
28. Ibid., p. 478.
29. Ibid., p. 478.
30. Ibid., p. 477.
31. Ibid., p. 479.
32. Ibid., p. 485.
33. Ibid., pp. 557–58.
34. Nietzsche, *Birth of Tragedy*, p. 77.
35. Ibid., p. 92.
36. Nietzsche, *Tragic Age*, p. 2.

37. Thomas Gould, "The Innocence of Oedipus," parts 1–3, *Arion*, 4:i; 4:iv; 5:iv.
38. *Oedipus Rex*, lines 1189–96 and the concluding lines.
39. W. B. Yeats, *A Vision* (New York: Macmillan, 1937), pp. 27–29.
40. Nietzsche, *Tragic Age*, pp. 16–17.
41. Nietzsche, *Good and Evil*, p. 48.
42. Nietzsche, *Twilight*, pp. 561ff.
43. Ibid., p. 486.
44. Ibid., p. 487.
45. Ibid., p. 488.
46. Nietzsche, *Good and Evil*, p. 47.
47. Nietzsche, *Twilight*, p. 494.
48. Nietzsche, *Good and Evil*, pp. 54–55.
49. Ibid., p. 75.
50. Ibid., p. 228.
51. Ibid., p. 32.
52. Sigmund Freud, *Totem and Taboo*, trans. James Strachey (New York: Norton, 1950), p. 90.
53. Sigmund Freud, *New Introductory Lectures on Psychoanalysis*, trans. W.J.H. Sprott (New York: Norton, 1933), p. 112.
54. Sigmund Freud, *Beyond the Pleasure Principle* (1920), trans. James Strachey (New York: Norton, 1961), p. 32.
55. Sigmund Freud, *The Ego and the Id*, trans. Joan Riviere (New York: Norton, 1960), p. 28.
56. Sigmund Freud, *General Introduction to Psychoanalysis*, trans. Joan Riviere (New York: Liveright, 1963), p. 290.
57. Lionel Trilling, "Freud and Literature," *The Liberal Imagination* (New York: Scribner's 1950), pp. 34ff.
58. Sigmund Freud, *An Outline of Psychoanalysis*, trans. James Strachey (New York: Norton, 1949), p. 15.
59. Freud; *New Introductory Lectures*, pp. 104–12.
60. Freud, *An Outline*, p. 19.
61. Freud, *Beyond the Pleasure Principle*, p. 36.
62. Freud, *General Introduction*, p. 289.
63. Ibid., pp. 289–96.
64. Freud, *Beyond the Pleasure Principle*, p. 34.
65. Freud, *Totem and Taboo*, p. 89.
66. Freud, *New Introductory Lectures*, pp. 105–7.
67. Freud, *An Outline*, p. 34.

68. Northrop Frye, *The Anatomy of Criticism* (Princeton: Princeton University Press, 1957), p. 353.
69. Claude Lévi-Strauss, *The Savage Mind* (London: Weidenfeld and Nicolson, 1966), p. 269.
70. Carl Jung, *Modern Man in Search of a Soul* (London: Routledge, 1973), p. 48.
71. Carl Jung and Carl Kerényi, *Essays on a Science of Mythology* (Princeton: Princeton University Press, 1973), pp. 1–2.
72. Claude Lévi-Strauss, *Tristes tropiques*, trans. John and Doreen Weightman (New York: Atheneum, 1974), p. 58.
73. Jung, "The Special Phenomenology of the Child-Archetype," *Science of Mythology*, p. 92.
74. Frank Kermode, *Modern Essays* (London: Fontana, 1970), p. 145.
75. John Macquarrie, *The Scope of De-mythologizing* (London: SMC Press, 1960), p. 33.
76. Fritz Buri, *Theology of Existence*, as translated in ibid.
77. Jung, *Four Archetypes*, trans. R.F.C. Hull (London: Routledge, 1972), pp. 38–39.
78. Fry wants to make certain that we catch the parallel to the contemporary situation. Aside from the title, *Thor, With Angels* also offers a few resonating lines like, "We went to early rite"— just to be safe.
79. D. H. Lawrence, *Apocalypse* (Harmondsworth: Penguin, 1974), pp. 7–8.
80. Ibid., p. 93.
81. Kirk, *Myth*, pp. 250–51.
82. Victor White, *Soul and Psyche* (New York: Harper & Row, 1960), p. 147.
83. D. H. Lawrence, *Women in Love* (New York: Bantam, 1969), p. 125.
84. Lawrence, *Apocalypse*, p. 114.
85. Ibid., p. 80.
86. Ibid., p. 62.
87. Ibid., p. 94.
88. D. H. Lawrence, *St. Mawr and the Man Who Died* (New York: Vintage, 1953), p. 185.
89. T. S. Eliot, "Baudelaire," *Selected Essays* (New York: Harcourt, Brace & World, 1964), p. 380.
90. Graham Hough, *The Dark Sun* (Aylsbury: Duckworth, 1972), pp. 240–53. Hough claims that this union has no cosmic im-

plications, yet Lawrence writes, "the time of the narcissus was past. . . . All changed, the blossom of the universe changed its petals and swung round to look another way."

91. Lawrence, *The Man Who Died*, p. 182.
92. Lawrence, *Apocalypse*, p. 124.
93. As quoted in Victor White, *Soul and Psyche*, pp. 113, 134.
94. Lawrence, *Women in Love*, pp. 14–15.
95. D. H. Lawrence, "The Risen Lord," *Assorted Articles* (New York: Knopf, 1930), p. 127.
96. Ibid., pp. 128–29, 131.
97. W. B. Yeats, *Wheels and Butterflies* (London: Macmillan, 1934), pp. 65–66.
98. Wallace Stevens, "A High-Toned Old Christian Lady," *The Palm at the End of the Mind* (New York: Vintage, 1972), p. 77.

VIII

1. Charles Maurras, *Anthinea d'Athènes à Florence* (Paris: Champion, 1913), pp. 102–3.
2. The argument of Charles Maurras' *Barbarie et poésie* (Paris: Champion, 1925); and cf. his *Le Conseil de Dante* (Versailles: Bibliothèque des grands auteurs, 1928).
3. See Maurras' *Prologue d'un essai sur la critique* (Paris: La Porte étroite, 1932).
4. Maurras' opinion of the Roman Catholic Church is often misconstrued. Maurras was not proposing that the church become more pagan, only that it always had been pagan and should remain so. See Joseph Vialatoux, *La Doctrine catholique et l'école de Maurras* (Lyons: n.p., 1927).
5. Ezra Pound, "Canto 45": the Usury Canto.
6. Ezra Pound, "Chronicles," *Blast*, 2 (July 1915), p. 85.
7. Ibid., pp. 85–86.
8. Ezra Pound, "The State," *The Exile*, Spring 1927, p. 1.
9. Noel Stock, *The Life of Ezra Pound* (New York: Avon, 1970), p. 212.
10. The source for this quotation is Hugh Kenner, in his 1973 interview for the Pound volume of *Occident*.
11. Ezra Pound, *Selected Prose, 1901–1965*, ed. William Cookson (London: Faber, 1973), p. 137.
12. It seems that even Pound's determination to include political

elements in his verse derived as much from a belief that such was necessary to great literature as from any didactic intentions. In a letter to Louis Dudek, Pound wrote of "The ENormous organized cowardice" of poets who pretend "that basic ethics is mere politics and 'unpoetic' / Minor poets evade, hide, do NOT face / what Dant and Shx / did / no one supposes Dant uncivic / Shx /was SO civic that any amount of tosh has been writ to shove idea that only Bacon, Lord Chancellor cd / have done it. That is the line between major and minor verse." See letter 60 (1959), *leaf is a LEAF*, ed. Louis Dudek (Montreal: DC Books, 1974).

13. Ezra Pound, "Murder by Capital," *The Criterion* 12, no. 49, p. 589.
14. Ibid.
15. Ibid., p. 592.
16. Ezra Pound, *Guide to Kulchur* (New York: New Directions, 1970), p. 249.
17. Ezra Pound, *Jefferson and/or Mussolini* (London: Nott, 1935), p. 85.
18. Pound, *Guide*, p. 256.
19. Cf. Cantos 45, 46, 51, and "Hugh Selwyn Mauberley," lines 21–24, 47–48. The ill effect of usury on art is explained and denounced with special vigor in *Guide*, pp. 27, 62, 184, 281, 345.
20. Pound, *Guide*. 301.
21. Pound, *Jefferson*, pp. 83, 106.
22. Pound, *Guide*, p. 299 (for example).
23. Ibid., pp. 261–62.
24. Good examples of *Cantos* techniques exist in both the *Guide* (esp. on pp. 151, 232–33) and *Jefferson* (pp. 54–55, 100). We even can read certain passages as explanations of how to approach some of *The Cantos'* peculiarities—as, for instance, on p. 138 of the *Guide*, where a large, blank space between two sections of text contains this comment: "This is where the present commentator suggests that his reader pause for reflection."
25. Pound, *Guide*, p. 36.
26. Pound, *Jefferson*, p. 74.
27. Pound, "America: Chances and Remedies," *New Age* (London) 13, 6 (5 June 1913), p. 143.
28. *Blast*, 1 (only issue of 1914), p. 153.
29. William Chace, *The Political Identities of Ezra Pound and T. S.*

Eliot (Stanford: Stanford University Press, 1974), pp. 30ff. The most startling revelation in this book is that Pound was briefly a supporter of Mao's revolutionary movement in China, until he discovered that Mao was anti-Confucian. Note also the number of times Pound invokes the name of Lenin in the same sentence with those of his protagonists in *Jefferson and/or Mussolini*. One important reason Pound rejected Marxism, it seems, was the association of fascism with the only respectable part of Europe (the Mediterranean); he found that the only comparable "possibilities of intelligence" were those in "Rhoosia! Mais voui," but it is obvious he did not think much of Slavic culture (*Jefferson*, p. 126).

30. Pound, *Jefferson*, p. 24.
31. Pound's principal essay on the Increments of Association and Cultural Heritage is *Social Credit: An Impact* (London: Nott, 1935).
32. For example, in *Guide*, p. 306, where Pound directs the reader to "Schopenhauer's admirable essay on style, and how you can tell a true man from a false one." He refers to "the Fascist style" in *A Visiting Card* (London: Peter Russell, 1952).
33. Pound, *Guide*, p. 134.
34. Pound, *Jefferson*, p. 35.
35. Ibid., pp. 57, 74.
36. Ibid., pp. 33–34.
37. Ibid., p. 125.
38. Ibid., p. 95.
39. Pound, *Guide*, p. 12.
40. 1911: "A Retrospect," in *Literary Essays of Ezra Pound*, ed. T. S. Eliot (New York: New Directions, 1935), p. 12. 1933: Pound, *Jefferson*, p. 127. 1940: Pound, "Canto 62." Pound was careful to distinguish the love of order from the will to power— he saw the latter as "vulgar, in the worst sense of the word" (*Jefferson*, p. 99).
41. "Analogy": Ernest Fenollosa, *The Chinese Written Character as a Medium for Poetry*, ed. Ezra Pound (San Francisco: City Lights, 1969), p. 22.
42. "Geometries" and "heavenly model": Pound, *Guide*, p. 130.
43. Pound, "Canto 74," excerpts.
44. W. H Auden, "Squares and Oblongs" in *Poets at Work*, ed. Charles Abbott (New York: Harcourt, Brace & Co., 1948), pp. 178–79.

45. Auden seems to apologize specifically for that attitude of mind in the passages quoted, as well as in his 1941 New Year Letter (London: Faber), p. 82: "Both their unique position in society and the unique nature of their work conspire to make artists less fitted for political thinking than most people."

46. Auden, "Squares and Oblongs," pp. 178–79.

47. John R. Harrison, The Reactionaries (London: Gollencz, 1966), p. 33.

48. Auden, "Squares and Oblongs," p. 175.

49. Ibid., p. 180.

50. Geoffrey Barraclough, Contemporary History (Harmondsworth: Penguin, 1967), pp. 243, 248.

51. Iris Murdoch, "The Sublime and the Beautiful Revisited," Yale Review 49, 2 (Dec. 1959), p. 257.

52. Robert Creeley: Contexts of Poetry, ed. Donald Allen (London: Calder and Boyars, 1973), pp. 9–10.

53. Stephen Spender, "Speaking of Books," New York Times Book Review, 1 Aug. 1954, p. 2.

54. Conversations with Claude Lévi-Strauss, ed. Georges Charbonnier (London: Jonathan Cape, 1973), pp. 30–31, 131.

55. Donald Davie, Pound (Bungay: Fontana Modern Masters, 1975), p. 108.

56. K. K. Ruthven, "The 'Fascism' of Modernist Writers," Southern Review (Adelaide, Australia), Sept. 1972, pp. 225, 230.

57. Davie, Pound, pp. 96–97.

58. Hannah Arendt, The Origins of Totalitarianism (New York: Harcourt, Brace & World, 1951), pp. 326–28.

59. Joseph Frank, "Spatial Form: Further Reflections," Critical Inquiry 5, 2 (Winter 1978), pp. 276–77.

60. Harold Rosenberg, The Tradition of the New (New York: McGraw-Hill, 1965), p. 176.

61. E. H. Gombrich, "Hegelianism without Metaphysics," In Search of Cultural History (Oxford: Clarendon, 1969), p. 30.

62. "LEAF": Pound, letter 54 (1953), leaf is a LEAF. "Hawk": Pound, "A Retrospect" (1912) in Literary Essays, p. 9.

63. Frank Kermode, The Sense of an Ending (London: Oxford University Press, 1967), p. 103.

64. Cf. also the Old Man's instruction to his son in Purgatory ("Study that tree") with these lines of Vladimir in Waiting for Godot: "Look at the tree," "The tree, look at the tree."

65. Frank Kermode, *Modern Essays* (London: Fontana, 1970), p. 64. Kermode's quotation of Eliot is from *To Criticize the Critic* (1965).

66. Erwin Panofsky, *Renaissance and Renascences in Western Art* (New York: Harper & Row, 1972), p. 113.

• INDEX •

150, 177, 179, 183, 185, 191,
226, 228, 231, 252, 257–59,
271, 292n.73
Rorty, Richard, 5
Rosenberg, Harold, 278
Rousseau, Jean-Jacques, 21, 30, 42,
58, 104, 129; *Confessions*, 35,
42, 195; *Contrat social*, 52; *Dis-
cours sur l'inégalité*, 42, 53;
Émile, 35, 53, 56; *Essai sur l'ori-
gine des langues*, 57; *Julie, ou La
Nouvelle Héloïse*, 5, 35–56, 69,
74, 130, 161, 189, 221, 256
Rudge, Olga, 266
Ruskin, John, 93, 100
Russell, George ("AE"), 149

Sainte-Beuve, C. A., 59
Saintsbury, George, 91
Sartre, Jean-Paul, 273
Saurin, Bernard Joseph, 114
Schiller, J.C.F. von, 295n.23
Schlegel, August Wilhelm, 112–13,
115, 121
Schlegel, Friedrich, 4, 6–7, 58–59,
144, 221, 235
Schliemann, Heinrich, 32
scholasticism, *see* Aquinas, St.
Thomas
Schopenhauer, Arthur, 118, 138,
312n.32
sciences and technology, 10, 23,
29, 58, 65–67, 84–85, 87, 100,
105, 119, 122, 140, 182, 190–
91, 193, 199–201, 204, 210,
214, 221–22, 225, 228, 231,
235–37, 240, 242–43, 278
Seidel, Michael, 184
Seznec, Jean, 7, 10, 63
Shaftesbury, Anthony Ashley
Cooper, Earl of, 80
Shakespeare, William, 68, 70, 73,
79, 85–86, 113, 116, 127, 138,
148, 189, 195–96, 198, 213,

281, 293n.84, 304n.22, 306n.46,
311n.12
Shaw, T. E., *see* Lawrence, T. E.
Shelley, Mary, 113
Shelley, Percy Bysshe, 60, 73, 76,
78, 80, 100, 113–16, 118, 120,
127–28, 136, 139, 260, 270, 272
Smith, Grover, 292n.75
Socrates, 39, 118–19, 225, 227–32,
239
solipsism, 91, 187, 189
Sophocles, 62, 77–78, 112, 232–
34, 237–39
Sparta, *see* Greece, ancient
Spencer, Herbert, 100
Spender, Stephen, 274
Spengler, Oswald, 244
Spinoza, Baruch, 187
Steiner, George, 6, 274
Stendhal, 70, 151, 153, 156, 159,
162
Stevens, Wallace, 143, 188, 221
Stock, Noel, 261, 267
Stockhausen, Karlheinz, 273
Stravinsky, 67, 128, 211
Stuart, James, *see* Dilettanti
Surrey, Henry Howard, Earl of, 74
Swift, Jonathan, 129
Swinburne, Algernon, 70, 72, 92
symbolisme, 59–61, 65, 69–70, 76,
80–82, 89, 97, 99, 105, 129–30,
142, 173–74, 216–17, 235, 267–
68, 272, 278

technology, *see* sciences and technology
Tennyson, Alfred Lord, 19, 72, 90,
100, 151–52, 154
Thackeray, William Makepeace,
172
theodicy, 26–29, 34, 43–44, 145,
151, 177, 182–83, 191, 196,
211, 215, 218, 220
theogony, 140, 178

old, 125–26, 297n.51; *The Land of Heart's Desire*, 128–32; *On Baile's Strand*, 131–33; *On the Boiler*, 133–34; *The Only Jealousy of Emer*, 121–22, 128; *Purgatory*, 132–35, 139, 280, 313n.64; "The Second Coming," 252; theater essays, 28–29, 122–23, 125–29, 133, 139; *A Vision*, 29, 233, 253; *Wheels and Butterflies*, 123; *Words Upon the Window Pane*, 125, 128–29, 139

Ziolkowski, Theodore, 251
Zionism, 32, 179–80, 183, 185

• Library of Congress Cataloging in Publication Data •

Perl, Jeffrey M.
The tradition of return.
Bibliography: p.   Includes index.
1. Literature, Modern—History and criticism. I. Title.
PN701.P4 1984   809'.03   84-42567
ISBN 0-691-06621-3

Jeffrey M. Perl is currently a Rockefeller Fellow and Assistant Professor of English and Comparative Literature at Columbia University